CST-30 NEW YORK STATE TEACHER CERTIFICATION SERIES

This is your
PASSBOOK for...

Multi-Subject: Teachers of Early Childhood (Birth-Gr. 2)

Test Preparation Study Guide
Questions & Answers

NATIONAL LEARNING CORPORATION®

COPYRIGHT NOTICE

This book is SOLELY intended for, is sold ONLY to, and its use is RESTRICTED to individual, bona fide applicants or candidates who qualify by virtue of having seriously filed applications for appropriate license, certificate, professional and/or promotional advancement, higher school matriculation, scholarship, or other legitimate requirements of education and/or governmental authorities.

This book is NOT intended for use, class instruction, tutoring, training, duplication, copying, reprinting, excerption, or adaptation, etc., by:

1) Other publishers
2) Proprietors and/or Instructors of "Coaching" and/or Preparatory Courses
3) Personnel and/or Training Divisions of commercial, industrial, and governmental organizations
4) Schools, colleges, or universities and/or their departments and staffs, including teachers and other personnel
5) Testing Agencies or Bureaus
6) Study groups which seek by the purchase of a single volume to copy and/or duplicate and/or adapt this material for use by the group as a whole without having purchased individual volumes for each of the members of the group
7) Et al.

Such persons would be in violation of appropriate Federal and State statutes.

PROVISION OF LICENSING AGREEMENTS – Recognized educational, commercial, industrial, and governmental institutions and organizations, and others legitimately engaged in educational pursuits, including training, testing, and measurement activities, may address request for a licensing agreement to the copyright owners, who will determine whether, and under what conditions, including fees and charges, the materials in this book may be used them. In other words, a licensing facility exists for the legitimate use of the material in this book on other than an individual basis. However, it is asseverated and affirmed here that the material in this book CANNOT be used without the receipt of the express permission of such a licensing agreement from the Publishers. Inquiries re licensing should be addressed to the company, attention rights and permissions department.

All rights reserved, including the right of reproduction in whole or in part, in any form or by any means, electronic or mechanical, including photocopying, recording, or by any information storage and retrieval system, without permission in writing from the Publisher.

Copyright © 2025 by
National Learning Corporation

212 Michael Drive, Syosset, NY 11791
(516) 921-8888 • www.passbooks.com
E-mail: info@passbooks.com

PASSBOOK® SERIES

THE *PASSBOOK® SERIES* has been created to prepare applicants and candidates for the ultimate academic battlefield – the examination room.

At some time in our lives, each and every one of us may be required to take an examination – for validation, matriculation, admission, qualification, registration, certification, or licensure.

Based on the assumption that every applicant or candidate has met the basic formal educational standards, has taken the required number of courses, and read the necessary texts, the *PASSBOOK® SERIES* furnishes the one special preparation which may assure passing with confidence, instead of failing with insecurity. Examination questions – together with answers – are furnished as the basic vehicle for study so that the mysteries of the examination and its compounding difficulties may be eliminated or diminished by a sure method.

This book is meant to help you pass your examination provided that you qualify and are serious in your objective.

The entire field is reviewed through the huge store of content information which is succinctly presented through a provocative and challenging approach – the question-and-answer method.

A climate of success is established by furnishing the correct answers at the end of each test.

You soon learn to recognize types of questions, forms of questions, and patterns of questioning. You may even begin to anticipate expected outcomes.

You perceive that many questions are repeated or adapted so that you can gain acute insights, which may enable you to score many sure points.

You learn how to confront new questions, or types of questions, and to attack them confidently and work out the correct answers.

You note objectives and emphases, and recognize pitfalls and dangers, so that you may make positive educational adjustments.

Moreover, you are kept fully informed in relation to new concepts, methods, practices, and directions in the field.

You discover that you are actually taking the examination all the time: you are preparing for the examination by "taking" an examination, not by reading extraneous and/or supererogatory textbooks.

In short, this PASSBOOK®, used directedly, should be an important factor in helping you to pass your test.

NEW YORK STATE TEACHER CERTIFICATION EXAMINATIONS™
INTRODUCTION

GENERAL INFORMATION

About the Testing Program

Those seeking a New York State teaching certificate for the common branch subjects in prekindergarten through grade 6 or for academic subjects in the secondary grades 7 through 12, i.e., English, a language other than English, mathematics, a science (biology, chemistry, earth science, physics), or social studies, must pass the New York State Teacher Certification Examinations (NYSTCE®) as part of the requirements for certification.

Those seeking a New York State teaching certificate in other areas may need to achieve qualifying scores on the NYSTCE® as indicated in the table which follows.

The New York State Teacher Certification Examinations™ program consists of the

- Liberal Arts and Sciences Test (LAST)
- Elementary and Secondary Assessment of Teaching Skills Written (ATS-W)
- Content Specialty Tests (CSTs)
- Language Proficiency Assessments (LPAs)
- Assessment of Teaching Skills - Performance (ATS-P) (Video)

These exams provide an objective basis of competency and skill for teaching in New York State.

For the requirements, check the summary table of testing requirements which follows.

Test Development

The New York State Teacher Certification Examinations™ are criterion referenced and objective based. A criterion-referenced test is designed to measure a candidate's knowledge and skills in relation to an established standard rather than in relation to the performance of other candidates. The purpose of these exams is to certify candidates who have demonstrated requisite knowledge and skills necessary for a public school teacher.

> The New York State Teacher Certification Examination C"NYSTCE.") program was developed and is administered by the New York State Education Department ("NYSED® ") and National Evaluation Systems, Inc. ("NES"), and this test preparation guide was neither developed in connection with these organizations, nor is it endorsed by them. The NES® and NYSTCE®names and logos are registered service marks of. National Evaluation Systems, Inc. for use with testing services and related products.

An individual's performance on a test is evaluated against an established standard. The passing score for each test is established by the New York State Commissioner of Education based on the professional judgments and recommendations of New York State educators. Examinees who do not pass a test may retake it at any of the subsequent scheduled test administrations.

Description of the Tests
The following is a description of the tests within the NYSTCE® program.

Liberal Arts and Sciences Test (LAST). The Liberal Arts and Sciences Test consists of multiple-choice test questions and a written assignment. Candidates are asked to demonstrate conceptual and analytical skills, critical-thinking and communication skills, and multicultural awareness. The test covers scientific and mathematical processes, historical and social scientific awareness, artistic expression and the humanities, communication skills, and written
         n analysis and expression. The Liberal Arts and Sciences Test is required for a provisional certificate.

Elementary and Secondary Versions of the Assessment of Teaching Skills - Written (ATS-W). There are two versions of the Assessment of Teaching Skills - Written (ATS-W). The elementary ATS-W should be taken by individuals seeking a PreK-6, common branch subject teaching certificate. The secondary ATS-W should be taken by individuals seeking a certificate for a secondary academic subject. Individuals seeking a certificate in other titles may take either the elementary or the secondary ATS-W. The ATS-W is required for a provisional certificate.

The elementary and secondary versions .of the Assessment of Teaching Skills - Written consists of multiple-choice test questions and a written assignment. These tests address knowledge of the learner, instructional planning and assessment, instructional delivery, and the professional environment.

Content Specialty Tests (CSTs). There are currently 21 Content Specialty Tests. For a complete list of test titles, see the list that follows.

The Content Specialty Tests (except Japanese, Russian, Mandarin, Cantonese, Hebrew, and Greek) contain multiple-choice test questions. The CSTs for languages other than English also include audiotaped listening and speaking components and writing components. The CSTs are required for a permanent certificate.

Language Proficiency Assessments (ELPA-C, ELPA-N, TLPAs). The Language Proficiency Assessments are required for ESOL certificates and for bilingual education extension certificates in New York State.

Assessment of Teaching Skills - Performance (ATS-P) (video). The Assessment of Teaching Skills - Performance (ATS-P) (video) is one requirement for individuals seeking a permanent New York State teaching certificate in specified areas. For this assessment, candidates are required to prepare a videotape of their instruction with students who are part of their regular teaching assignments in grades PreK through 12. The teaching skills assessed by the ATS-P (video) are defined by the five objectives in the Instructional Delivery subarea of the Assessment of Teaching Skills test framework.

From the official announcement for instructional purposes

TESTS

Test (Test Code)

Liberal Arts and Sciences Test (LAST) (01)
Elementary Assessment of Teaching Skills - Written (ATS-W) (90)
Secondary Assessment of Teaching Skills - Written (ATS-W) (91)
Elementary Education (02)
English (03)
Mathematics (04)
Social Studies (05)
Biology (06)
Chemistry (07)
Earth Science (08)
Physics (09)
Early Childhood (21)
Latin (10)
Cantonese (11)
French (12)
German (13)
Greek (14)
Hebrew (15)
Italian (16)
Japanese (17)
Mandarin (18)
Russian (19)
Spanish (20)
English to Speakers of Other Languages (ESOL) (22)
English Language Proficiency Assessment for Classroom Personnel (ELPA-C) (23)
English Language Proficiency Assessment for Nonclassroom Personnel (ELPA-N) (25)
Target Language Proficiency Assessment - Spanish (24)
Target Language Proficiency Assessment other than Spanish

NEW YORK STATE TEACHER CERTIFICATION TESTING REQUIREMENTS

(Commissioner's Regulation) Teaching Certificates	Current Requirements		Projected Requirements
(8 NYCRR 80.15) PreK-6, Common Branch Subjects	LAST ATS-W CST (Elementary Education) ATS-P	Provisional Provisional Permanent Permanent	Same as current requirements
7-9 Extension	Same as base certificate, PLUS: CST in academic subject	 Permanent	
Early Childhood Annotation (PreK-3)	CST in annotation	Permanent	
(8 NYCRR 80.16) 7-12 Academic Subjects, e.g., English, Language other than English, Mathematics, Science (Biology, Chemistry, Earth Science, Physics), Social Studies	LAST ATS-W CST (in academic subject) ATS-P	Provisional Provisional Permanent Permanent	Same as current requirements
5-6 Extension	Same as base certificate		
(8 NYCRR 80.9) Bilingual Education [Extension]	Same as base certificate, PLUS: LPA in English (oral)* LPA in Target Language (oral & written)*	 Prov./Perm. Prov./Perm.	Same as current requirements
(8 NYCRR 80.10) English to speakers of other languages (ESOL)	LAST* ATS-W* LPA in English (oral)* CST* (ESOL) ATS-P*	Provisional Provisional Provisional Permanent Permanent	Same as current requirements
(8 NYCRR 80.5) Occupational Subjects, e.g. Agricultural Subjects, Business/Distributive Education, Health Occupations, Trade Subjects, Technical Subjects, Home Economics Subjects	Baccalaureate-based certificates: LAST + ATS-W or NTE Core Battery Associate & non-degree-based certificate titles: ATS-W or NTE Core Battery	 Provisional Permanent	Baccalaureate-based certificates: LAST Provisional ATS-W Provisional CST Permanent ATS-P Permanent Associate & non-degree-based certificate titles ATS-W Provisional ATS-P Permanent

NEW YORK STATE TEACHER CERTIFICATION TESTING REQUIREMENTS

(Commissioner's Regulation) Teaching Certificates	Current Requirements		Projected Requirements	
(8 NYCRR 80.6) Special Education, e.g. Special Education, Blind/ Partially Sighted, Deaf/ Hearing Impaired ——————————— Speech/Hearing Handicapped	LAST & ATS-W or NTE Core Battery	Provisional	Same as for PreK-6 or 7-12 certificate, PLUS: Special Education Supplement to ATS-W	Provisional
			Special Education supplement to ATS-P	Permanent
(8 NYCRR 80.7) Reading	LAST & ATS-W or NTE Core Battery	Provisional	Same as for PreK-6 or 7-12 certificate, PLUS: CST in Reading	Permanent
(8 NYCRR 80.8) School Media Specialist	LAST + ATS-W or NTE Core Battery	Provisional	LAST ATS-W CST ATS-P	Provisional Provisional Permanent Permanent
(8 NYCRR 80.17) Special Subjects, e.g. Art, Business/Distributive Education, Dance, Health, Home Economics, Music, Physical Education, Recreation, Speech, Technology Education	LAST + ATS-W or NTE Core Battery	Provisional	LAST ATS-W CST ATS-P	Provisional Provisional Permanent Permanent

```
LAST  = Liberal Arts & Sciences Test
ATS-W = Assessment of Teaching Skills - Written
CST   = Content Specialty Test
ATS-P = Assessment of Teaching Skills - Performance (video)
LPA   = Language Proficiency Assessment
```

FOR FURTHER INFORMATION

If you have questions regarding which test(s) you must take, contact the teacher certification contact person at your college or:

NEW YORK STATE EDUCATION DEPARTMENT
OFFICE OF TEACHING
CULTURAL EDUCATION CENTER
ALBANY, N.Y. 12230

TELEPHONE: (518) 474-3901
9:00-11:45 A.M., 12:45-4:30 P.M. Eastern Time

Relay center telephone number for the deaf within New York State: 1-800-622-1220

Nationwide AT&T Relay Operator for the Deaf: 1-800-855-2880 (TTY)

If you have questions regarding the Test Registration, Administration Procedures, Admission Ticket, or Score Report, contact:

NYSTCE
NATIONAL EVALUATION SYSTEMS, INC.
30 GATEHOUSE ROAD
P.O. BOX 660
AMHERST, MA 01004-9008

TELEPHONE: (413) 256-2882
9:00 A.M. - 5:00 P.M. Eastern Time

Telephone number for the deaf: (413) 256-8032 (TTY)

NEW YORK STATE TEACHER CERTIFICATION EXAMINATIONS™

FIELDS 211/212/245: MULTI-SUBJECT: TEACHERS OF EARLY CHILDHOOD (BIRTH–GRADE 2)
ASSESSMENT DESIGN

This assessment consists of three parts, administered as three separate tests. Part One: Literacy and English Language Arts and Part Two: Mathematics are newly developed tests. Part Three: Arts and Sciences is a test using content from the previously administered Multi-Subject Content Specialty Test (CST) (field 002). In order to pass the overall assessment, candidates are required to achieve a score that meets or exceeds a separate performance standard for each part. Part Three is shared by all four Multi-Subject assessments; therefore, candidates seeking Multi-Subject certificates for more than one grade level need to pass Part Three only once.

Parts One and Two each consist of selected-response items and one extended constructed-response item. The constructed-response item, designed to measure candidates' pedagogical content knowledge, is scenario-based and requires an extended written response based on the analysis of multiple samples of student-based evidence. Part Three consists of selected-response items only.

As indicated in the tables that follow, for Part One the selected-response items count for 70% of the total test score and the constructed-response item counts for 30% of the total test score. For Part Two the selected-response items count for 80% of the total test score and the constructed-response item counts for 20% of the total test score. Each selected-response item counts the same toward the total test score. The percentage of the total test score derived from the constructed-response item is also indicated in the tables that follow.

The total testing times are 120 minutes for Part One, 135 minutes for Part Two, and 60 minutes for Part Three. The following estimates were used to determine the total test time:

- Part One: The selected-response items are designed with the expectation of response time up to 60 minutes, and the constructed-response item is designed with the expectation of a response up to 60 minutes.

- Part Two: The selected-response items are designed with the expectation of response time up to 75 minutes, and the constructed-response item is designed with the expectation of a response up to 60 minutes.

- Part Three: The selected-response items are designed with the expectation of response time up to 60 minutes.

Further information regarding the content of each competency can be found in the assessment framework.

FIELDS 211/212/245: MULTI-SUBJECT: TEACHERS OF EARLY CHILDHOOD (BIRTH–GRADE 2) ASSESSMENT DESIGN

Part One: Literacy and English Language Arts

Competency	Selected-Response		Constructed-Response	
	Approximate Number of Items	Approximate Percentage of Test Score	Number of Items	Approximate Percentage of Test Score
0001 Knowledge of Literacy & Language Arts	17	30%	--	--
0002 Instruction in Foundational Literacy Skills	17	30%	--	--
0003 Instruction in English Language Arts	6	10%	--	--
0004 Analysis, Synthesis, and Application	--	--	1	30%
Total	40	70%	1	30%

Part Two: Mathematics

Competency	Selected-Response		Constructed-Response	
	Approximate Number of Items	Approximate Percentage of Test Score	Number of Items	Approximate Percentage of Test Score
0001 Number and Operations	10	20%	--	--
0002 Operations and Algebraic Thinking	15	30%	--	--
0003 Measurement, Geometry, and Data	10	20%	--	--
0004 Instruction in Mathematics	5	10%	--	--
0005 Analysis, Synthesis, and Application	--	--	1	20%
Total	40	80%	1	20%

FIELDS 211/212/245: MULTI-SUBJECT: TEACHERS OF EARLY CHILDHOOD (BIRTH–GRADE 2) ASSESSMENT DESIGN

Part Three: Arts and Sciences

Competency		Selected-Response		Constructed-Response	
		Approximate Number of Items	Approximate Percentage of Test Score	Number of Items	Approximate Percentage of Test Score
0001	Science and Technology	16	40%	--	--
0002	Social Studies	16	40%	--	--
0003	Fine Arts, Health and Fitness, Family and Consumer Science, and Career Development	8	20%	--	--
	Total	40	100%	0	0%

HOW TO TAKE A TEST

I. YOU MUST PASS AN EXAMINATION

A. WHAT EVERY CANDIDATE SHOULD KNOW

Examination applicants often ask us for help in preparing for the written test. What can I study in advance? What kinds of questions will be asked? How will the test be given? How will the papers be graded?

As an applicant for a civil service examination, you may be wondering about some of these things. Our purpose here is to suggest effective methods of advance study and to describe civil service examinations.

Your chances for success on this examination can be increased if you know how to prepare. Those "pre-examination jitters" can be reduced if you know what to expect. You can even experience an adventure in good citizenship if you know why civil service exams are given.

B. WHY ARE CIVIL SERVICE EXAMINATIONS GIVEN?

Civil service examinations are important to you in two ways. As a citizen, you want public jobs filled by employees who know how to do their work. As a job seeker, you want a fair chance to compete for that job on an equal footing with other candidates. The best-known means of accomplishing this two-fold goal is the competitive examination.

Exams are widely publicized throughout the nation. They may be administered for jobs in federal, state, city, municipal, town or village governments or agencies.

Any citizen may apply, with some limitations, such as the age or residence of applicants. Your experience and education may be reviewed to see whether you meet the requirements for the particular examination. When these requirements exist, they are reasonable and applied consistently to all applicants. Thus, a competitive examination may cause you some uneasiness now, but it is your privilege and safeguard.

C. HOW ARE CIVIL SERVICE EXAMS DEVELOPED?

Examinations are carefully written by trained technicians who are specialists in the field known as "psychological measurement," in consultation with recognized authorities in the field of work that the test will cover. These experts recommend the subject matter areas or skills to be tested; only those knowledges or skills important to your success on the job are included. The most reliable books and source materials available are used as references. Together, the experts and technicians judge the difficulty level of the questions.

Test technicians know how to phrase questions so that the problem is clearly stated. Their ethics do not permit "trick" or "catch" questions. Questions may have been tried out on sample groups, or subjected to statistical analysis, to determine their usefulness.

Written tests are often used in combination with performance tests, ratings of training and experience, and oral interviews. All of these measures combine to form the best-known means of finding the right person for the right job.

II. HOW TO PASS THE WRITTEN TEST

A. NATURE OF THE EXAMINATION

To prepare intelligently for civil service examinations, you should know how they differ from school examinations you have taken. In school you were assigned certain definite pages to read or subjects to cover. The examination questions were quite detailed and usually emphasized memory. Civil service exams, on the other hand, try to discover your present ability to perform the duties of a position, plus your potentiality to learn these duties. In other words, a civil service exam attempts to predict how successful you will be. Questions cover such a broad area that they cannot be as minute and detailed as school exam questions.

In the public service similar kinds of work, or positions, are grouped together in one "class." This process is known as *position-classification*. All the positions in a class are paid according to the salary range for that class. One class title covers all of these positions, and they are all tested by the same examination.

B. FOUR BASIC STEPS

1) Study the announcement

How, then, can you know what subjects to study? Our best answer is: "Learn as much as possible about the class of positions for which you've applied." The exam will test the knowledge, skills and abilities needed to do the work.

Your most valuable source of information about the position you want is the official exam announcement. This announcement lists the training and experience qualifications. Check these standards and apply only if you come reasonably close to meeting them.

The brief description of the position in the examination announcement offers some clues to the subjects which will be tested. Think about the job itself. Review the duties in your mind. Can you perform them, or are there some in which you are rusty? Fill in the blank spots in your preparation.

Many jurisdictions preview the written test in the exam announcement by including a section called "Knowledge and Abilities Required," "Scope of the Examination," or some similar heading. Here you will find out specifically what fields will be tested.

2) Review your own background

Once you learn in general what the position is all about, and what you need to know to do the work, ask yourself which subjects you already know fairly well and which need improvement. You may wonder whether to concentrate on improving your strong areas or on building some background in your fields of weakness. When the announcement has specified "some knowledge" or "considerable knowledge," or has used adjectives like "beginning principles of..." or "advanced ... methods," you can get a clue as to the number and difficulty of questions to be asked in any given field. More questions, and hence broader coverage, would be included for those subjects which are more important in the work. Now weigh your strengths and weaknesses against the job requirements and prepare accordingly.

3) Determine the level of the position

Another way to tell how intensively you should prepare is to understand the level of the job for which you are applying. Is it the entering level? In other words, is this the position in which beginners in a field of work are hired? Or is it an intermediate or advanced level? Sometimes this is indicated by such words as "Junior" or "Senior" in the class title. Other jurisdictions use Roman numerals to designate the level – Clerk I, Clerk II, for example. The word "Supervisor" sometimes appears in the title. If the level is not indicated by the title, check the description of duties. Will you be working under very close supervision, or will you have responsibility for independent decisions in this work?

4) Choose appropriate study materials

Now that you know the subjects to be examined and the relative amount of each subject to be covered, you can choose suitable study materials. For beginning level jobs, or even advanced ones, if you have a pronounced weakness in some aspect of your training, read a modern, standard textbook in that field. Be sure it is up to date and has general coverage. Such books are normally available at your library, and the librarian will be glad to help you locate one. For entry-level positions, questions of appropriate difficulty are chosen – neither highly advanced questions, nor those too simple. Such questions require careful thought but not advanced training.

If the position for which you are applying is technical or advanced, you will read more advanced, specialized material. If you are already familiar with the basic principles of your field, elementary textbooks would waste your time. Concentrate on advanced textbooks and technical periodicals. Think through the concepts and review difficult problems in your field.

These are all general sources. You can get more ideas on your own initiative, following these leads. For example, training manuals and publications of the government agency which employs workers in your field can be useful, particularly for technical and professional positions. A letter or visit to the government department involved may result in more specific study suggestions, and certainly will provide you with a more definite idea of the exact nature of the position you are seeking.

III. KINDS OF TESTS

Tests are used for purposes other than measuring knowledge and ability to perform specified duties. For some positions, it is equally important to test ability to make adjustments to new situations or to profit from training. In others, basic mental abilities not dependent on information are essential. Questions which test these things may not appear as pertinent to the duties of the position as those which test for knowledge and information. Yet they are often highly important parts of a fair examination. For very general questions, it is almost impossible to help you direct your study efforts. What we can do is to point out some of the more common of these general abilities needed in public service positions and describe some typical questions.

1) General information

Broad, general information has been found useful for predicting job success in some kinds of work. This is tested in a variety of ways, from vocabulary lists to questions about current events. Basic background in some field of work, such as sociology or economics, may be sampled in a group of questions. Often these are principles which have become familiar to most persons through exposure rather than through formal training. It is difficult to advise you how to study for these questions; being alert to the world around you is our best suggestion.

2) Verbal ability

An example of an ability needed in many positions is verbal or language ability. Verbal ability is, in brief, the ability to use and understand words. Vocabulary and grammar tests are typical measures of this ability. Reading comprehension or paragraph interpretation questions are common in many kinds of civil service tests. You are given a paragraph of written material and asked to find its central meaning.

3) Numerical ability

Number skills can be tested by the familiar arithmetic problem, by checking paired lists of numbers to see which are alike and which are different, or by interpreting charts and graphs. In the latter test, a graph may be printed in the test booklet which you are asked to use as the basis for answering questions.

4) Observation

A popular test for law-enforcement positions is the observation test. A picture is shown to you for several minutes, then taken away. Questions about the picture test your ability to observe both details and larger elements.

5) Following directions

In many positions in the public service, the employee must be able to carry out written instructions dependably and accurately. You may be given a chart with several columns, each column listing a variety of information. The questions require you to carry out directions involving the information given in the chart.

6) Skills and aptitudes

Performance tests effectively measure some manual skills and aptitudes. When the skill is one in which you are trained, such as typing or shorthand, you can practice. These tests are often very much like those given in business school or high school courses. For many of the other skills and aptitudes, however, no short-time preparation can be made. Skills and abilities natural to you or that you have developed throughout your lifetime are being tested.

Many of the general questions just described provide all the data needed to answer the questions and ask you to use your reasoning ability to find the answers. Your best preparation for these tests, as well as for tests of facts and ideas, is to be at your physical and mental best. You, no doubt, have your own methods of getting into an exam-taking mood and keeping "in shape." The next section lists some ideas on this subject.

IV. KINDS OF QUESTIONS

Only rarely is the "essay" question, which you answer in narrative form, used in civil service tests. Civil service tests are usually of the short-answer type. Full instructions for answering these questions will be given to you at the examination. But in case this is your first experience with short-answer questions and separate answer sheets, here is what you need to know:

1) Multiple-choice Questions

Most popular of the short-answer questions is the "multiple choice" or "best answer" question. It can be used, for example, to test for factual knowledge, ability to solve problems or judgment in meeting situations found at work.

A multiple-choice question is normally one of three types—
- It can begin with an incomplete statement followed by several possible endings. You are to find the one ending which *best* completes the statement, although some of the others may not be entirely wrong.
- It can also be a complete statement in the form of a question which is answered by choosing one of the statements listed.

- It can be in the form of a problem – again you select the best answer.

Here is an example of a multiple-choice question with a discussion which should give you some clues as to the method for choosing the right answer:

When an employee has a complaint about his assignment, the action which will *best* help him overcome his difficulty is to
  A. discuss his difficulty with his coworkers
  B. take the problem to the head of the organization
  C. take the problem to the person who gave him the assignment
  D. say nothing to anyone about his complaint

In answering this question, you should study each of the choices to find which is best. Consider choice "A" – Certainly an employee may discuss his complaint with fellow employees, but no change or improvement can result, and the complaint remains unresolved. Choice "B" is a poor choice since the head of the organization probably does not know what assignment you have been given, and taking your problem to him is known as "going over the head" of the supervisor. The supervisor, or person who made the assignment, is the person who can clarify it or correct any injustice. Choice "C" is, therefore, correct. To say nothing, as in choice "D," is unwise. Supervisors have and interest in knowing the problems employees are facing, and the employee is seeking a solution to his problem.

2) True/False Questions

The "true/false" or "right/wrong" form of question is sometimes used. Here a complete statement is given. Your job is to decide whether the statement is right or wrong.

SAMPLE: A roaming cell-phone call to a nearby city costs less than a non-roaming call to a distant city.

This statement is wrong, or false, since roaming calls are more expensive.

This is not a complete list of all possible question forms, although most of the others are variations of these common types. You will always get complete directions for answering questions. Be sure you understand *how* to mark your answers – ask questions until you do.

V. RECORDING YOUR ANSWERS

Computer terminals are used more and more today for many different kinds of exams.

For an examination with very few applicants, you may be told to record your answers in the test booklet itself. Separate answer sheets are much more common. If this separate answer sheet is to be scored by machine – and this is often the case – it is highly important that you mark your answers correctly in order to get credit.

An electronic scoring machine is often used in civil service offices because of the speed with which papers can be scored. Machine-scored answer sheets must be marked with a pencil, which will be given to you. This pencil has a high graphite content which responds to the electronic scoring machine. As a matter of fact, stray dots may register as answers, so do not let your pencil rest on the answer sheet while you are pondering the correct answer. Also, if your pencil lead breaks or is otherwise defective, ask for another.

Since the answer sheet will be dropped in a slot in the scoring machine, be careful not to bend the corners or get the paper crumpled.

The answer sheet normally has five vertical columns of numbers, with 30 numbers to a column. These numbers correspond to the question numbers in your test booklet. After each number, going across the page are four or five pairs of dotted lines. These short dotted lines have small letters or numbers above them. The first two pairs may also have a "T" or "F" above the letters. This indicates that the first two pairs only are to be used if the questions are of the true-false type. If the questions are multiple choice, disregard the "T" and "F" and pay attention only to the small letters or numbers.

Answer your questions in the manner of the sample that follows:

32. The largest city in the United States is
    A. Washington, D.C.
    B. New York City
    C. Chicago
    D. Detroit
    E. San Francisco

1) Choose the answer you think is best. (New York City is the largest, so "B" is correct.)
2) Find the row of dotted lines numbered the same as the question you are answering. (Find row number 32)
3) Find the pair of dotted lines corresponding to the answer. (Find the pair of lines under the mark "B.")
4) Make a solid black mark between the dotted lines.

VI. BEFORE THE TEST

Common sense will help you find procedures to follow to get ready for an examination. Too many of us, however, overlook these sensible measures. Indeed, nervousness and fatigue have been found to be the most serious reasons why applicants fail to do their best on civil service tests. Here is a list of reminders:

- Begin your preparation early – Don't wait until the last minute to go scurrying around for books and materials or to find out what the position is all about.
- Prepare continuously – An hour a night for a week is better than an all-night cram session. This has been definitely established. What is more, a night a week for a month will return better dividends than crowding your study into a shorter period of time.
- Locate the place of the exam – You have been sent a notice telling you when and where to report for the examination. If the location is in a different town or otherwise unfamiliar to you, it would be well to inquire the best route and learn something about the building.
- Relax the night before the test – Allow your mind to rest. Do not study at all that night. Plan some mild recreation or diversion; then go to bed early and get a good night's sleep.
- Get up early enough to make a leisurely trip to the place for the test – This way unforeseen events, traffic snarls, unfamiliar buildings, etc. will not upset you.
- Dress comfortably – A written test is not a fashion show. You will be known by number and not by name, so wear something comfortable.

- Leave excess paraphernalia at home – Shopping bags and odd bundles will get in your way. You need bring only the items mentioned in the official notice you received; usually everything you need is provided. Do not bring reference books to the exam. They will only confuse those last minutes and be taken away from you when in the test room.
- Arrive somewhat ahead of time – If because of transportation schedules you must get there very early, bring a newspaper or magazine to take your mind off yourself while waiting.
- Locate the examination room – When you have found the proper room, you will be directed to the seat or part of the room where you will sit. Sometimes you are given a sheet of instructions to read while you are waiting. Do not fill out any forms until you are told to do so; just read them and be prepared.
- Relax and prepare to listen to the instructions
- If you have any physical problem that may keep you from doing your best, be sure to tell the test administrator. If you are sick or in poor health, you really cannot do your best on the exam. You can come back and take the test some other time.

VII. AT THE TEST

The day of the test is here and you have the test booklet in your hand. The temptation to get going is very strong. Caution! There is more to success than knowing the right answers. You must know how to identify your papers and understand variations in the type of short-answer question used in this particular examination. Follow these suggestions for maximum results from your efforts:

1) Cooperate with the monitor
The test administrator has a duty to create a situation in which you can be as much at ease as possible. He will give instructions, tell you when to begin, check to see that you are marking your answer sheet correctly, and so on. He is not there to guard you, although he will see that your competitors do not take unfair advantage. He wants to help you do your best.

2) Listen to all instructions
Don't jump the gun! Wait until you understand all directions. In most civil service tests you get more time than you need to answer the questions. So don't be in a hurry. Read each word of instructions until you clearly understand the meaning. Study the examples, listen to all announcements and follow directions. Ask questions if you do not understand what to do.

3) Identify your papers
Civil service exams are usually identified by number only. You will be assigned a number; you must not put your name on your test papers. Be sure to copy your number correctly. Since more than one exam may be given, copy your exact examination title.

4) Plan your time
Unless you are told that a test is a "speed" or "rate of work" test, speed itself is usually not important. Time enough to answer all the questions will be provided, but this does not mean that you have all day. An overall time limit has been set. Divide the total time (in minutes) by the number of questions to determine the approximate time you have for each question.

5) Do not linger over difficult questions

If you come across a difficult question, mark it with a paper clip (useful to have along) and come back to it when you have been through the booklet. One caution if you do this – be sure to skip a number on your answer sheet as well. Check often to be sure that you have not lost your place and that you are marking in the row numbered the same as the question you are answering.

6) Read the questions

Be sure you know what the question asks! Many capable people are unsuccessful because they failed to *read* the questions correctly.

7) Answer all questions

Unless you have been instructed that a penalty will be deducted for incorrect answers, it is better to guess than to omit a question.

8) Speed tests

It is often better NOT to guess on speed tests. It has been found that on timed tests people are tempted to spend the last few seconds before time is called in marking answers at random – without even reading them – in the hope of picking up a few extra points. To discourage this practice, the instructions may warn you that your score will be "corrected" for guessing. That is, a penalty will be applied. The incorrect answers will be deducted from the correct ones, or some other penalty formula will be used.

9) Review your answers

If you finish before time is called, go back to the questions you guessed or omitted to give them further thought. Review other answers if you have time.

10) Return your test materials

If you are ready to leave before others have finished or time is called, take ALL your materials to the monitor and leave quietly. Never take any test material with you. The monitor can discover whose papers are not complete, and taking a test booklet may be grounds for disqualification.

VIII. EXAMINATION TECHNIQUES

1) Read the general instructions carefully. These are usually printed on the first page of the exam booklet. As a rule, these instructions refer to the timing of the examination; the fact that you should not start work until the signal and must stop work at a signal, etc. If there are any *special* instructions, such as a choice of questions to be answered, make sure that you note this instruction carefully.

2) When you are ready to start work on the examination, that is as soon as the signal has been given, read the instructions to each question booklet, underline any key words or phrases, such as *least, best, outline, describe* and the like. In this way you will tend to answer as requested rather than discover on reviewing your paper that you *listed without describing*, that you selected the *worst* choice rather than the *best* choice, etc.

3) If the examination is of the objective or multiple-choice type – that is, each question will also give a series of possible answers: A, B, C or D, and you are called upon to select the best answer and write the letter next to that answer on your answer paper – it is advisable to start answering each question in turn. There may be anywhere from 50 to 100 such questions in the three or four hours allotted and you can see how much time would be taken if you read through all the questions before beginning to answer any. Furthermore, if you come across a question or group of questions which you know would be difficult to answer, it would undoubtedly affect your handling of all the other questions.

4) If the examination is of the essay type and contains but a few questions, it is a moot point as to whether you should read all the questions before starting to answer any one. Of course, if you are given a choice – say five out of seven and the like – then it is essential to read all the questions so you can eliminate the two that are most difficult. If, however, you are asked to answer all the questions, there may be danger in trying to answer the easiest one first because you may find that you will spend too much time on it. The best technique is to answer the first question, then proceed to the second, etc.

5) Time your answers. Before the exam begins, write down the time it started, then add the time allowed for the examination and write down the time it must be completed, then divide the time available somewhat as follows:
   - If 3-1/2 hours are allowed, that would be 210 minutes. If you have 80 objective-type questions, that would be an average of 2-1/2 minutes per question. Allow yourself no more than 2 minutes per question, or a total of 160 minutes, which will permit about 50 minutes to review.
   - If for the time allotment of 210 minutes there are 7 essay questions to answer, that would average about 30 minutes a question. Give yourself only 25 minutes per question so that you have about 35 minutes to review.

6) The most important instruction is to *read each question* and make sure you know what is wanted. The second most important instruction is to *time yourself properly* so that you answer every question. The third most important instruction is to *answer every question*. Guess if you have to but include something for each question. Remember that you will receive no credit for a blank and will probably receive some credit if you write something in answer to an essay question. If you guess a letter – say "B" for a multiple-choice question – you may have guessed right. If you leave a blank as an answer to a multiple-choice question, the examiners may respect your feelings but it will not add a point to your score. Some exams may penalize you for wrong answers, so in such cases *only*, you may not want to guess unless you have some basis for your answer.

7) Suggestions
   a. Objective-type questions
      1. Examine the question booklet for proper sequence of pages and questions
      2. Read all instructions carefully
      3. Skip any question which seems too difficult; return to it after all other questions have been answered
      4. Apportion your time properly; do not spend too much time on any single question or group of questions

5. Note and underline key words – *all, most, fewest, least, best, worst, same, opposite,* etc.
6. Pay particular attention to negatives
7. Note unusual option, e.g., unduly long, short, complex, different or similar in content to the body of the question
8. Observe the use of "hedging" words – *probably, may, most likely,* etc.
9. Make sure that your answer is put next to the same number as the question
10. Do not second-guess unless you have good reason to believe the second answer is definitely more correct
11. Cross out original answer if you decide another answer is more accurate; do not erase until you are ready to hand your paper in
12. Answer all questions; guess unless instructed otherwise
13. Leave time for review

   b. Essay questions
1. Read each question carefully
2. Determine exactly what is wanted. Underline key words or phrases.
3. Decide on outline or paragraph answer
4. Include many different points and elements unless asked to develop any one or two points or elements
5. Show impartiality by giving pros and cons unless directed to select one side only
6. Make and write down any assumptions you find necessary to answer the questions
7. Watch your English, grammar, punctuation and choice of words
8. Time your answers; don't crowd material

8) Answering the essay question

Most essay questions can be answered by framing the specific response around several key words or ideas. Here are a few such key words or ideas:

M's: manpower, materials, methods, money, management
P's: purpose, program, policy, plan, procedure, practice, problems, pitfalls, personnel, public relations

   a. Six basic steps in handling problems:
1. Preliminary plan and background development
2. Collect information, data and facts
3. Analyze and interpret information, data and facts
4. Analyze and develop solutions as well as make recommendations
5. Prepare report and sell recommendations
6. Install recommendations and follow up effectiveness

   b. Pitfalls to avoid
1. *Taking things for granted* – A statement of the situation does not necessarily imply that each of the elements is necessarily true; for example, a complaint may be invalid and biased so that all that can be taken for granted is that a complaint has been registered

2. *Considering only one side of a situation* – Wherever possible, indicate several alternatives and then point out the reasons you selected the best one
3. *Failing to indicate follow up* – Whenever your answer indicates action on your part, make certain that you will take proper follow-up action to see how successful your recommendations, procedures or actions turn out to be
4. *Taking too long in answering any single question* – Remember to time your answers properly

IX. AFTER THE TEST

Scoring procedures differ in detail among civil service jurisdictions although the general principles are the same. Whether the papers are hand-scored or graded by machine we have described, they are nearly always graded by number. That is, the person who marks the paper knows only the number – never the name – of the applicant. Not until all the papers have been graded will they be matched with names. If other tests, such as training and experience or oral interview ratings have been given, scores will be combined. Different parts of the examination usually have different weights. For example, the written test might count 60 percent of the final grade, and a rating of training and experience 40 percent. In many jurisdictions, veterans will have a certain number of points added to their grades.

After the final grade has been determined, the names are placed in grade order and an eligible list is established. There are various methods for resolving ties between those who get the same final grade – probably the most common is to place first the name of the person whose application was received first. Job offers are made from the eligible list in the order the names appear on it. You will be notified of your grade and your rank as soon as all these computations have been made. This will be done as rapidly as possible.

People who are found to meet the requirements in the announcement are called "eligibles." Their names are put on a list of eligible candidates. An eligible's chances of getting a job depend on how high he stands on this list and how fast agencies are filling jobs from the list.

When a job is to be filled from a list of eligibles, the agency asks for the names of people on the list of eligibles for that job. When the civil service commission receives this request, it sends to the agency the names of the three people highest on this list. Or, if the job to be filled has specialized requirements, the office sends the agency the names of the top three persons who meet these requirements from the general list.

The appointing officer makes a choice from among the three people whose names were sent to him. If the selected person accepts the appointment, the names of the others are put back on the list to be considered for future openings.

That is the rule in hiring from all kinds of eligible lists, whether they are for typist, carpenter, chemist, or something else. For every vacancy, the appointing officer has his choice of any one of the top three eligibles on the list. This explains why the person whose name is on top of the list sometimes does not get an appointment when some of the persons lower on the list do. If the appointing officer chooses the second or third eligible, the No. 1 eligible does not get a job at once, but stays on the list until he is appointed or the list is terminated.

X. HOW TO PASS THE INTERVIEW TEST

The examination for which you applied requires an oral interview test. You have already taken the written test and you are now being called for the interview test – the final part of the formal examination.

You may think that it is not possible to prepare for an interview test and that there are no procedures to follow during an interview. Our purpose is to point out some things you can do in advance that will help you and some good rules to follow and pitfalls to avoid while you are being interviewed.

What is an interview supposed to test?

The written examination is designed to test the technical knowledge and competence of the candidate; the oral is designed to evaluate intangible qualities, not readily measured otherwise, and to establish a list showing the relative fitness of each candidate – as measured against his competitors – for the position sought. Scoring is not on the basis of "right" and "wrong," but on a sliding scale of values ranging from "not passable" to "outstanding." As a matter of fact, it is possible to achieve a relatively low score without a single "incorrect" answer because of evident weakness in the qualities being measured.

Occasionally, an examination may consist entirely of an oral test – either an individual or a group oral. In such cases, information is sought concerning the technical knowledges and abilities of the candidate, since there has been no written examination for this purpose. More commonly, however, an oral test is used to supplement a written examination.

Who conducts interviews?

The composition of oral boards varies among different jurisdictions. In nearly all, a representative of the personnel department serves as chairman. One of the members of the board may be a representative of the department in which the candidate would work. In some cases, "outside experts" are used, and, frequently, a businessman or some other representative of the general public is asked to serve. Labor and management or other special groups may be represented. The aim is to secure the services of experts in the appropriate field.

However the board is composed, it is a good idea (and not at all improper or unethical) to ascertain in advance of the interview who the members are and what groups they represent. When you are introduced to them, you will have some idea of their backgrounds and interests, and at least you will not stutter and stammer over their names.

What should be done before the interview?

While knowledge about the board members is useful and takes some of the surprise element out of the interview, there is other preparation which is more substantive. It *is* possible to prepare for an oral interview – in several ways:

1) Keep a copy of your application and review it carefully before the interview

This may be the only document before the oral board, and the starting point of the interview. Know what education and experience you have listed there, and the sequence and dates of all of it. Sometimes the board will ask you to review the highlights of your experience for them; you should not have to hem and haw doing it.

2) Study the class specification and the examination announcement

Usually, the oral board has one or both of these to guide them. The qualities, characteristics or knowledges required by the position sought are stated in these documents. They offer valuable clues as to the nature of the oral interview. For example, if the job involves supervisory responsibilities, the announcement will usually indicate that knowledge of modern supervisory methods and the qualifications of the candidate as a supervisor will be tested. If so, you can expect such questions, frequently in the form of a hypothetical situation which you are expected to solve. NEVER go into an oral without knowledge of the duties and responsibilities of the job you seek.

3) Think through each qualification required

Try to visualize the kind of questions you would ask if you were a board member. How well could you answer them? Try especially to appraise your own knowledge and background in each area, *measured against the job sought*, and identify any areas in which you are weak. Be critical and realistic – do not flatter yourself.

4) Do some general reading in areas in which you feel you may be weak

For example, if the job involves supervision and your past experience has NOT, some general reading in supervisory methods and practices, particularly in the field of human relations, might be useful. Do NOT study agency procedures or detailed manuals. The oral board will be testing your understanding and capacity, not your memory.

5) Get a good night's sleep and watch your general health and mental attitude

You will want a clear head at the interview. Take care of a cold or any other minor ailment, and of course, no hangovers.

What should be done on the day of the interview?

Now comes the day of the interview itself. Give yourself plenty of time to get there. Plan to arrive somewhat ahead of the scheduled time, particularly if your appointment is in the fore part of the day. If a previous candidate fails to appear, the board might be ready for you a bit early. By early afternoon an oral board is almost invariably behind schedule if there are many candidates, and you may have to wait. Take along a book or magazine to read, or your application to review, but leave any extraneous material in the waiting room when you go in for your interview. In any event, relax and compose yourself.

The matter of dress is important. The board is forming impressions about you – from your experience, your manners, your attitude, and your appearance. Give your personal appearance careful attention. Dress your best, but not your flashiest. Choose conservative, appropriate clothing, and be sure it is immaculate. This is a business interview, and your appearance should indicate that you regard it as such. Besides, being well groomed and properly dressed will help boost your confidence.

Sooner or later, someone will call your name and escort you into the interview room. *This is it.* From here on you are on your own. It is too late for any more preparation. But remember, you asked for this opportunity to prove your fitness, and you are here because your request was granted.

What happens when you go in?

The usual sequence of events will be as follows: The clerk (who is often the board stenographer) will introduce you to the chairman of the oral board, who will introduce you to the other members of the board. Acknowledge the introductions before you sit down. Do not be surprised if you find a microphone facing you or a stenotypist sitting by. Oral interviews are usually recorded in the event of an appeal or other review.

Usually the chairman of the board will open the interview by reviewing the highlights of your education and work experience from your application – primarily for the benefit of the other members of the board, as well as to get the material into the record. Do not interrupt or comment unless there is an error or significant misinterpretation; if that is the case, do not hesitate. But do not quibble about insignificant matters. Also, he will usually ask you some question about your education, experience or your present job – partly to get you to start talking and to establish the interviewing "rapport." He may start the actual questioning, or turn it over to one of the other members. Frequently, each member undertakes the questioning on a particular area, one in which he is perhaps most competent, so you can expect each member to participate in the examination. Because time is limited, you may also expect some rather abrupt switches in the direction the questioning takes, so do not be upset by it. Normally, a board member will not pursue a single line of questioning unless he discovers a particular strength or weakness.

After each member has participated, the chairman will usually ask whether any member has any further questions, then will ask you if you have anything you wish to add. Unless you are expecting this question, it may floor you. Worse, it may start you off on an extended, extemporaneous speech. The board is not usually seeking more information. The question is principally to offer you a last opportunity to present further qualifications or to indicate that you have nothing to add. So, if you feel that a significant qualification or characteristic has been overlooked, it is proper to point it out in a sentence or so. Do not compliment the board on the thoroughness of their examination – they have been sketchy, and you know it. If you wish, merely say, "No thank you, I have nothing further to add." This is a point where you can "talk yourself out" of a good impression or fail to present an important bit of information. Remember, *you close the interview yourself.*

The chairman will then say, "That is all, Mr. _____, thank you." Do not be startled; the interview is over, and quicker than you think. Thank him, gather your belongings and take your leave. Save your sigh of relief for the other side of the door.

How to put your best foot forward
Throughout this entire process, you may feel that the board individually and collectively is trying to pierce your defenses, seek out your hidden weaknesses and embarrass and confuse you. Actually, this is not true. They are obliged to make an appraisal of your qualifications for the job you are seeking, and they want to see you in your best light. Remember, they must interview all candidates and a non-cooperative candidate may become a failure in spite of their best efforts to bring out his qualifications. Here are 15 suggestions that will help you:

1) Be natural – Keep your attitude confident, not cocky
If you are not confident that you can do the job, do not expect the board to be. Do not apologize for your weaknesses, try to bring out your strong points. The board is interested in a positive, not negative, presentation. Cockiness will antagonize any board member and make him wonder if you are covering up a weakness by a false show of strength.

2) Get comfortable, but don't lounge or sprawl
Sit erectly but not stiffly. A careless posture may lead the board to conclude that you are careless in other things, or at least that you are not impressed by the importance of the occasion. Either conclusion is natural, even if incorrect. Do not fuss with your clothing, a pencil or an ashtray. Your hands may occasionally be useful to emphasize a point; do not let them become a point of distraction.

3) Do not wisecrack or make small talk
This is a serious situation, and your attitude should show that you consider it as such. Further, the time of the board is limited – they do not want to waste it, and neither should you.

4) Do not exaggerate your experience or abilities

In the first place, from information in the application or other interviews and sources, the board may know more about you than you think. Secondly, you probably will not get away with it. An experienced board is rather adept at spotting such a situation, so do not take the chance.

5) If you know a board member, do not make a point of it, yet do not hide it

Certainly you are not fooling him, and probably not the other members of the board. Do not try to take advantage of your acquaintanceship – it will probably do you little good.

6) Do not dominate the interview

Let the board do that. They will give you the clues – do not assume that you have to do all the talking. Realize that the board has a number of questions to ask you, and do not try to take up all the interview time by showing off your extensive knowledge of the answer to the first one.

7) Be attentive

You only have 20 minutes or so, and you should keep your attention at its sharpest throughout. When a member is addressing a problem or question to you, give him your undivided attention. Address your reply principally to him, but do not exclude the other board members.

8) Do not interrupt

A board member may be stating a problem for you to analyze. He will ask you a question when the time comes. Let him state the problem, and wait for the question.

9) Make sure you understand the question

Do not try to answer until you are sure what the question is. If it is not clear, restate it in your own words or ask the board member to clarify it for you. However, do not haggle about minor elements.

10) Reply promptly but not hastily

A common entry on oral board rating sheets is "candidate responded readily," or "candidate hesitated in replies." Respond as promptly and quickly as you can, but do not jump to a hasty, ill-considered answer.

11) Do not be peremptory in your answers

A brief answer is proper – but do not fire your answer back. That is a losing game from your point of view. The board member can probably ask questions much faster than you can answer them.

12) Do not try to create the answer you think the board member wants

He is interested in what kind of mind you have and how it works – not in playing games. Furthermore, he can usually spot this practice and will actually grade you down on it.

13) Do not switch sides in your reply merely to agree with a board member

Frequently, a member will take a contrary position merely to draw you out and to see if you are willing and able to defend your point of view. Do not start a debate, yet do not surrender a good position. If a position is worth taking, it is worth defending.

14) Do not be afraid to admit an error in judgment if you are shown to be wrong

The board knows that you are forced to reply without any opportunity for careful consideration. Your answer may be demonstrably wrong. If so, admit it and get on with the interview.

15) Do not dwell at length on your present job

The opening question may relate to your present assignment. Answer the question but do not go into an extended discussion. You are being examined for a *new* job, not your present one. As a matter of fact, try to phrase ALL your answers in terms of the job for which you are being examined.

Basis of Rating

Probably you will forget most of these "do's" and "don'ts" when you walk into the oral interview room. Even remembering them all will not ensure you a passing grade. Perhaps you did not have the qualifications in the first place. But remembering them will help you to put your best foot forward, without treading on the toes of the board members.

Rumor and popular opinion to the contrary notwithstanding, an oral board wants you to make the best appearance possible. They know you are under pressure – but they also want to see how you respond to it as a guide to what your reaction would be under the pressures of the job you seek. They will be influenced by the degree of poise you display, the personal traits you show and the manner in which you respond.

ABOUT THIS BOOK

This book contains tests divided into Examination Sections. Go through each test, answering every question in the margin. We have also attached a sample answer sheet at the back of the book that can be removed and used. At the end of each test look at the answer key and check your answers. On the ones you got wrong, look at the right answer choice and learn. Do not fill in the answers first. Do not memorize the questions and answers, but understand the answer and principles involved. On your test, the questions will likely be different from the samples. Questions are changed and new ones added. If you understand these past questions you should have success with any changes that arise. Tests may consist of several types of questions. We have additional books on each subject should more study be advisable or necessary for you. Finally, the more you study, the better prepared you will be. This book is intended to be the last thing you study before you walk into the examination room. Prior study of relevant texts is also recommended. NLC publishes some of these in our Fundamental Series. Knowledge and good sense are important factors in passing your exam. Good luck also helps. So now study this Passbook, absorb the material contained within and take that knowledge into the examination. Then do your best to pass that exam.

EXAMINATION SECTION

EXAMINATION SECTION
TEST 1

DIRECTIONS: Each question or incomplete statement is followed by several suggested answers or completions. Select the one that BEST answers the question or completes the statement. *PRINT THE LETTER OF THE CORRECT ANSWER IN THE SPACE AT THE RIGHT.*

1. The time of day MOST suitable for bathing a baby is

    A. just before feeding him
    B. just after feeding him
    C. early in the day
    D. at any time most convenient for the mother

2. Of the following, the BEST cure for diaper rash is to

    A. avoid the use of fabric softeners in laundering
    B. expose the rash to air and sunlight
    C. use waterproof pants over the diaper
    D. dry diapers slowly at a low temperature in laundering

3. Except for the consistency of food, the diet of a baby resembles that of an older child by the time he is _____ old.

    A. 6 weeks   B. 2 months   C. 3 months   D. 6 months

4. During the first three to five days of life, a normal baby loses

    A. two to three ounces of weight
    B. from several ounces to a pound of weight
    C. as much as two pounds of weight
    D. no weight

5. Toddlers at play

    A. generally amuse themselves
    B. need someone to play games with them
    C. need constant direction
    D. enjoy telling stories

6. During pregnancy, the first baby tooth starts to form during the _____ or _____ month.

    A. first; second   B. third; fourth
    C. sixth; seventh   D. eighth; ninth

7. The croup tent provides

    A. oxygen to relieve dyspnea
    B. warm moist air
    C. cool moist air
    D. cool dry air

8. Emetics used to reduce laryngeal spasms in croup are given PRIMARILY for the purpose of

   A. drying up bronchial secretions
   B. producing sleep
   C. inducing vomiting
   D. dilating the bronchi

9. An envelope-type wrap that covers a baby's hands and feet, as well as his body, is called a

   A. sacque   B. Gertrude   C. bunting   D. crawler

10. The crust that sometimes forms on babies' scalps is called

    A. acne
    B. cradle cap
    C. eczema
    D. prickly heat

11. The MOST satisfactory filling for a crib mattress is

    A. cotton
    B. hair
    C. soft foam rubber
    D. cotton and innersprings

12. By far, the MOST common disrupter of the newborn's slumber is

    A. hunger pain
    B. his need for close, warm contact and rhythmic movement
    C. his need to exercise his lungs
    D. the *startle reflex*

13. Of the following, the MOST helpful when *burping* a baby at feeding is to

    A. thump him on the back
    B. avoid letting him suck on an empty bottle
    C. encourage relaxation by gentle patting or rubbing
    D. keep the bottle neck well-filled

14. The *soft spots* that can be felt in the newborn infant's skull are called the

    A. suture lines
    B. fontanels
    C. occipital sutures
    D. parietal cavities

15. A young baby's sleep position should be rotated in order to

    A. prevent misshaping of soft bones
    B. encourage him to roll from side to side
    C. make complete relaxation possible
    D. teach him to adjust

16. Of the following, the MOST advantageous sleep position for a baby is on his

    A. stomach   B. back   C. right side   D. left side

17. In a newborn baby, the *Darwinian reflex*

    A. is set off by a touch on the child's lips
    B. gives the child an extra supply of oxygen
    C. is aroused by a sudden noise or loss of support
    D. makes the child's hands grasp anything touching his palm

18. The number of *milk* teeth which a baby usually has is 18.____

    A. 12 B. 16 C. 20 D. 24

19. In an infant, intense crying which nothing seems to help is PROBABLY a sign of 19.____

    A. colic
    B. indigestion
    C. too tightly binding garments
    D. possible injury from a pin

20. To habituate pupils in safety procedure, 20.____

    A. discuss the problem
    B. motivate them to want to practice safety
    C. insist on repetitive processes
    D. excuse occasional exceptions

21. Of the following, the STRONGEST influence on the personality of a child during his first three years is the 21.____

    A. playmates with whom he agrees
    B. economic status of the family
    C. social status of the family
    D. relationships with the members of his family

22. Of the following, the toy MOST suitable for a toddler is a(n) 22.____

    A. airplane   B. pair of blunt scissors
    C. wheelbarrow   D. small football

23. When a child becomes temporarily boisterous and irritable, the parents should 23.____

    A. divert his attention
    B. punish him
    C. cajol him
    D. try to ascertain the reason for the behavior

24. The BEST reason why school children should have a weekly allowance is that they may 24.____

    A. buy their own lunches
    B. learn how to use money
    C. learn to save money
    D. be popular with their friends

25. Among early indications of social consciousness of the infant, the FIRST is 25.____

    A. protest at being alone
    B. cooing at other infants
    C. the smile of recognition
    D. the demand for attention

26. A PRIMARY need of the infant is

   A. affection and security
   B. constant attention
   C. rigid regularity of schedule
   D. adequate discipline

27. Of the following, the LEAST satisfactory corrective measure when dealing with children is

   A. sending to bed
   B. restriction
   C. isolation
   D. deprivation

28. In a child's development, body control occurs FIRST in the muscles of the

   A. trunk
   B. leg
   C. head
   D. arm and hand

29. If a teenage girl is careless about putting her clothes away,

   A. put the clothing away for her
   B. tolerate the situation
   C. inspire her to be neat
   D. lecture her

30. A two-year-old child that refuses to eat lunch should

   A. be forced to eat
   B. be appeased
   C. not be forced to eat and the food should be removed without comment after a reasonable time has passed
   D. be scolded

31. Thumbsucking should be eliminated by

   A. satisfying the physical and emotional needs
   B. mechanical restraints
   C. applying distasteful compounds
   D. punishment

32. When Susan, a five-year-old, delights in telling fantastic stories, she should be

   A. punished
   B. psychoanalyzed
   C. ignored
   D. ridiculed

33. For 12-year-old children, an allowance

   A. may be used as a training device
   B. should be provided
   C. encourages a distorted sense of values
   D. provides a means of disciplinary control

34. Lefthandedness

   A. is an inherited trait
   B. should be corrected
   C. indicates a shortcoming
   D. is a conditioned reflex

35. To reduce fears in children, parents should

    A. give affection
    B. lecture them
    C. shield them
    D. provide safeguards

36. When a new baby is expected, to encourage a sense of belonging, older children should be allowed

    A. to anticipate another playmate
    B. no knowledge of the new baby
    C. to know but not talk about the new baby
    D. to share in the preparations

37. To ease an older child's adjustment to a new baby in the home, it is BEST to

    A. assure him that he is loved equally with the baby
    B. bolster his ego by reminding him of his baby days
    C. explain his responsibilities in helping to care for the new baby
    D. give him full attention when mother first arrives home with the new baby

38. Food cooked to suit the taste of an adult often proves to be unpleasant to a child because

    A. the child has a keener sense of taste than an adult has
    B. a child needs to be protected from eating foods he is not able to digest
    C. such foods are indigestible for him
    D. he needs to be taught to eat everything

39. In general, the _____ child will grow up to be most liberal.

    A. youngest
    B. middle
    C. oldest
    D. one cannot determine

40. In general, the _____ child will grow up to be most rigid.

    A. youngest
    B. middle
    C. oldest
    D. one cannot determine

KEY (CORRECT ANSWERS)

1. D	11. B	21. D	31. A
2. B	12. A	22. D	32. C
3. D	13. C	23. D	33. A
4. B	14. B	24. B	34. A
5. A	15. A	25. C	35. A
6. B	16. A	26. A	36. D
7. B	17. D	27. A	37. D
8. C	18. C	28. C	38. A
9. C	19. A	29. C	39. A
10. B	20. B	30. C	40. C

TEST 2

DIRECTIONS: Each question or incomplete statement is followed by several suggested answers or completions. Select the one that BEST answers the question or completes the statement. *PRINT THE LETTER OF THE CORRECT ANSWER IN THE SPACE AT THE RIGHT.*

1. For a child, the REAL purpose of play is to   1.____
   A. keep busy   B. provide exercise
   C. provide self-expression   D. discover abilities

2. Making a simple doll of yarn is a creative play experience enjoyed by the   2.____
   A. 3-year-old girl   B. 4-5-year-old girl
   C. 4-5-year-old child   D. 3-year-old child

3. An ideal kind of play for the child before meals and before bedtime is   3.____
   A. dramatic play   B. quiet amusements
   C. construction play   D. neighborhood games

4. To encourage good behavior in children, one should use   4.____
   A. candy rewards
   B. punishment for mistakes
   C. reasoning
   D. praise and approval for good behavior

5. A toy suitable for a child from infancy to two years of age should be   5.____
   A. free of sharp corners   B. small things to climb on
   C. colored crayons   D. easily broken

6. A child usually laces his own shoes at the age of _____ years.   6.____
   A. 3   B. 4   C. 5   D. 6

7. Girls' interest in clothes reaches its peak at about _____ years of age.   7.____
   A. 10   B. 12   C. 14   D. 16

8. In a child's speech development, his grammatical usage is reasonably accurate by the 8.____
   age of _____ years.
   A. 5   B. 3   C. 7   D. 9

9. A child should be able to pedal a tricycle at _____ year(s).   9.____
   A. 1   B. 2   C. 3   D. 4

10. The BEST antidote for jealousy in a child is to   10.____
    A. point out his defects to him
    B. extend love, overtly
    C. present an older sibling as a model
    D. fawn on a younger sibling

11. Books for the pre-school child should deal with

    A. science
    B. songs and games
    C. adventure
    D. everyday activities

12. Five-year olds enjoy kindergarten because they have

    A. ability to communicate
    B. capacity to move about
    C. receptiveness to new ideas
    D. developed a desire for sociability

13. A toy suitable for a two-year-old child is a(n)

    A. tinker toy
    B. erector set
    C. Punch and Judy puppet
    D. push-pull toy

14. Of the following, the MOST effective in training a child in obedience is

    A. consistency
    B. attention to comfort
    C. a firm, loud voice
    D. punishment for failure

15. Self-consciousness is a form of

    A. egotism   B. altruism   C. stoicism   D. pedantism

16. In young children, fear is MOST frequently accompanied by

    A. emotional shock
    B. screaming
    C. hiding
    D. investigating

17. In general, of the following, the factor which is MOST important in the development of emotional stability in children is

    A. adequate toys and playmates
    B. complete freedom of choice
    C. strict discipline
    D. happy family life

18. The drinking of coffee and carbonated drinks by children is discouraged MAINLY because these drinks

    A. are stimulants
    B. increase calorie intake
    C. are substituted by children for essential foods
    D. disturb the child's digestive system

19. Among the following statements concerning child feeding, the FALLACIOUS statement is:

    A. Hunger is the chief stimulus to willingness to eat
    B. Given free choice, children will choose a sound diet from a selection of foods
    C. Given free choice, children usually select a high carbohydrate diet washed down with palatable liquids
    D. Forcing usually results in stubborn refusal to eat

20. Stuttering in children is USUALLY associated with

    A. vitamin deficiency
    B. mental deficiency
    C. emotional conflict
    D. imitation of other stutterers

21. A child's tendency to pattern after his parents is known as

    A. identification
    B. projection
    C. compensation
    D. substitution

22. MOST educators agree that righthandedness should be

    A. disregarded if the child indicates a preference for the left hand
    B. forced
    C. encouraged in all actions
    D. encouraged for writing only

23. Parents should provide opportunities to habituate control of small muscles of the arms when the child

    A. eats solid food
    B. makes an effort to feed himself
    C. eats in restaurants
    D. attends school

24. Concerning a six-year-old child, parents who insist on absolute perfection may

    A. hamper future accomplishments
    B. encourage good habits
    C. increase mutual love
    D. destroy imitative performance

25. The mother of a family should engage in social activities outside the home because they will

    A. prepare her for earning a living should necessity arise
    B. help her to *grow* with her husband
    C. provide a means of solving the children's problems
    D. broaden her own viewpoints and continue development of her own personality

26. The BEST method of managing family finances is for the breadwinner to

    A. dole out the money when it is needed
    B. turn over all control to the spouse
    C. provide an allowance for each member of the family to use as he pleases
    D. plan cooperatively with the entire family

27. The home can BEST benefit the mental health of its members through

    A. development of attitudes which result in appropriate emotional expression
    B. an elementary knowledge of psychiatry
    C. a check on the psychosomatics of the older members
    D. regular physical check-ups

28. Toilet training should be

   A. started early
   B. geared to the child's ability
   C. based on age
   D. introduced promptly in a firm businesslike manner

29. When training a child in the use of his hands, one may avoid emotional tensions in the child by remembering that

   A. during the first few months, babies are ambidextrous
   B. it is a simple matter to change from the use of the left to the right hand
   C. it is a risky business to try to change from the use of the left to the right hand if the left has been established as the dominant one
   D. feelings of insecurity result if a child is allowed to develop lefthandedness

30. When a child expresses fear of darkness on retiring, the BEST procedure is to

   A. make light of his fears
   B. compel him to accept the darkness
   C. provide a dim light
   D. shame him for his fears

31. Studies comparing the desirability of feeding to premature infants formulas warmed to body temperature and those given directly on removal from the refrigerator show

   A. no significant difference
   B. disturbed sleep following intake of cold formula
   C. regurgitation following intake of cold formula
   D. slower weight gain with cold feeding

32. An envelope-type wrap covering a baby's hands and feet, as well as his body, is called a

   A. bunting   B. crawler   C. Gertrude   D. sacque

33. The water for the baby's bath should be _____ ° F.

   A. 90   B. 95   C. 100   D. 105

34. At the end of one year, the weight of an infant in relation to its birth weight should be

   A. an increase of 12 ounces monthly
   B. double
   C. 20 pounds more
   D. triple

35. Breastfeeding

   A. is unimportant
   B. is a drain on the mother
   C. increases infant development
   D. provides temporary immunity

36. Non-conforming young children should be

    A. observed and trained while they are young
    B. permitted to outgrow their undesirable traits by themselves
    C. punished at rare intervals
    D. the subject of discussion between members of the family circle without others being present

37. A growing child should NOT drink coffee because it

    A. acts as a stimulant
    B. is habit-forming
    C. reduces milk intake
    D. spoils the appetite

38. An underweight child should be fed

    A. more bread
    B. greater quantities of all foods eaten
    C. starchy desserts
    D. fatty meat cuts

39. Anorexia is BEST treated by

    A. peer pressure
    B. parents
    C. school counseling
    D. medical intervention

40. Personality development is principally affected by

    A. genetics
    B. social experiences
    C. cultural background
    D. school

KEY (CORRECT ANSWERS)

1. C	11. D	21. A	31. A
2. C	12. D	22. A	32. A
3. B	13. D	23. B	33. C
4. D	14. A	24. A	34. D
5. A	15. A	25. D	35. C
6. C	16. C	26. D	36. A
7. C	17. D	27. A	37. C
8. A	18. C	28. B	38. B
9. C	19. B	29. C	39. D
10. B	20. C	30. C	40. A

EXAMINATION SECTION
TEST 1

DIRECTIONS: Each question or incomplete statement is followed by several suggested answers or completions. Select the one that BEST answers the question or completes the statement. *PRINT THE LETTER OF THE CORRECT ANSWER IN THE SPACE AT THE RIGHT.*

1. Normal reflexes during the neonatal period include

   A. moro
   B. grasp
   C. stepping
   D. all of the above

   1.____

2. The milestone MOST likely to occur at 12 weeks of age is the infant's

   A. sustaining social contact
   B. laughing out loud
   C. rolling over
   D. sitting with pelvic support

   2.____

3. A newborn infant CANNOT

   A. turn his head
   B. touch a surface with his nose
   C. lift his head to the plane of the body
   D. flex around his supporting hand

   3.____

4. The age at which an infant starts to sustain his head in the plane of the body is APPROXIMATELY _____ month(s).

   A. one
   B. two
   C. three
   D. four

   4.____

5. At 4 months of age, an infant can do all of the following EXCEPT

   A. sit with a truncal support
   B. show displeasure if social contact is broken
   C. roll over
   D. none of the above

   5.____

6. An infant starts using pincer movement at APPROXIMATELY _____ of age.

   A. five
   B. six
   C. eight
   D. nine

   6.____

7. At what age can a child imitate a number or letter figure? _____ months.

   A. 18
   B. 30
   C. 36
   D. None of the above

   7.____

8. Which of the following is a cognitive milestone achieved by a child at 28 weeks?

   A. Releasing one cube into a cup after demonstration
   B. Raking at a pallet
   C. Uncovering a hidden object
   D. Knowing one or more words and their meanings

   8.____

9. A 3-month-old infant can do all of the following EXCEPT

   A. listen to music
   B. creep-crawl
   C. fail to grasp
   D. sustain social contact

   9.____

10. Unassisted pincer movement develops at the age of _____ months.

    A. four   B. six   C. eight   D. twelve

11. At 6 months of age, developmental milestones do NOT include the child's

    A. putting a pellet into a bottle
    B. releasing two cubes into a cup
    C. scribbling spontaneously
    D. enjoying a simple ball game

12. Which of the following is NOT a normal accomplishment of a child at 18 months of age?

    A. Learning to say *no*
    B. Listening to stories while looking at the pictures
    C. Identifying one or more body parts
    D. Kissing parent with a pucker

13. Normal milestones at 2 months of age include the infant's doing each of the following EXCEPT

    A. reaching at objects
    B. smiling on social contact
    C. attending to voices and coos
    D. following a moving object to 180 visually

14. A 15-month-old child can do all of the following EXCEPT

    A. walk alone
    B. crawl up stairs
    C. imitate a stroke of crayon
    D. make a tower of 3 cubes

15. During the second year of life, weight gain averages _____ kg per year.

    A. 1   B. 2.5   C. 3.5   D. 5

16. During the second year of life, height gain averages APPROXIMATELY _____ centimeters per year.

    A. 2   B. 6   C. 10   D. 15

17. At what age does a child usually reach double the length of his birth length? _____ year(s).

    A. 1   B. 2   C. 3   D. 4

18. A 15-month-old child can make a tower of _____ cubes.

    A. 3   B. 5   C. 7   D. 9

19. A 4-year-old child generally CANNOT

    A. throw a ball   B. climb well
    C. copy a triangle   D. hop on one foot

20. Which of the following is NOT considered a normal motor milestone for a child 3 years of age?

    A. Building a 10-cube tower
    B. Copying a circle
    C. Copying a square
    D. Attempting to draw a person

21. A normally developing 2-year-old child can do all of the following EXCEPT

    A. handle a spoon well
    B. alternate feet while going upstairs
    C. fold paper imitatively
    D. climb on furniture

22. At what age can a child with normal social and cognitive development know his or her own age and sex?
    At _____ months of age.

    A. 18   B. 24   C. 30   D. 36

23. A 3-year-old child can do all of the following EXCEPT

    A. alternate feet while going downstairs
    B. ride a tricycle
    C. hop on one foot
    D. repeat three numbers

24. Nuts, pitted fruits, and popcorn should not be given to a toddler PRIMARILY because they

    A. have almost no food value for a toddler
    B. can cause tooth cavities
    C. will affect the child's appetite
    D. are easily aspirated

25. All of the following statements describe toddlers' well-known sleeping patterns EXCEPT:

    A. Toddlers' sleep needs average 12 hours per day.
    B. A toddler typically discontinues daytime naps around age 3.
    C. A toddler typically sleeps through the night and has at least three daytime naps.
    D. A consistent bedtime ritual helps prepare a toddler for sleep.

26. The one of the following immunizations that is NOT necessary for a toddler to receive is

    A. MMR (measles, mumps, and rubella)
    B. DPT-4, OPV-3 (if not given earlier), PRP-D
    C. HBPV (hemophilus influenzae type B polysaccharide vaccine)
    D. DPT-5, OPV-4

27. Which of the following statements about toddlers' physical growth and development is NOT correct?

    A. Bow-leggedness typically persists through toddlerhood since the legs must bear the weight of the relatively large trunk.
    B. Growth of about 3 inches per year and an average height of 34 inches at age 2 years is normal for toddlers.
    C. Gain of about 4 to 6 lbs. per year and an average weight of 27 lbs. at age 2 years is normal for toddlers.
    D. In toddlers, height and weight increase in a linear fashion.

28. All of the following information about toddlers' psycho-motor milestones is correct EXCEPT:

    A. Sensory changes increase as proximodistal sensations heighten.
    B. The toddler typically begins to walk by age 12 to 15 months, to run by age 2 years, and to walk backward and hop on one foot by age 3 years.
    C. By 24 months of age, a toddler usually achieves fairly good bowel and bladder control.
    D. The toddler usually cannot alternate feet when climbing stairs.

29. All of the following describe normal height and weight changes in children of 3 to 6 years of age EXCEPT:

    A. Gain of 6 to 8 lbs. per year
    B. Average height of 37 inches at age 3, 40 1/2 inches at age 4, and 43 inches at age 5
    C. Growth of 2 1/2 to 3 inches per year
    D. Average weight of 32 lbs. at age 3, 37 lbs. at age 4, and 41 lbs. at age 5

30. Which of the following is NOT a true fact about psycho-motor milestones of children age 3 to 6 years?
    A preschooler

    A. demonstrates increased skill in balancing; by age 4 or 5, he or she can balance on alternate feet with eyes closed
    B. alternates feet when climbing stairs, indicating increased balance and coordination
    C. can successfully perform jobs such as using scissors
    D. is still not skilled enough to tie his or her shoelaces

KEY (CORRECT ANSWERS)

1.	D	16.	B
2.	A	17.	D
3.	C	18.	A
4.	B	19.	C
5.	C	20.	C
6.	D	21.	B
7.	C	22.	D
8.	B	23.	C
9.	B	24.	D
10.	D	25.	C
11.	C	26.	D
12.	B	27.	D
13.	A	28.	C
14.	C	29.	A
15.	B	30.	D

TEST 2

DIRECTIONS: Each question or incomplete statement is followed by several suggested answers or completions. Select the one that BEST answers the question or completes the statement. *PRINT THE LETTER OF THE CORRECT ANSWER IN THE SPACE AT THE RIGHT.*

1. Toys play a useful role in a child's development. All of the following factors should be taken into consideration while selecting a toy for a toddler EXCEPT

   A. expense
   B. durability
   C. safety
   D. weight

2. All of the following are appropriate and important components for disciplining a toddler EXCEPT

   A. distraction
   B. admonishment
   C. explanation
   D. praise

3. Which of the following statements MOST accurately describes the toilet training of a toddler?

   A. Bowel control is accomplished by 18 months.
   B. Daytime bladder control is achieved by 12 to 24 months.
   C. Nightime bladder control is achieved by 24 to 36 months.
   D. Toilet training is usually completed by 4 1/2 years.

4. A toddler's daily nutritional needs from the four basic food groups do NOT include

   A. two servings from the meat group, 2 tablespoons per serving
   B. four servings from the fruit and vegetable group, 2 tablespoons per serving
   C. seven or more servings of breads and cereals, 1 slice of bread or 3/4 to 1 cup of cereal per serving
   D. 3 cups of milk or milk products

5. John and Peter, both 3 years of age, are fighting over a toy train.
   Which of the following interventions would be the MOST appropriate in this situation?

   A. Admonish them for fighting and tell them to share the train.
   B. Tell them to stop fighting and that there are enough toys to play with, and give Peter puzzles.
   C. Without saying anything, take the train away from the boys and place them in separate parts of the room, giving them some other toys to play with.
   D. Find another train and tell them that they can each have one.

6. Which of the following characteristics is NOT typical of a toddler's language development?

   A. Begins to use short sentences at 18 months to 2 years
   B. Can remember and repeat 3 numbers by 3 years
   C. Answers questions with multi-word sentences
   D. After knowing own name by 12 months, gives first name by 24 months and full name by 3 years

7. A child commonly experiences more fears during the preschool period than at any other time.
All of the following are good examples of preschoolers' common fears EXCEPT

   A. being left alone
   B. body mutilation
   C. small animals like rabbits, cats, etc.
   D. objects associated with painful experiences

8. In a conflict situation among preschoolers, which of the following disciplinary principles would be considered the BEST nursing intervention to help the child relieve intensity, regain control, and think about his or her behavior?

   A. Explaining to the child the negative aspects of the conflict
   B. Admonishing the child for the conflict
   C. Distracting the child by providing him with one of the toys he or she likes most
   D. Giving the child a short time-out of 1 minute per year of age

9. All of the following are findings of Freud's theory of psychosexual development of toddlers EXCEPT:

   A. The toddler experiences nothing else but a deep frustration as he or she gains control over containing and releasing bodily waste.
   B. In this stage, the child's focus shifts from the mouth to the anal area, with emphasis on bowel control as he or she gains neuromuscular control over the anal sphincter.
   C. In the *anal stage,* typically extending from age 8 months to 4 years, the erogenous zone is the anus and buttocks, and sexual activity centers on expulsion and retention of bodily waste.
   D. The conflict between *holding on* and *letting go* gradually resolves as bowel training progresses; resolution occurs once control is firmly established.

10. It is NOT true that a toddler of age 15 to 18 months

    A. does not have any signs of temper tantrums yet
    B. walks sideways and backwards
    C. imitates simple things
    D. pulls a toy while walking

11. Which of the following statements about toddlers' play activities is NOT correct?

    A. For a toddler, play is a major socializing medium.
    B. Play typically is parallel - beside rather than with another child.
    C. Push-pull toys help enhance walking skills.
    D. Because of a toddler's long attention span, he or she does not change toys often.

12. Of the following, the INCORRECT statement about toddlers' language and socialization patterns is:

    A. A toddler tends to ask many *what* questions
    B. A toddler typically begins to use longer sentences and has a vocabulary of about 500 words by age 2
    C. A toddler's social interaction is dominated by ritualism, negativism, and independence

D. Confidence in separating from parents continues to grow

13. Common fears of toddlers include all of the following EXCEPT

    A. loss of parents, separation anxiety
    B. stranger anxiety
    C. musical toys' noises
    D. large animals

14. Discipline strategies are affected by a toddler's temperament.
    Which of the following disciplinary approaches would likely be the MOST effective for a *difficult* child?

    A. Sustained eye contact and a stern voice
    B. A friendly warning to curtail activities with structured time-out if necessary
    C. Time for gradual introduction to new situations
    D. A quick spanking with explanation for misbehavior

15. The toddler's feeling that commonly develops after a new baby is born, stemming from a sense of *dethronement* since he or she no longer is the sole focus of his parent's attention, is known as

    A. identification
    B. mitleiden
    C. sibling rivalry
    D. motivation

16. All of the following are considered as important interventions to prevent injuries in toddlers EXCEPT:

    A. Instruct parents to keep crib rails up, place gates across stairways, keep screens secure on all windows, and supervise the toddler at play
    B. Instruct parents never to forget about tightening the car safety belt while riding a toddler around in a car
    C. Teach parents to place all toxic substances up high and locked; secure safety caps on medications; and remove all small, easily aspirated objects from the child's environment
    D. Instruct parents to avoid using table covers to prevent spilling of hot foods or liquids by the child on himself or herself

17. Which of the following statements is NOT part of Piaget's Theory of Cognitive Development of toddlers?

    A. The theory is expressed in two phases, i.e., the Sensorimotor phase and the Preconceptual phase.
    B. The first stage of the Sensorimotor phase explains the primary circular reactions at the age of 12 to 14 months.
    C. The second stage of the Sensorimotor phase explains the beginning of thought at the age of 18 to 24 months, during which time the toddler begins to devise new means for accomplishing tasks through mental calculations.
    D. In the Preconceptual phase, extending from about age 2 to 4 years, the child uses representational thought to recall the past, represent the present, and anticipate the future.

18. According to Kohlberg's Theory of Moral Development of toddlers, moral judgment is a cognitive process that develops gradually at all of these levels EXCEPT the _____ level.

    A. paraconventional
    B. preconventional
    C. conventional
    D. postconventional

19. The Denver Developmental Screening Test (DDST) evaluates a child's _____ development.

    A. social
    B. motor
    C. physical
    D. all of the above

20. According to Erikson's theory of psychosocial development, the toddler begins to master all of the following EXCEPT

    A. individuation
    B. control of bodily functions
    C. control of the sense of autonomy, and moves on to master the task of initiative
    D. acquisition of socially acceptable behavior

21. Kohlberg's Theory of Moral Development for preschoolers does NOT include the finding that

    A. a preschooler is in the preconventional phase of moral development, which extends from 5 to 8 years of age
    B. in this phase, conscience emerges and the emphasis is on external control
    C. a preschooler's preconventional phase of moral development extends from age 4 to 10 years
    D. a preschooler's moral standards are those of others, and he or she observes them either to avoid punishment or to reap rewards

22. Which of the following statements is FALSE concerning the language skills of a preschooler?

    A. A preschooler's vocabulary typically increases to about 1300 words by age 3.
    B. By age 5, a preschooler's vocabulary typically increases to about 2100 words.
    C. A preschooler may talk incessantly and ask many *why* questions.
    D. By age 3, a child usually talks in three- or four-word sentences.

23. Which of the following is considered MOST appropriate to aid gross motor development of a preschooler?

    A. Dress-up clothes
    B. Paints, paper, and crayons
    C. Swimming
    D. Field trips to museums and parks

24. A preschooler needs regular interaction with agemates to help develop _____ skills.

    A. creative
    B. imaginative
    C. motor
    D. social

25. According to Erikson's Theory of Psychosocial Development, between 3 and 6 years of age, a child faces a psycho-social crisis which Erikson terms _____ vs. _____ .

    A. definitive; initiative
    B. initiative; terminative
    C. terminative; fear
    D. initiative; guilt

26. According to Erikson's Theory, the development of a sense of guilt occurs when the child is made to feel that his or her imagination and activities are unacceptable.
Guilt, anxiety, and fear result when the child's thoughts and actions clash with parents'

    A. guilt
    B. fear
    C. anxiety
    D. expectations

27. Freud terms his Theory of Psychosexual Development of Preschoolers all of the following EXCEPT the _____ stage.

    A. phallic
    B. oedipal
    C. oediphallic
    D. all of the above

28. In the phallic stage of Freud's theory, extending from about age 3 to 7, the child's pleasure centers on

    A. the attention given by the parents
    B. friendship with children of the opposite sex
    C. genitalia and masturbation
    D. all of the above

29. Piaget, who defines his Theory of Cognitive Development for preschoolers as a stage of preconceptual thoughts, classifies his theory in two phases, i.e., preconceptual phase and intuitive phase.
He includes all of the following activities in the preconceptual phase, which extends from age 2 to 4, EXCEPT

    A. making simple classifications
    B. reasoning from specific to specific
    C. exhibiting egocentric thinking
    D. forming concepts that are complete and logical

30. According to the intuitive phase of Piaget's theory, which extends from age 4 to 7, it is NOT correct that a preschooler

    A. becomes capable of classifying, quantifying, and relating objects
    B. exhibits intuitive thought processes
    C. is aware of the principles behind classifying and relating objects
    D. uses many words appropriately but without a real knowledge of their meaning

KEY (CORRECT ANSWERS)

1.	A	16.	B
2.	B	17.	B
3.	A	18.	A
4.	C	19.	D
5.	D	20.	C
6.	C	21.	A
7.	C	22.	A
8.	D	23.	C
9.	A	24.	D
10.	A	25.	D
11.	D	26.	D
12.	B	27.	C
13.	C	28.	C
14.	B	29.	D
15.	C	30.	C

EXAMINATION SECTION
TEST 1

DIRECTIONS: Each question or incomplete statement is followed by several suggested answers or completions. Select the one that BEST answers the question or completes the statement. *PRINT THE LETTER OF THE CORRECT ANSWER IN THE SPACE AT THE RIGHT.*

1. In Freud's theory, the aspect of personality that operates according to the pleasure principle is called the

    A. id
    B. ego
    C. superego
    D. unconditioned stimulus

    1._____

2. The soundness with which a test measures what it is intended to measure is referred to as its

    A. validity
    B. reliability
    C. positive correlation
    D. statistical significance

    2._____

3. When two treatments combine to have an effect that is greater than the sum of the individual treatment effects, we say that there is a _____ effect.

    A. main
    B. synergistic
    C. teratogen
    D. developmental systems

    3._____

4. According to psychologist Kurt Lewin, *There is nothing so practical as a good*

    A. fact
    B. theory
    C. assumption
    D. 5-cent cigar

    4._____

5. A researcher designs a study in which he will give candy to one group of children for breakfast, and eggs and cereal to a second group. He then plans to test the children's physical endurance during gym class at 9:30 in the morning.
Regarding this study, we can say that the type of food is the

    A. control variable
    B. dependent variable
    C. independent variable
    D. sample

    5._____

6. In Pavlov's classic experiments with dogs, the bell was the

    A. unconditioned stimulus
    B. conditioned stimulus
    C. unconditioned response
    D. conditioned response

    6._____

7. The practice of rooming-in allows the

    A. father to stay in the hospital room overnight
    B. hospital to double-up on rooms to save costs
    C. mother to stay at home to have the baby
    D. baby to be with the mother whenever the mother wishes

    7._____

8. Which of the following is a statement fundamental to social learning theory?

    A. Many behaviors are learned gradually through shaping.
    B. Many behaviors are learned quickly through observation and imitation (modelling).
    C. The frequency of a desired behavior is affected by rewards contingent on the behavior.
    D. Knowledge is constructed as a result of interaction between the individual and the environment.

    8._____

9. The belief that racial mixing results in inferior offspring is contradicted by the idea of

   A. paradigms
   B. critical periods
   C. hybrid vigor
   D. natural selection

10. Betty Rubin's newborn snuggles near his mom's breast and turns his head several times to find a good nursing position. Just then the phone rings loudly and he startles, throws his arms out and loses his comfortable position. Which two reflexes are illustrated in order of appearance?

    A. Babinski and Moro
    B. Rooting and Moro
    C. Rooting and Babinski
    D. Moro and Babinski

11. When looking at theories and applying them, they are NOT

    A. things that evolve over time
    B. facts
    C. systematic and organized assumptions
    D. affected by the theorist's social context

12. One reason for having a control group in an experimental study is to

    A. keep the children in the experimental group from controlling the outcome
    B. check to see if events external to the study made the experimental group score high or low
    C. see what happens to children who are initially different from the control group
    D. make the experiment a case study

13. A limited time period when rapid development takes place in an organ, a part of the body, or a behavior is referred to as a(n)

    A. age of viability
    B. developmental pull
    C. critical period
    D. pseudodevelopmental phase

14. Mrs. Jann says her new baby wants to learn things just because they are interesting. Who would agree with her?

    A. Freud   B. Skinner   C. Watson   D. Piaget

15. Every gene is a sequence of

    A. somatic cells
    B. trophoblasts
    C. DMA
    D. chorionics

16. An individual's tendency to discount information that is not consistent with what he or she already believes is an example of

    A. negation bias
    B. confirmatory bias
    C. blind procedure
    D. construct validity

17. During the first half of the 20th century, there were a number of movements designed to improve humankind by eliminating, sterilizing, or forbidding marriage to individuals perceived to be inferior. These are classified as

    A. ego-defense
    B. classical conditioning
    C. social interactionist
    D. eugenics

18. Reflexes such as rooting, Babinski, Moro, and tonic neck   18.____
    A. develop slowly during the neonatal and infancy periods
    B. replace the voluntary movements made by infants at birth
    C. begin to appear after neonates are able to maintain a normal body temperature
    D. are typically replaced by voluntary behaviors during the first year of life

19. Piaget indicated that babies know about the world through their interactions with objects. 19.____
    He called this

    A. object reality
    B. object permanence
    C. sensorimotor intelligence
    D. state interaction

20. Which of the following statements is based on a *behavioral* view of child development?   20.____

    A. Children seek stimulation.
    B. You may play with your toys after you have cleaned up your room.
    C. Children need to work out their emotional conflicts through dramatic play.
    D. Leave her alone; she'll grow out of it.

21. Alcohol and cigarette smoke are examples of environmental agents that adversely affect   21.____
    prenatal development. They are called

    A. anoxias   B. perinatals
    C. surrogates   D. teratogens

22. Which of the following is an important focus in the development systems approach to   22.____
    child development?

    A. Mutual interaction throughout many levels of organization
    B. Neurological maturation
    C. Equilibration
    D. Progression from one stage to the next

23. Which of the following is NOT an example of a social biological effect?   23.____
    A

    A. child's exposure to high levels of lead resulting in a lowered IQ
    B. child born with fetal alcohol syndrome
    C. child who develops a fear of dogs after being bitten
    D. man living near Chernobyl whose sperm have chromosomal damage

24. A child who is learning soccer skills might be guided through the zone of proximal devel- 24.____
    opment by

    A. having the child practice with a more skilled peer
    B. receiving a reinforcement for each skill level mastered
    C. exposure to unconditioned stimuli
    D. shaping successive approximations to the target behavior

25. Do infants who sleep separately from their mothers grow up to be more independent 25._____
    than those who sleep with their mothers?

    A. Yes
    B. No
    C. There is no research on this
    D. There is no definitive answer according to research done

---

KEY (CORRECT ANSWERS)

1. A	11. B
2. A	12. B
3. B	13. C
4. B	14. D
5. C	15. C
6. B	16. B
7. D	17. D
8. B	18. D
9. C	19. C
10. B	20. B

21. D
22. A
23. C
24. A
25. D

TEST 2

DIRECTIONS: Each question or incomplete statement is followed by several suggested answers or completions. Select the one that BEST answers the question or completes the statement. *PRINT THE LETTER OF THE CORRECT ANSWER IN THE SPACE AT THE RIGHT.*

1. Depth perception is

    A. formed from concepts
    B. learned by habituation
    C. innate
    D. modeled from parents

    1._____

2. Grammatical errors are common in the language of preschoolers. Which of the following is appropriate advice for how to handle grammatical errors?

    A. Use a direct approach by saying *No,* then telling them how they should say the sentence
    B. With each error, ask a question about what the child said, using the correct use of the word in the question
    C. Say, *Please try saying that sentence again*
    D. Listen for content and use the correct grammar in conversational responses to the child

    2._____

3. The Chess and Thomas longitudinal study of easy, difficult, and slow-to-warm-up children suggests that the _____ is critical for successful child rearing.

    A. goodness-of-fit between child temperament and parental interaction styles
    B. genetic temperament of the child matters more than the initial parenting style
    C. initial parenting style matters more than the early temperament of the child
    D. child's genetics and peer group

    3._____

4. Preschooler Seth Thomas is counting a dozen blocks on the table. He touches them all, some twice, and ends up with a count of 15. What kind of counting error is he making?

    A. Coordination
    B. Hierarchical
    C. Partitioning
    D. Tagging

    4._____

5. Which of the following is NOT a good example of functional autonomy?

    A. Brushing your teeth
    B. Good manners
    C. Bulimia
    D. Breathing

    5._____

6. Which of the following is most likely to promote locomotor development in 4-month-old infants?

    A. Placing them in a stomach-down prone position on the floor
    B. Laying them on their backs and encouraging spontaneous leg exercises
    C. Providing lots of pillows to permit climbing and more upright positioning
    D. Stimulating after 6 months since development isn't facilitated until then

    6._____

7. The degree to which a 9-month-old exhibits stranger anxiety can be reduced by

    A. the mother being in constant contact with her baby
    B. the child's inability to crawl or walk away
    C. social referencing
    D. social games

    7._____

8. According to a research study, when mothers brought their babies in for a doctor's examination, it was found that the group of mothers who stood closest to their babies had more early contact with their children. It is difficult to argue that this means that these mothers had bonded better with their children because the outcome measure lacks _____ validity.

   A. predictive
   B. face
   C. external
   D. internal

9. Which of the following are characteristics of infant-directed or child-directed speech (CDS)?

   A. More narrow pitch range
   B. Less contrast between high and low pitches
   C. Longer pauses between words
   D. All of the above

10. According to analysis of Maccoby's study on infants' babbling, does babbling relate to or predict later intelligence?

    A. *Yes,* for boys only
    B. *Yes,* for girls only
    C. *Yes,* for both boys and girls
    D. *No*; when boys and girls are separated, there is no relation

11. Which of the following is the most noticeable change in appearance during the preschool years?

    A. Protruding stomach
    B. Rapid growth of legs and trunk
    C. Fast growth in height
    D. Weight gained faster than during year one

12. During the preschool years, there are many changes in motor development. Which of the following is NOT an accurate statement about motor development changes?

    A. Fine motor development of the fingers allows marked improvement in coloring, cutting, and pasting.
    B. Because their center of gravity moves up, they are more coordinated in climbing and jumping.
    C. Jumping ability improves markedly in part due to thrusting their arms forward rather than *winging* their arms in a jump.
    D. In climbing ladders and jungle gyms, there is a change from marked-time climbing to alternating feet.

13. Which of the following was found to be a productive way to overcome attachment difficulties between mothers and babies during the first year of life?

    A. Trying to get the baby to imitate the mother's actions
    B. Soliciting the baby's attention when he looked away
    C. Teaching the mother to choose appropriate responses to the baby's signals
    D. Teaching the mother to plan a regular schedule of activities in order to establish a routine with the infant

14. In number conservation tasks, most preschoolers judge which row has more objects by

    A. the length of the row
    B. counting the objects in the display
    C. making another row that is identical to the first and counting objects as they make the second row
    D. compensation

15. By 6 years of age, when most children enter first grade, their vocabularies range from about _____ words.

    A. 3,000-6,000
    B. 7,000-9,000
    C. 10,000-14,000
    D. 15,000-20,000

16. Baby Shemirah now has the ability to imagine actions in her head. Piaget would say that this ability allows a strong concept of

    A. object permanence
    B. imagination
    C. habituation
    D. fixation

17. A significantly slower than average rate of growth that is due to feeding and caregiving problems rather than to disease or heredity is termed

    A. encropresis
    B. failure-to-thrive
    C. slow-growth syndrome
    D. maturational lag

18. Two-month-old baby Watson looks longer at his own mother than he does at the occasional sitter, visiting grandma, or the bookmobile delivery woman. This recognition is based upon his mother's

    A. facial features
    B. hairline
    C. eye contact
    D. voice cues

19. At age 11 months, Missy started saying *da-da* rather than her usual *dadadada*. According to developmental linguists, she is now

    A. overextending
    B. babbling
    C. modifying
    D. using a protoword

20. Peter and his younger sister Sally were playing *house,* Peter told Sally to set the table while he cooked the turkey, showing her how to count the forks and napkins. Then he asked her to think of a good desert.
    Peter is _____ his sister's pretend play abilities.

    A. categorizing
    B. scaffolding
    C. modeling
    D. decentrizing

21. Jill can't take another point of view and tells you what the child sitting on the other side of the mountain can see. Piaget would say that she is

    A. hierarchical
    B. self-centered
    C. identity-bound
    D. egocentric

22. Many 3-year-old children were quite frightened by the dinosaur movie, JURASSIC PARK. 22.____
The reason is that younger children

    A. can't centrate on film
    B. can't distinguish appearance from reality
    C. have highly tuned emotional systems
    D. have too much imagination

23. Which of the following is supported by research on infant and toddler development? 23.____

    A. The weight of the brain's cortex is unaffected by environmental factors.
    B. It is fairly easy to separate the effects of malnourishment and stimulation deprivation.
    C. About 10% of the adult's brain weight develops during the first two years.
    D. A stimulating environment can produce more growth of brain cells.

24. Selma is 3 years old. Her dad has read TEDDY BEAR, TEDDY BEAR to her many times. 24.____
Now Selma can *read* it aloud with inflection, even though she isn't actually reading the
words. Selma is a(n) _____ reader.

    A. beginning   B. coded
    C. emergent   D. syllabic

25. Which of the following is true concerning hearing problems in infants? 25.____

    A. It is difficult for infants to learn sign language.
    B. When deaf children learn sign language, they learn it at a slower rate than hearing children learn oral language.
    C. If infants make vocal sounds, they must be able to hear them.
    D. Infants learning sign language babble in sign just as hearing infants babble orally.

KEY (CORRECT ANSWERS)

1. C	11. B
2. D	12. B
3. A	13. C
4. C	14. A
5. D	15. C
6. A	16. A
7. C	17. B
8. B	18. B
9. C	19. D
10. B	20. B

21. D
22. B
23. D
24. C
25. D

TEST 3

DIRECTIONS: Each question or incomplete statement is followed by several suggested answers or completions. Select the one that BEST answers the question or completes the statement. *PRINT THE LETTER OF THE CORRECT ANSWER IN THE SPACE AT THE RIGHT.*

1. Kohlberg called the first level of moral development *preconventional*. At this level, children make moral decisions

    A. based on what is expected of them by society
    B. based on a simple set of philosophical principles
    C. on the basis of self-interest
    D. on the basis of living up to what close family members expect of them

    1.____

2. The ability to attend to the form rather than the meaning of language is called

    A. phonological awareness
    B. metalinguistic awareness
    C. multisyllabic interpretations
    D. word boundary interpretations

    2.____

3. Emotions can have positive or negative natures. This is called the

    A. target   B. valence   C. surrogate   D. polarity

    3.____

4. Which of the following illustrates the secular growth trend?

    A. April is an Olympic champion in running and hasn't begun her menstrual period, even at age 15.
    B. June is very uncomfortable with her transition to adulthood based mainly on her individual perceptions.
    C. August is beginning her menstrual period at age 11, and her great-grandmother, who didn't begin until 15, is quite concerned.
    D. October is not faring very well in academics or social situations and her doctor wants her checked for secondary characteristics.

    4.____

5. Carl has not seen the word *unbending* before, but he knows what *bending* means. Since he also understands *un*, he will be able to figure out what *unbending* means by

    A. understanding the word from its grammatical structure
    B. inferring word meaning from morphological knowledge
    C. learning from the suffix information
    D. getting the meaning from context

    5.____

6. When Maria finally realizes that she will always be a girl, even if she cuts her hair or changes her clothes, we say she has achieved

    A. gender identity   B. gender constancy
    C. gender typing   D. sex-role structure

    6.____

7. Why does Piaget label the thinking of school-age children as *concrete operational*?

    A. As long as they can see what they are talking about, or are familiar with it, they can think logically.
    B. While they cannot think abstractly, they can cement abstract ideas together if they make sense.
    C. Since the structure is basic or concrete, the thinking process can only be basic.
    D. They can juggle variables and contemplate possibilities about situations that exist only in their minds.

8. In the 3-kinds-of-memory-store model, which memory is our *working memory*?

    A. Sensory   B. Long-term
    C. Short-term   D. Intermediate

9. Carrie, a third grade girl, according to the research on beliefs and expectations is most likely to

    A. respond to failure by increasing her efforts
    B. believe that when she fails, she can expect more reinforcement from her teacher
    C. attribute failure to a lack of ability
    D. attribute her poor performance to nonintellectual aspects of her work

10. Race was examined as a risk factor in Sameroff's study because

    A. research has demonstrated that children from different races vary in their risk-taking behavior
    B. race is related to many negative outcomes in our society, even if it does not cause them
    C. minority children mature earlier, which puts them at risk
    D. experiments have demonstrated a causal relationship between race and cognitive performance

11. In regard to socialization and moral development, _____ is the process whereby adult values are adopted as the child's own, and _____ explains why the child adopts, the characteristics of the same-sex parent.

    A. social responsiveness; proximity seeking
    B. proximity seeking; social responsiveness
    C. identification; internalization
    D. internalization; identification

12. Cleo's dad decided to ignore Cleo's whining about not wanting to go to bed. Eventually she stopped whining. One night she smiled as she was putting on her pajamas, and her dad said, *My, I do like to see those nice bedtime smiles*. Cleo became happier about bedtime.
    Her clever dad first used a(n) _____ procedure, then a(n) _____ procedure.

    A. social cognition; reinforcement
    B. extinction; reinforcement
    C. extinction; exhortation
    D. social cognition; exhortation

13. Sternberg's triarchic theory of intelligence differentiates between which three aspects of mental ability?

    A. Verbal, quantitative, analytical
    B. Analytical, creative, practical
    C. Logical-mathematical, bodily-kinesthetic, interpersonal
    D. Memory, convergent, divergent

14. _____ are the primary engines of development,

    A. Chaos and individualism
    B. Continuity and change
    C. Proximal processes
    D. Peer groups

15. What is the level of intelligence for most ADHD children?

    A. Above normal
    B. Normal
    C. Below normal
    D. No data available

16. Which of the following best describes brain growth during the school-age years?

    A. Brain weight equals adult levels by age 6.
    B. Brain myelination is complete by age 7.
    C. Brain lateralization begins at age 6.
    D. The head grows quickly during the school-age years.

17. Sally is going through tremendous physical changes and is increasing in height and weight very quickly. However, she has not yet reached menarche.
    What term do we give to this period of development?

    A. Puberty
    B. Juvenescence
    C. Pubescence
    D. Presexagesimal

18. Changes that occurred in diary recordings from the late 19th century to the early 20th century were from
    I. no explicit sexual content in entries in the 19th century to entries discussing heterosexual and homosexual behaviors in the 20th century
    II. strong family loyalty apparent in entries in the 19th century to disregard for parents and thoughts of running away in the 20th century
    III. entries planning to make alterations in one's character in the 19th century to plans to make alterations in one's outer appearances in the 20th century

    The CORRECT answer is:

    A. I only   B. II only   C. I, III   D. I, II, III

19. Over the course of this century, the ratio of youths to adults has

    A. steadily increased
    B. steadily decreased
    C. both decreased and increased
    D. mirrored the secular growth trend

20. Which of the following is a secondary sex characteristic?

    A. Ovulation
    B. Menstruation
    C. Axillary hair
    D. Muscle development

21. Some data shows that little girls don't imitate Batman and Power Rangers nearly as much as little boys do. According to Bandura, this occurs because

    A. girls are innately less aggressive
    B. boys have more imagination
    C. girls don't perceive themselves as similar to the models
    D. boys don't want to be perceived as *sissies*

22. Sue's preschool teacher said to her, *You're spending so much time on those drawings, and they are so colorful! Won't they look niee on the art wall!* Sue sees herself as an artist, and returns to the painting area every day. Her teacher has used

    A. verbal prompting   B. response cost
    C. positive attribution   D. social cognizing

23. Studies of children who have been exposed to violence show all but one of the following:

    A. Exposure to violence decreases children's future orientation
    B. Real news on television helps children to understand that violence is not a major threat
    C. Children's confidence is declining for believing that adults can protect them from violence
    D. Children are becoming desensitive to violence

24. What does current research point to as the primary problem in dyslexia?

    A. Language processing   B. Vision problems
    C. Visual-motor problems   D. Low intelligence

25. Arnold Sameroff's study of the accumulation of risk factors shows that

    A. each accumulation of an additional risk factor in a child's environment was related to an equal decrease in the child's later IQ
    B. categorical programs are likely to be the most successful at dealing with the accumulation of risk factors
    C. some risk factors put a child at much greater risk for a decreased IQ than others
    D. children with one or two risk factors had only slightly lower later IQs than those with no risk factors

KEY (CORRECT ANSWERS)

1. C
2. B
3. B
4. C
5. B

6. B
7. A
8. C
9. C
10. B

11. D
12. B
13. B
14. C
15. B

16. A
17. C
18. C
19. C
20. C

21. C
22. C
23. B
24. A
25. D

EXAMINATION SECTION
TEST 1

DIRECTIONS: Each question or incomplete statement is followed by several suggested answers or completions. Select the one that BEST answers the question or completes the statement. *PRINT THE LETTER OF THE CORRECT ANSWER IN THE SPACE AT THE RIGHT.*

1. Which one of the following statements is TRUE with respect to the development of language ability?

    A. Boys tend to talk a little earlier than girls.
    B. Twins tend to talk earlier than single children.
    C. The amount of stimulation in the home environment is a relatively unimportant factor in the development of language.
    D. Children who talk earliest generally prove to be most intelligent when tested at a later age.

    1.____

2. Which of the following statements is LEAST likely to be TRUE of first-grade children as compared with fifth graders?

    A. There is much concern for group welfare and group approval.
    B. There is little concern for order and neatness.
    C. Some regular routines give security to children of this age.
    D. There is little intermingling of boys and girls in their play activities.

    2.____

3. Reasoning begins to develop in children during the period of the _____ years.

    A. pre-school
    B. primary school
    C. intermediate school
    D. high school

    3.____

4. Growth

    A. is saltatory
    B. proceeds most rapidly during the adolescent years
    C. follows an orderly genetic sequence in the emergence of behavior patterns
    D. depends entirely on maturation

    4.____

5. When the individual perceives relationships, observes which things belong together, and which things do not, or observes the relation between means and ends, he is said to

    A. introspect
    B. remember
    C. learn by "insight"
    D. possess eidetic imagery

    5.____

6. Investigators have found a small but consistent superiority of females over males in _____ ability.

    A. artistic
    B. linguistic
    C. arithmetical
    D. reasoning

    6.____

7. Mental development and physical development are _____ correlated.

    A. highly
    B. perfectly
    C. only very slightly
    D. not in the least

    7.____

8. Which of the following statements is MOST in agreement with modern theories of child development? Growth is a(n)

   A. continuous process, uniform in rate
   B. continuous process, but it is not uniform in rate
   C. predictable process, but so highly individual that group generalizations should not be attempted
   D. unpredictable process in which patterns are difficult to establish

9. Generally, which of the following influences exerts the GREATEST impact on the development of the self-concept in fifteen-year-old individuals?

   A. Acceptance by their friends and classmates
   B. Acceptance by their teachers
   C. Ideals and aspirations
   D. Knowledge of their abilities from school experiences

10. In comparing boys and girls as to the period of peak body growth, called the "prepuberal growth spurt," it can be said that, on the average,

    A. girls precede boys by about eighteen months
    B. the phenomenon occurs in both sexes at about the same time
    C. boys precede girls by about one year
    D. girls precede boys by about six months

11. As a child grows older, outwardly visible signs of emotion become

    A. more intense
    B. more common
    C. less frequent
    D. less important

12. Fairy tales are MOST popular with children whose age is

    A. 3 years
    B. 5 years
    C. 7 years
    D. 9 years

13. Of the following, the MOST suitable active game for seven-year-old children is

    A. London Bridge
    B. Looby-Loo
    C. dodge ball
    D. Cobbler, Mend My Shoe

14. All of the following are characteristic of the typical four-year-old EXCEPT

    A. his attention span is short
    B. his coordination is not well-developed
    C. he is not likely to be interested in people
    D. he is not likely to share things with other children

15. Of the following physical characteristics of the pre-kindergarten child, the one which is INCORRECT is that he

    A. begins to develop small muscle control
    B. is susceptible to communicable diseases
    C. is usually near-sighted
    D. needs frequent rest

16. Of the following, the GREATEST factor in the motor development of a five-year-old child is 16.____

    A. steady practice
    B. mental ability
    C. maturation
    D. home environment

17. Of the following, the statement which BEST describes the child of kindergarten age is that he 17.____

    A. is adept at projecting himself into other places and times
    B. is incapable of any flights of imagination
    C. seldom questions anything in his physical environment
    D. is bound to the here and now by his stage of organic development, as well as by his limited experience

18. Of the following, the PRIME reason why five-year-olds are often willing to share their things is that they 18.____

    A. seek adult approval
    B. have no interest in possessions
    C. have no use for them
    D. prefer companions to possessions

19. Research tends to show that all of the following are TRUE of development of language in children of pre-school and elementary school age EXCEPT that 19.____

    A. girls tend to be poorer than boys in clarity of enunciation and freedom from speech defects
    B. the number of basic words known increases by several thousands per year
    C. the length of responses tends to increase with the age of the child
    D. the average length of sentences spoken by girls is greater than it is for boys of the same age

20. Of the following, the natural sequence of language growth is 20.____

    A. listening, reading, speaking, writing
    B. reading, listening, speaking, writing
    C. listening, speaking, reading, writing
    D. listening, speaking, writing, reading

21. Of the following parts of speech, the one which predominates in the vocabulary of a child beginning to speak is 21.____

    A. adjectives
    B. nouns
    C. verbs
    D. pronouns

22. All of the following are known for writings in the area of child growth and development EXCEPT 22.____

    A. Frances Ilg
    B. Anna B. Comstock
    C. Arnold Gesell
    D. Maria Montessori

23. All of the following are characteristic of the average seven-year-old EXCEPT that he 23.____

    A. likes to bat and pitch a ball
    B. fits easily into organized group play

C. enjoys alternate periods of activity and inactivity
D. shows more interest in some activities and tries fewer new ventures than the four-year-old

24. All of the following statements regarding language arts in early childhood education are true EXCEPT

    A. if a number of children wander away while the teacher is reading a story, it may be that they have had too many sedentary activities that day
    B. storytelling - as opposed to story reading - should be undertaken only when the teacher feels she is unable to read the story with sufficient dramatic expression to maintain the children's interest
    C. listening to rhythmic poetry affords much enjoyment to young children
    D. the line between fantasy and reality is generally not sharply defined in the mind of the four-year-old child

25. All of the following statements concerning social relationships in the early school years are usually true EXCEPT

    A. groups are small and shift rapidly
    B. friends are selected because of propinquity and the accident of sharing objects
    C. children play and work with others to satisfy personal rather than social desires
    D. friends are selected on the basis of belonging to the same sex

26. In general, the language development of girls is

    A. more rapid than that of boys
    B. less rapid than that of boys
    C. equal to that of boys
    D. more rapid than that of boys in oral communication, but slower in written communication

27. Defense mechanisms are used

    A. *most frequently* by average children
    B. *less frequently* by slow learners than by average children
    C. *more frequently* by slow learners than by average children
    D. *by all children* regardless of level of ability

28. Research in child development shows that all children have

    A. a single, fixed design of growth
    B. individual potentialities for various patterns of growth
    C. equal abilities for growth in all areas
    D. no consistent growth patterns

29. The period designated as "early childhood"

    A. is a period when memory is high
    B. is a time of very rapid growth
    C. is relatively unimportant so far as learning is concerned
    D. is a time when there is little change in physical structure

30. Of the following, the one MOST characteristic of the normally developing adolescent is   30.____

    A. continuous need for parental support
    B. development of emotional maturity
    C. desire for constant domination by siblings
    D. freedom from peer group identification

31. The normal child on entering school knows the meaning of about   31.____

    A. 500 words   B. 1,000 words
    C. 2,000 words   D. 3,000 words

32. For a four-year-old child, the events of the present are   32.____

    A. less vivid than those of the past
    B. less vivid than those of the future
    C. more vivid than those of the past or future
    D. as vivid as those of the past or future

33. The EARLIEST aesthetic experiences of the young child are likely to occur in play with   33.____

    A. blocks and paints
    B. games and toys
    C. swings, see-saws, and sliding ponds
    D. kitchen and household utensils

34. Of the following characteristics of child development, the one MOST closely related to the 10-12 age group is   34.____

    A. difficulty with gross motor coordination
    B. eagerness for peer approval
    C. anxiety to please the teacher
    D. interest in the immediate environment

35. The one of the following which is a psychological principle which can BEST be described as a situation in which an individual experiences some ambivalence and indecisiveness in choosing one or more desired objects or goals is   35.____

    A. task-orientation   B. conflict
    C. apathy   D. projection

36. The treatment method which allows or encourages the client to express his charged feelings around a pressing emotional need is known as   36.____

    A. exploring   B. synthesizing
    C. catharsis   D. ventilating

37. The emotional release that results from recall of a previously forgotten painful experience is known as   37.____

    A. introjection   B. abreaction
    C. sublimation   D. free association

38. The action whereby an individual directs his aggression against an innocent bystander rather than expressing it against the source of his difficulties is called

    A. displacement
    B. projection
    C. introjection
    D. abreaction

39. An attempt to attribute emotionally caused behavior to reasonable factors MORE acceptable to the individual is known as

    A. projection
    B. rationalization
    C. introjection
    D. free association

40. The unconscious application of elements of the experiences in a former relationship to a new relationship is known as

    A. projection
    B. abreaction
    C. transference
    D. sublimation

41. In reference to learning, most children will tend to set goals for themselves which are

    A. similar to those of their peers
    B. different from those of their peers
    C. too difficult or complex
    D. too easy or too low

42. Children involved in initial learning tend to do significantly better on problems where the rule or principle is

    A. given or stated
    B. independently derived
    C. minimized
    D. neglected

43. Studies of sensory deprivation during infancy indicate that lack of stimulation during this period is most likely to result in

    A. low frustration tolerance
    B. poor psychomotor coordination
    C. lack of emotional responsiveness
    D. delayed intellectual development

44. When do coordination and convergence of the eyes begin to develop in the infant?

    A. Immediately after birth
    B. After one week
    C. After two weeks
    D. After three weeks

45. In the IOWA studies of children's reactions to frustration, which one of the following reactions was LEAST observed?

    A. Regression
    B. Aggression
    C. Resignation
    D. Accommodation

46. Dick, who is 14 years old, has been given a curfew of midnight. Arriving home at 2:30 A.M., he explains his decision to come in late was based on the fact that everyone his age stays out that late. He is using

    A. compensation
    B. denial
    C. displacement
    D. rationalization

47. By virtue of his earlier interaction with his mother, a child may display affectional responses to other adults.
    This is an example of

    A. secondary reinforcement
    B. stimulus generalization
    C. response diffusion
    D. learned mediation

48. Which one of the following BEST illustrates the distinction between "performance" and "competence" as drawn by contemporary psycholinguists?

    A. A child can vocalize before he can speak.
    B. A child's motor development depends upon language acquisition.
    C. A child is more limited in language production than in language comprehension.
    D. A child acquires language to meet his need to function as an effective person.

49. Bruner and Page, among others, contend that children can learn anything that adults can. Ausubel, in his writings,

    A. extends the contention
    B. modifies the contention
    C. rejects the contention
    D. supports the contention

50. An 8-year-old pupil is told by his teacher that he cannot join his group in play because he needs to practice writing. The boy starts crying, drops to the floor, sobs heavily and strikes the floor with hands and legs. The behavior exhibited by the boy is an example of

    A. repression
    B. identification
    C. aggression
    D. regression

KEY (CORRECT ANSWERS)

1. D	11. C	21. B	31. B	41. A
2. A	12. C	22. B	32. C	42. A
3. A	13. C	23. B	33. A	43. D
4. C	14. C	24. B	34. B	44. A
5. C	15. C	25. A	35. B	45. D
6. B	16. C	26. A	36. D	46. D
7. C	17. D	27. D	37. B	47. B
8. B	18. A	28. B	38. A	48. C
9. A	19. A	29. B	39. B	49. C
10. A	20. C	30. B	40. C	50. D

EXAMINATION SECTION
TEST 1

DIRECTIONS: Each question or incomplete statement is followed by several suggested answers or completions. Select the one that BEST answers the question or completes the statement. *PRINT THE LETTER OF THE CORRECT ANSWER IN THE SPACE AT THE RIGHT.*

1. Of the following, the area of greatest similarity among children is in their

    A. inherited traits
    B. rates of development
    C. sequences of development
    D. patterns of growth dimensions
    E. perceptual and conceptual development

    1.____

2. Of the following, which is the MOST significant factor in determining the choice of friends among children between the ages of six and ten?

    A. Mutual interests
    B. Similar personality traits
    C. Conveniently close location
    D. Social and economic standing of parents
    E. Physical maturity

    2.____

3. Joe Flirp is a great health education teacher, to a large extent, because the boys model themselves after him. The foregoing illustrates the psychological mechanism of

    A. sublimation   B. displacement
    C. regression   D. identification
    E. projection

    3.____

4. "You're much too authoritarian," said the principal to the teacher. "And I won't stand for that in my school." The principal is demonstrating the psychological mechanism of

    A. sublimation   B. conversion
    C. projection   D. identification
    E. displaced aggression

    4.____

5. Margaret Snorble, unhappy because of her lack of friendship, devoted all her energy to studying. She became the number one student in her grade. Margaret is demonstrating the psychological mechanism of

    A. sublimation   B. conversion
    C. introjection   D. fantasy
    E. rationalization

    5.____

6. Joanie asked for apple pie and was told that there was none left. "Oh well," said she, "give me peach pie. I like it better anyway." Joanie is demonstrating the psychological mechanism of

    A. regression   B. displacement
    C. rationalization   D. sublimation
    E. recidivism

    6.____

7. The principal had just left after telling Miss Jones she had to improve the quality of her lesson plans. Tears came to her eyes; she stamped her foot several times, pounded on the desk and then broke into uncontrolled sobbing. Miss Jones' behavior is an example of the psychological mechanism of

   A. introjection
   B. projection
   C. sublimation
   D. regression
   E. displaced hostility

8. Of the following statements concerning praise and punishment, which is LEAST in accord with modern psychological principles?

   A. When a child is bad, spank him.
   B. When a child is bad, say, "If you're not good, I won't love you any more."
   C. When a child is good, give him something to show your approval.
   D. When a child is good, say, "That's O.K. Let's try to do better next time."
   E. When a child is good, do not over-reinforce him.

9. Defining personality as the end-product of our habit systems expresses a concept most characteristic of a psychological orientation termed

   A. behavioristic
   B. psychoanalytic
   C. Gestalt
   D. personalistic
   E. structuralistic

10. Studies on intelligence and creativity have yielded findings which indicate that

    A. the two characteristics are completely independent
    B. they are independent for subjects of high average ability and above
    C. they are negatively correlated
    D. for all practical purposes, measuring one trait is essentially the same as measuring the other
    E. the two characteristics vary in pattern, depending on the particular individual being tested

11. A five-year-old is walking with his father and notes that there is a full moon. He says, "Daddy, the moon is following us." What type of thinking is exemplified by the child's comment?

    A. Syncretism
    B. Centralism
    C. Autism
    D. Primatism
    E. Egocentrism

12. The process whereby an individual develops great sympathy towards another in order to conceal from himself certain malicious feelings toward this person, is known as

    A. rationalization
    B. intropunitiveness
    C. extrapunitiveness
    D. reaction formation
    E. introjection

13. Paranoia is best understood in terms of the mechanism of

    A. projection
    B. regression
    C. hostility
    D. reaction formation
    E. sublimation

14. The MOST practicable procedure yet found to identify persons who are not giving honest answers in a personality inventory is to

    A. include a set of items which sound good but which few honest persons would answer in the "good" direction
    B. repeat the inventory at a later date
    C. check the consistency of the response to different items
    D. tell the individual to try to make himself appear normal, then neurotic
    E. repeat certain questions in slightly different form throughout the test

15. Johnny, a twelve-year-old handicapped child, suddenly begins to suck his thumb and wet his bed soon after his newborn brother is brought home from the hospital. This psychological mechanism is known as

    A. introjection
    B. sublimation
    C. repression
    D. regression
    E. compensation

16. Six- and seven-year-old children are interested primarily in stories about

    A. family and school activities
    B. fairies and elves
    C. adventures on land and sea
    D. science and nature
    E. cowboys and Indians

17. The use of rewards is MOST productive in learning to the extent that they

    A. are concrete
    B. are used economically
    C. are delayed
    D. correspond to the work that has been done
    E. fulfill a need of the learner

18. In order to increase the chances that learned responses will be applied to new problem situations, the teacher should attempt, whenever possible, to

    A. provide clear objectives
    B. use concrete materials
    C. generalize patterns of response
    D. integrate subject matter areas
    E. use examples from everyday life

19. The pupil's readiness for any learning situation is the sum of all his characteristics which make him more likely to respond one way than another. Of these characteristics, the MOST important one generally is his

    A. interests
    B. physical health
    C. previous experience
    D. maturity
    E. perceptivity

20. It is generally assumed by clinical psychologists that the MOST serious behavior problems are manifested by children who

A. are most retarded B. are most withdrawn
C. are most aggressive D. cannot read
E. are overly dependent

21. Finger painting is enjoyed by many children. As a mechanism of adjustment, interest in finger painting may be looked upon as a form of

   A. projection B. conversion
   C. self-expression D. sublimation
   E. displacement

22. Personal problems in adjustment are MOST likely to arise in adolescent groups of

   A. early maturing girls and boys
   B. late maturing girls and boys
   C. early maturing girls and late maturing boys
   D. late maturing girls and early maturing boys
   E. all early and late maturing girls and boys

23. In establishing identity and sex role, the adolescent is MOST likely to be influenced by

   A. parents B. siblings
   C. peers D. ministers
   E. movie and baseball stars

24. Which one of the following judgments about parent-teenager relationships is FALSE?

   A. A parent's approval of work well done and overt pride in his child's accomplishment mean a great deal to the teenager, even though the latter may make light of it.
   B. To enhance ultimately the young person's self-respect, it is a good idea to criticize and question him as much as possible.
   C. Giving a teenager abundant opportunity to relate with a group has a positive effect on his school achievement.
   D. A parent's recognition and appreciation of good school progress, without exerting heavy pressure, serves to aid in maintaining this good record of accomplishment.
   E. A parent's realization that a major aspect of adolescent social development is the shift in interest and involvement from the family to the outside, with a concomitant desire and need for independence.

25. In learning theory terms, the psychoanalytic mechanism of displacement may be seen as an illustration of

   A. reinforcement B. discrimination
   C. extinction D. generalization
   E. assimilation

26. When an illness is described as psychosomatic, it means that the symptoms

   A. are psychological, but physiological factors contribute
   B. are physiological, but psychological factors contribute
   C. and all contributing factors are psychological
   D. and all contributing factors are physiological
   E. are both physiological and psychological

27. Most pronounced cases of bullying and aggressiveness are the result of efforts on the child's part to

A. impress adults with his strength
B. gain the attention of those around him
C. reach a level of achievement that is beyond him
D. compensate for deep feelings of inadequacy
E. create a "real-self" which corresponds to an "ideal-self"

28. Suzanne has received more votes than any other girl for student senate member. If she is typical of most of the girls who win this kind of recognition, she probably differs MOST from the average girl in the school in   28.____

    A. being emotionally more mature and balanced
    B. showing less competitive and aggressive tendencies
    C. making innovations without permission
    D. exhibiting more concern for herself and less awareness of the needs and problems of others
    E. being somewhat superior in aptitude and achievement

29. "I know what my parents expect of me; I know what teachers demand. I know what the other fellows in my crowd want me to do. I have a dim idea of what my girl wants from me. But I don't know what I want for myself." This statement illustrates the central adolescent problem of   29.____

    A. configuration
    B. peer group conformity
    C. acculturation
    D. introspection and inversion
    E. identity

30. The imaginative transposing of oneself into the thinking, feeling, and acting of another, and so structuring the world as he does, is an accurate definition of   30.____

    A. empathy   B. rapport
    C. conditioning   D. exclusion
    E. projection

31. A common change in the personality defenses of the adolescent child is the development of   31.____

    A. greater intellectualism and isolation of affect
    B. a tendency toward avoidance and denial
    C. suspicion and withdrawal
    D. repression and depression
    E. greater empathy and awareness of others

32. Tom has applied for several college scholarships, but has not obtained any. He says that none of the colleges really examine the candidates carefully or fairly. Which defense mechanism is he manifesting? That of   32.____

    A. rationalization   B. projection
    C. sublimation   D. repression
    E. introspection

33. When a person says, "I am so fond of you," when you know he actually dislikes you, there is reason to suspect that he is using the defense mechanism of   33.____

A. introjection B. projection
C. rationalization D. compensation
E. reaction formation

34. Of the following self-concepts, the MOST desirable one for a child to develop from the standpoint of mental health is

   A. whatever I do is good
   B. if I fail at something, it isn't important
   C. I know I have limitations; no one is perfect
   D. I must always be alert to my weaknesses
   E. I am capable of reaching my goals

35. Studies of children's fantasies show that, in the average elementary school child, fantasies

   A. play no significant part in his life
   B. will still be active but are becoming tempered with reality
   C. are an indication of an unsettled inner life
   D. are an indication that the child is unable to face his problems
   E. encourage the child to retreat from the demands of the world of reality

36. In collecting data for identifying pupil problems, information which compares a child to his peer group is called

   A. ideographic B. psychogenic
   C. psychodiagnostic D. normative
   E. sociometric

37. Of the following, what is the effect of a child's self-concept upon his behavior?

   A. It shifts and/or distorts the perceptions that act as stimuli to behavior.
   B. It functions principally in matters where conformity to or violation of the social code is involved.
   C. Its influence is best described by the Freudian concept of superego.
   D. It enables him to put his best foot forward.
   E. It helps the child to learn who he really is.

38. Compared to a group of unselected children of the same age, sex and race, gifted children, on the average,

   A. have a higher incidence of visual defects
   B. reach puberty later
   C. are taller, heavier and stronger
   D. show more personality problems
   E. are better "mixers"

39. Roger, who has a morbid fear of attending school and has been absent all year, is described as suffering from a(n)

   A. psychosis B. phobia
   C. inversion D. regression
   E. psychopathy

40. The term AMBIVALENT is used to describe a child who

    A. is given to creating dissension among others
    B. makes a statement and later amplifies it with conscious intent
    C. seems to be daydreaming while actually alert
    D. is aggressive at times and friendly at other times
    E. fearful in manner but overpowering in action

41. Transference is an important aspect of

    A. test construction
    B. grade placement
    C. anecdotal record keeping
    D. superior intelligence
    E. therapy

42. The term commonly used in statistics to refer to the average of a group of scores is the

    A. range
    B. mode
    C. central tendency
    D. median
    E. mean

43. A wound or injury to the emotions is called

    A. an illusion
    B. a trauma
    C. hysteria
    D. a delusion
    E. a syndrome

44. A child is psychotic who has a(n)

    A. urge toward some inappropriate sexual behavior
    B. nervous disorder of a functional type
    C. prolonged form of mental derangement
    D. inhibition in his social behavior
    E. physiogenic disorder

45. Individual differences in persons begin to be noticeable

    A. from birth onward
    B. after the child enters school
    C. when the child begins to communicate
    D. after visual-motor coordination has been achieved
    E. when the child begins to participate in competitive sports

46. In which one of the following statements is the mechanism of identification operating?

    A. "I'm not a good ballplayer, but I get good grades in arithmetic."
    B. "My teacher is always picking on me."
    C. "John was mad at me, but I'm bigger, so he pushed Sally, she's smaller."
    D. "I like blue dresses; my teacher wears blue a lot."
    E. "Of course I lost the tennis match; I was using a defective racket!"

47. In developing good character traits in young children, the BEST of the following techniques is probably

A. short dramatic discussions on good behavior
B. TV programs which have good behavior as "the moral"
C. administration of a personality test and follow-up discussion of the results
D. the desired type of behavior on the part of the adults with whom the children come into contact regularly
E. the emulation of outstanding personalities in the news, including athletes and actors

48. The term which MOST clearly expresses the psychological basis of modern educational practice is   48.___

    A. atomistic
    B. structuralistic
    C. analytic
    D. behavioristic
    E. organismic

49. Of the following possible first steps for helping an awkward child overcome his fear of playground activities, the one which is usually BEST is to   49.___

    A. give him some easy task connected with the game, "keeping score," for example
    B. send him to another classroom during the game period
    C. insist that he get into the game and play immediately
    D. allow him to work or do something else, alone
    E. encourage him to observe the game for a while with the hope that he will soon be motivated to play

50. Of the following, the MOST important consideration in distinguishing anxiety from fear is the   50.___

    A. intensity of the emotion
    B. extent of relation to subjective as distinguished from objective conditions
    C. strength of the personality organization of the one who is affected
    D. actuality of danger
    E. direction of the emotion

KEY (CORRECT ANSWERS)

1. C	11. E	21. D	31. A	41. E
2. C	12. D	22. C	32. A	42. E
3. D	13. A	23. C	33. E	43. B
4. C	14. A	24. B	34. E	44. C
5. A	15. D	25. D	35. B	45. A
6. C	16. A	26. B	36. D	46. D
7. D	17. E	27. D	37. A	47. D
8. B	18. C	28. C	38. C	48. E
9. A	19. D	29. E	39. B	49. A
10. B	20. B	30. A	40. D	50. B

TEST 2

DIRECTIONS: Each question or incomplete statement is followed by several suggested answers or completions. Select the one that BEST answers the question or completes the statement. *PRINT THE LETTER OF THE CORRECT ANSWER IN THE SPACE AT THE RIGHT.*

1. Research on sex differences in reading achievement indicates that

    A. more boys than girls suffer reading disabilities
    B. more girls than boys suffer reading disabilities
    C. there are no appreciable sex differences in reading achievement
    D. more boys than girls suffer reading disabilities in the elementary grades, but more girls than boys suffer reading disabilities in the secondary grades
    E. all such studies are statistically unreliable

2. Studies have shown that the ratio of reading disability among boys as compared to girls is

    A. 4 to 1
    B. 3 to 1
    C. 2 to 1
    D. equal
    E. slightly greater

3. The pecularities of language behavior in the schizophrenic arise from his extreme need of a feeling of

    A. personal security
    B. self-denial
    C. disarticulation
    D. isolation
    E. grandeur

4. Of the following, the LEAST effective way of dealing with children's fears is

    A. explaining and reassuring
    B. helping the child to face the feared situation
    C. simply ignoring the child's fear
    D. setting examples of fearlessness
    E. looking to the causes of the fear

5. The age at which individuals cease to grow in intellectual ability is

    A. 13 years
    B. 16 years
    C. 21 years
    D. 29 years
    E. probably none of these

6. Personality is the result of

    A. inheritance only
    B. environment only
    C. both inheritance and environment
    D. neither inheritance nor environment
    E. inheritance to a greater extent than environment

53

7. Children's groups about the age of two typically show 7.____
   - A. much cooperation
   - B. sex segregation
   - C. parallel activity
   - D. all of these
   - E. none of these

8. Play and reading interests of boys and girls will be found to be MOST different at the age of 8.____
   - A. three years
   - B. six years
   - C. ten years
   - D. twelve years
   - E. eighteen years

9. As children in groups with very limited environments, such as canal-boat dwellers, "hollow-folk," etc., grow older, their I.Q. is found to 9.____
   - A. increase
   - B. increase greatly
   - C. stay the same
   - D. decrease
   - E. vary widely and irregularly

10. A child reared in isolation will NOT naturally 10.____
    - A. eat
    - B. sleep
    - C. talk
    - D. take shelter
    - E. investigate his surroundings

11. Although young children are egocentric, it has been found that social development 11.____
    - A. is common among two-year-olds
    - B. is well under way at the age of four
    - C. is well under way at the age of five
    - D. is not noticeable until the sixth-year level
    - E. varies so greatly among children that it cannot be approximated at any one age

12. The rate and pattern of early motor development of children depend *mainly* upon 12.____
    - A. experience
    - B. acculturation
    - C. maturation
    - D. training
    - E. personal aptitude

13. For optimum individual and social growth, children should be encouraged to 13.____
    - A. initiate their own activities
    - B. accept the choices and decisions of their peers
    - C. learn to play alone
    - D. respect the leaders in the class
    - E. participate in clubs and groups led by children of their own age

14. Most young adolescents 14.____

    A. struggle to establish themselves as important members of the family but question family controls
    B. struggle to establish themselves as important members of the family and accept family controls without question
    C. are content with secondary roles in the family provided the family relinquishes all controls over them
    D. prefer to be told what to do by parents in order to be relieved of all responsibility for making decisions
    E. accept family controls when the rules are set by the father, but question and often disobey controls set by the mother

15. Because boys and girls of junior high school age become increasingly interested in the opposite sex, the teacher should 15.____

    A. seat them apart so that they can concentrate on their work
    B. encourage "dating"
    C. group the students with members of their own sex for all committee work
    D. forbid the use of all cosmetics in class
    E. teach the social amenities

16. On the whole, if junior high school children are treated as responsible young people, 16.____

    A. they will do what is expected of them
    B. they will react by giggling
    C. the teacher will lose control of the class
    D. their parents will object because they are not yet ready for responsibility
    E. they will assume that they are not amenable to ordinary school regulations

17. The adolescent is MOST likely to seek the greatest emotional support and understanding from 17.____

    A. idealized adults
    B. isolated activity
    C. religious authorities
    D. heterosexual interactions
    E. the peer culture

18. Emotional reactions are so important in behavior disorders because they are 18.____

    A. very intense
    B. not readily changed from infancy to adulthood
    C. varying in form from person to person
    D. so easily learned
    E. difficult to communicate and share socially

19. At the adolescent level, "adjustment" usually depends MOST strongly on having 19.____

    A. respect from parents
    B. adequate sex education
    C. average school achievement or better
    D. warm approval from teachers
    E. acceptance from peers

20. The fantasies of a child are MOST often used by a psychologist as a clue to his

   A. level of maturity
   B. inner needs
   C. social adjustment
   D. intelligence
   E. emotional stability

21.
   I. The social and emotional adjustment of the child of six to eight depends in a major way on the security of the home.
   II. Children tend to form stereotypes and to focus on the unusual.
   The CORRECT answer is:

   A. Both I and II are correct
   B. Both I and II are incorrect
   C. I is correct; II is incorrect
   D. I is incorrect; II is correct
   E. One cannot draw a conclusion

22. The psychological climate of the home which influences adjustment of the child is MOST closely related to the

   A. number of children in the home
   B. educational level of the parents
   C. occupational level of the father
   D. attitudes of the parents
   E. socio-economic status of the family

23. Of the following characteristics, the one MOST generally found among children just entering the junior high schools is

   A. a tendency of boys and girls to seek each other's company
   B. the acceptance of parent and teacher opinion with little question
   C. the popularity of guessing games, puzzles, and games of choice
   D. a preference for highly organized competitive team play
   E. a conscientious and ardent effort to achieve academic success

24. Studies of child growth indicate that

   A. the onset of puberty adversely effects the child's motor coordination
   B. mentally retarded children are usually above norms in physical growth
   C. each child has his own growth pattern
   D. mental growth and physical growth are highly correlated
   E. physical growth and emotional stability are highly correlated

25. Which of the following statements is LEAST likely to be TRUE of first grade children as compared with fifth graders?

   A. There is much concern for group welfare and group approval.
   B. There is little concern for order and neatness.
   C. Some regular routines give security to children of this age.
   D. There is little intermingling of boys and girls in their play activities.
   E. There is a dislike for oral reading.

26. Most differences in play activities and interests between boys and girls in the elementary school years can probably be attributed to

   A. inherent biological differences
   B. inherent emotional differences
   C. instinctual influences
   D. cultural influences
   E. inherent intellectual differences

27. As part of the socialization process, the phenomenon of ambivalence is at its highest intensity during the

   A. toddler years
   B. preschool years
   C. early school years
   D. intermediate school years
   E. high school years

28. In early childhood, the individual tends to pattern himself on or to identify himself MOST generally with

   A. glamorous or romantic figures
   B. age contemporaries
   C. characters in movies or on TV
   D. parents or parent substitutes
   E. teachers

29. With respect to physical growth, superior children as compared with children of average intelligence are

   A. markedly inferior   B. slightly inferior
   C. slightly superior   D. about average
   E. markedly superior

30. Wishes of children of elementary school age deal mainly with

   A. improvement of their own inner strength, character or intelligence
   B. exploitation of family relationships
   C. possessions, pleasant experiences, privileges, opportunities for enjoyment
   D. improvement of their personal appearance
   E. improvement of their physical strength and prowess

31. With reference to emotional stability, intellectually gifted children as a group compared to average children are

   A. generally inferior   B. unpredictably related
   C. generally superior   D. predictably related
   E. the same

32. In comparing the rate of biological growth for boys and girls between the ages of 5-7 and 7-10, the latter period shows

   A. a slightly more accelerated rate than the former
   B. a slightly less accelerated rate than the former
   C. a rate equal to the former period

D. a markedly more accelerated rate than the former
E. a markedly less accelerated rate than the former

33. Of the following, the MOST important determinant of leadership in pre-adolescent children is the child's

   A. self-confidence
   B. sex
   C. physical attractiveness
   D. socio-economic status
   E. mental abilities

34. Marked improvement in a child's ability to draw a man over a period of time is MOST likely to be related to

   A. better social adjustment
   B. maturational effect
   C. the overcoming of a reading disability
   D. recovery from an illness
   E. better muscular coordination

35. As a means of changing the current behavior pattern of an adolescent, which of the following forces will generally prove to be MOST potent? Disapproval of the behavior pattern by

   A. the adolescent's parents
   B. an adult he admires
   C. a group of his peers
   D. his classroom teacher
   E. a close sibling

36. Of the following, the characteristic that is MOST important in determining an individual's status in a group of pre-adolescent girls is her

   A. school achievement
   B. socio-economic status
   C. ability to make friends
   D. intelligence
   E. physical appearance

37. The main advantage of the cross-sectional study over the longitudinal study in child development research is that the former

   A. permits an analysis of the growth of each child
   B. allows for an examination of individual and child growth increments
   C. allows for a detailed analysis of the interrelations among growth processes
   D. involves fewer sampling difficulties
   E. yields more accurate results by studying a larger sample

38. The greatest "social distance" in boy-girl relationships has been found to be during the ages

   A. 13 to 17 years
   B. 9 to 13 years
   C. 2 to 5 years
   D. 5 to 9 years
   E. 17 to 19 years

39. Of the following, the MOST frequent reason why two 11-year old boys stop "being friends" is

    A. lack of agreement concerning activities to be undertaken
    B. lack of recent contact
    C. parental disapproval
    D. a clash of personalities
    E. changing interests

40. A recent comprehensive survey of child-rearing patterns in America found mothers of the working class when compared in their toilet-training practices with mothers of the upper-middle class to be

    A. more permissive
    B. more accepting
    C. more severe
    D. more indifferent
    E. more uninformed

41. The leisure time activities of the typical pre-adolescent boys' group is mainly given over to

    A. a succession of activities suited to a changing number of players
    B. just "hanging around with the boys"
    C. games governed by a highly organized series of rules
    D. aimless circulation over a relatively large area looking for something to do
    E. a succession of activities suited to a limited number of players and games governed by few, if any, rules

42. Of the following, the MOST important symptom indicative of the social and emotional maladjustment of problem pupils is

    A. whispering and fooling while work is going on
    B. association with a gang
    C. destroying your neighbor's work
    D. inability to assume responsibility
    E. shyness and daydreaming

43. Of the following types of behavior, psychiatrists consider the MOST serious to be

    A. profanity
    B. smoking
    C. unsociability
    D. whispering in class
    E. dependence

44. The MOST impelling reason for young adolescents' use of slang is

    A. ignorance
    B. hearing it at home
    C. the desire to attain peer status through its use
    D. the attraction of its colorful expressions
    E. rebellion against the accepted media of speech

45. Sibling rivalry is the term used to describe the competitive feeling between two or more individuals who

    A. are in the same school grade
    B. are children of the same parents
    C. have similar goals of achievement
    D. are in the same chronological age group
    E. are identical twins

45.___

KEY (CORRECT ANSWERS)

1. A	11. B	21. A	31. C	41. A
2. B	12. B	22. D	32. B	42. B
3. A	13. B	23. C	33. A	43. C
4. C	14. A	24. C	34. A	44. C
5. E	15. E	25. A	35. C	45. B
6. C	16. A	26. D	36. C	
7. C	17. E	27. B	37. D	
8. D	18. E	28. D	38. B	
9. D	19. E	29. C	39. B	
10. C	20. B	30. C	40. C	

EXAMINATION SECTION
TEST 1

DIRECTIONS: Each question or incomplete statement is followed by several suggested answers or completions. Select the one that BEST answers the question or completes the statement. *PRINT THE LETTER OF THE CORRECT ANSWER IN THE SPACE AT THE RIGHT.*

1. The peer group serves the individual in the socialization process by
    A. showing him how to relate to other groups
    B. showing him how to be mature
    C. helping him to achieve an identity for himself
    D. helping him accept the discipline of his family

2. The age at which intelligence tests yield the MOST reliable prediction of future academic performance is
    A. 2-4   B. 4-6   C. 6-8   D. 12-14

3. Many studies have explored the effects of maternal deprivation on children. The findings indicate that such deprived children are MOST likely to be
    A. independent and active
    B. inert, withdrawn, mentally retarded and physically inferior
    C. less prone to infectious diseases because there is less danger of infection from others
    D. socially responsive to other adults

4. Of the following, which is MOST characteristic of the late maturing adolescent boy?
    A. Better adjustment to his age mates
    B. Greater independence of others
    C. Better acceptance of discipline
    D. Consistently negative evaluation of himself

5. Of the following, the major cause of juvenile delinquency is
    A. parental rejection   B. poverty
    C. culture conflict   D. inferior biological structure

6. In the recent research and study concerning the learning of disadvantaged youth, the MOST important single finding has been that
    A. the pre-school is the level of education which must be expanded
    B. the mother is the key factor in the enrichment of the socially disadvantaged
    C. the model the child identifies with must be well chosen
    D. little can be done for delinquent girls after seventeen years of age

7. An author who concerns himself with the "epigenetic principle of gradual unfoldings," the principle that the successive differentiations made during a lifetime provide a person with a developmental concept of self, is
    A. Esther Lloyd-Jones   B. Erik Erikson
    C. John Dewey   D. Edmund G. Williamson

8. The belief that power and status motives are MORE significant for behavior than broadly sexual motives was advocated by

    A. Freud
    B. Adler
    C. Jung
    D. Rank

9. Of all children, what percentage is generally considered to be mentally retarded?

    A. .5   B. 3.0   C. 10.0   D. 15.0

10. Studies of social acceptance show that gifted children are

    A. less socially acceptable than the average
    B. more socially acceptable than the retarded but less socially acceptable than the average
    C. more socially acceptable than the average and far more than the retarded
    D. no more socially accepted than the average

11. Of the following, the major characteristic of autistic type schizophrenic children is

    A. psychosomatic symptoms
    B. extreme withdrawal tendencies
    C. psychopathic symptoms
    D. extreme suspiciousness of adults

12. Of the following, the protective test MOST useful in studying the body-image of crippled children is the

    A. CHILDREN'S APPERCEPTION TEST
    B. BLACKY TEST
    C. MACHOVER DRAW-A-PERSON
    D. HOUSE-TREE-PERSON

13. The MOST serious problem for the cerebral palsied which contributes to learning difficulty in school, next to speech, is

    A. defective vision
    B. left-handedness
    C. hearing
    D. hand and eye coordination

14. Of the following symptoms, which is MOST characteristic of brain damaged children?

    A. Perseveration
    B. Echolalia
    C. Hallucinations
    D. Anorexia

15. Of the following, the organization that would be MOST helpful in working with a child suffering from athetosis would be the

    A. Association for the Help of Retarded Children
    B. United Cerebral Palsy Association
    C. Parents' Association for CRMD
    D. League for Epilepsy

16. The behavior patterns that develop during adolescence are

    A. genetically determined
    B. culturally determined
    C. physiologically determined
    D. found in all societies

17. According to Erikson, if a child has his needs thoroughly satisfied during his childhood, he is *most likely* to be an adolescent who is

    A. over-demanding
    B. unable to meet frustration
    C. over-achieving
    D. successful in personal-social development

17.____

18. Research evidence on girls' fears indicates that their fears during the oepidal period involve the type of anxiety known as

    A. separation
    B. fixation
    C. castration
    D. deprivation

18.____

19. In the University of Chicago study on identical twins reared apart, the GREATEST similarity found was in

    A. intelligence
    B. vocational choice
    C. personality
    D. physical appearance

19.____

20. In which of the following groups of adolescents are personal problems in adjustment MOST likely to arise?

    A. Early maturing boys and girls
    B. Late maturing boys and girls
    C. Early maturing girls and late maturing boys
    D. Late maturing girls and early maturing boys

20.____

21. The adolescent gang structure fulfills the unsatisfied needs of lower class youth through his acquisition of

    A. social skills
    B. intellectual and vocational interests
    C. athletic skills
    D. sanctions for his own aggression

21.____

22. The major limitation of the sociogram and sociometric test is that it does NOT disclose the

    A. status of the individual
    B. variety of choice
    C. organization pattern
    D. factors underlying choice

22.____

23. In establishing identity and sex role, the adolescent is MOST likely to be influenced by which of the following?

    A. Parents
    B. Siblings
    C. Peers
    D. Teachers

23.____

24. Studies on the characteristics of intellectually dull adolescents indicate

    A. inferior physical development on the part of the dull as compared with normal children
    B. more frequent eye, ear and speech defects among the dull children
    C. no clear social or emotional difference between dull and normal children
    D. all of the above characteristics to be true

25. "I made the varsity basketball and football teams but the coach cut me off the track squad." This statement embodies which of the following ego-defense mechanisms?

    A. Projection
    B. Sublimation
    C. Repression
    D. Regression

26. Considering the various informal groups which exist in a school system, such as faculty friendship groups, student clubs, cliques, and gangs, it is noticeable that the members of each group tend to possess common information and common ideas in many respects. These group beliefs exist because

    A. of the initial self-selection of the group by its members
    B. information is filtered through group leaders
    C. members are subjected to the same range of information
    D. all of the above are true

27. Of the following, the information that a sociogram does NOT reveal is the

    A. general pattern of group organization
    B. network of group communication
    C. reasons for choices and rejections
    D. relative strength of choice status of individual members

28. The weaknesses in cross-sectional studies of adolescents lie in the fact that

    A. only those who survive through the high school are sampled
    B. only the lower levels of the socio-economic groups are sampled
    C. only some interrelationships of the aspects of growth are studied
    D. the lower levels of ability are also sampled

29. The stimulus-response theory of learning explains behavior in terms of

    A. subliminal motivational cues
    B. heredity and environment
    C. physiological processes
    D. learning by insight

30. Of the following, the major weakness of a sociometric test of social acceptability that asks only for positive choices is that it

    A. has a bad mental hygiene effect on the class
    B. crystallizes the groups' opinions of each other
    C. will give a good picture of the children in the middle range of acceptability
    D. fails to distinguish between the "overlooked" children and those who are rejected

31. In "Jonesville," middle class adolescents asked to name their best friends usually chose someone

    A. of their own social class
    B. of higher status than their own
    C. below them in social status
    D. they liked for personal reasons; their choices were distributed among all social classes

32. A common change in the personality defenses of the adolescent child is the development of

    A. greater intellectualism and isolation of affect
    B. a tendency toward avoidance and denial
    C. suspicion and withdrawal
    D. repression and literal-mindedness

33. Studies on the development of sex characteristics during pubescent growth indicate that

    A. the sequence in the development of sex characteristics is marked by great consistency
    B. the age at which specific sex characteristics appear is quite reliable
    C. the only differences in the age occurrence of specific characteristics is due to sex differences
    D. there is little range in size or variability of sex characteristics

34. Adler, Horney, and Rank are deviationists from which one of the following theories?

    A. Psychoanalytical   B. Rogerian
    C. Communications   D. Neobehavioral

35. All of the following are identified with behavioral counseling EXCEPT

    A. Williamson   B. Skinner
    C. Eysenck   D. Krumboltz

36. All of the following associations are correct EXCEPT

    A. endomorphy - softness and spherical appearance
    B. mesomorphy - hard and rectangular physique with a predominance of bone and muscle
    C. ectomorphy - a linear and fragile physique
    D. gynandromorphy - a physique that represents an exaggeration of sexual characteristics associated with the given sex

37. Psychiatrists generally agree that the three characteristics *usually* combined in a severely troubled child are

    A. laziness, hostility, withdrawal
    B. slight height, overweight, pallor
    C. lack of relatedness, a speech problem, an eating problem
    D. undernourishment, fatigue, lack of coordination

38. Directing an emotion toward a safe or acceptable object as a substitute for a dangerous or unacceptable object is a fairly good definition for which one of the following defense mechanisms?

    A. Displacement
    B. Repression
    C. Identification
    D. Rationalization

39. The "latency period" as a concept of psychoanalysis has reference to the

    A. years between early childhood and adolescence
    B. period during which successful toilet training (accommodation to time, place and manner) is normally achieved
    C. period during which the oedipal strivings reach their peak
    D. period of pubertal development

40. An unpopular girl frequently calls attention to the social deficiencies in others. Her behavior illustrates

    A. regression
    B. projection
    C. repression
    D. rationalization

41. Which one of the following was NOT supported by Kurt Lewin's research?

    A. People are more apt to change if they participate in a decision to change.
    B. It is easier to change individuals in a group situation rather than singly.
    C. Change brought about through groups was more lasting than that brought about singly.
    D. While pressures of group members upon individuals were very strong, they were not as influential as those of group leaders.

42. A six-year-old child should normally be expected to do all of the following EXCEPT

    A. play simple games
    B. put on a sweater without help
    C. draw with a crayon
    D. write in sentences

43. An educational television program developed especially for pre-school age children is

    A. Learning Your A B C's
    B. Sesame Street
    C. The Number Game
    D. The Partridge Family

44. Which of the following statements concerning masturbation in children is NOT true?

    A. Excessive masturbation can injure a child's genitals.
    B. Masturbation is practiced by most children at some point of their development.
    C. Masturbation may be a symptom of tenseness and nervousness in a child.
    D. There tends to be an increased urge to masturbate during adolescence.

45. A child's rate of physical growth is MOST rapid during the period

    A. from birth to two years
    B. from six to nine years
    C. of pre-adolescence
    D. of adolescence

46. In planning activities for a group of ten-year-old children, the children's counselor should

   A. encourage the children to participate in the planning
   B. schedule activities that are the easiest to plan
   C. realize that children at this age like to watch television
   D. insist that each child participate in each activity

47. A child of twelve would be MOST likely to find an outlet for his aggressive tendencies in

   A. watching television
   B. participating in athletics
   C. reading a history book
   D. playing checkers

48. Of the following, the statement which MOST accurately describes the physical development of boys and girls during adolescence is that

   A. girls generally mature earlier than boys
   B. boys generally mature earlier than girls
   C. boys and girls generally mature at about the same age
   D. physically active boys and girls generally mature earlier than physically inactive ones

49. The average child has not developed all the many abilities needed for beginning reading until the age of about

   A. two   B. four   C. six   D. eight

50. Which of the following situations indicates that the child is probably emotionally disturbed?

   A. A five-year-old girl suddenly starts behaving like a baby after the birth of her sister.
   B. A four-year-old boy keeps asking for his father, although he has been told repeatedly that his father has died.
   C. A ten-year-old boy has refused to play with other children since he first entered school five years ago.
   D. All of the above

KEY (CORRECT ANSWERS)

1. C	11. B	21. D	31. B	41. D
2. C	12. C	22. D	32. A	42. D
3. B	13. D	23. C	33. A	43. B
4. D	14. A	24. D	34. A	44. A
5. A	15. B	25. A	35. A	45. A
6. A	16. B	26. D	36. D	46. A
7. B	17. D	27. C	37. C	47. B
8. B	18. C	28. A	38. A	48. A
9. B	19. D	29. C	39. A	49. C
10. C	20. C	30. D	40. B	50. C

TEST 2

DIRECTIONS: Each question or incomplete statement is followed by several suggested answers or completions. Select the one that BEST answers the question or completes the statement. *PRINT THE LETTER OF THE CORRECT ANSWER IN THE SPACE AT THE RIGHT.*

1. The process by which children take to themselves the values, the thinking, and social behavior of their parents is called

    A. projection
    B. identification
    C. fixation
    D. sublimation

2. Of the following, the characteristic that MOST clearly differentiates primary drives from secondary drives is that primary drives

    A. are related to biological needs that must be satisfied
    B. are learned early in the developmental cycle
    C. are derived from complex patterns of behavior
    D. may be observed after biological needs have been met

3. Spitz and Goldfarb, in two different studies, have suggested that children who will have predictably lower I.Q's are those reared in

    A. institutions
    B. broken homes
    C. foster homes
    D. middle class homes

4. One of the MOST common fears of early childhood is the fear of

    A. animals
    B. being separated from parents
    C. being rejected by peers
    D. having too much independence

5. The average child shows the FIRST signs of laughing responses

    A. before the age of six months
    B. between the ages of six months and one year
    C. at the age of about one year
    D. at the age of about fifteen months

6. A child is LEAST likely to choose a child of the opposite sex to play with at the age of

    A. two
    B. four
    C. seven
    D. ten

7. When toilet training a two-year-old child, the children's counselor should

    A. scold the child when she wets her pants
    B. take the child to the bathroom only when she asks to go
    C. have the child sit on the toilet for long periods of time
    D. keep the toilet training routine free from tension

8. The average child of three years MOST often shows his anger by

   A. breaking things
   B. crying
   C. threatening his mother
   D. sulking

9. Children at the age of two or three occasionally have temper tantrums when they do not get what they want. Of the following, the BEST method for a children's counselor to use when faced with a temper tantrum by a two-year-old child in her group is to

   A. allow the child to have what he wants
   B. try to reason with the child by explaining why he cannot have what he wants
   C. wait until the worst of the temper tantrum is over and then make a friendly gesture toward the child
   D. order the child to stop this behavior

10. All of the following are good principles to follow in administering punishment to a three-year-old child EXCEPT the

    A. punishment should be administered immediately after the incident of bad behavior
    B. child should be punished only if he understands why his behavior was bad
    C. specific punishment should be appropriate to the specific case of bad behavior
    D. punishment should be administered in an impartial manner

11. Helen, a 14-year-old girl, has two younger sisters who are more successful than she in school. Her mother complains that at home Helen constantly makes remarks intended to hurt their feelings. Helen's behavior is BEST characterized as a form of

    A. compulsion
    B. sublimation
    C. rationalization
    D. projection

12. Overlearning is primarily an outgrowth of

    A. removal of inhibitions
    B. additional practice
    C. strong motivation
    D. fear of failure

13. "The mind responds to relationships, not to fixed stimuli" is associated with the movement in psychology known as

    A. associationism
    B. behaviorism
    C. Gestalt psychology
    D. functionalism

14. Which one of the following is an example of "projection"?

    A. Calling other people hostile although the hostility is within oneself
    B. Playing sick in order to avoid responsibility
    C. Kicking the desk when one really wants to kick the teacher
    D. Giving other than the true reason for one's behavior

15. The basketball player who was dropped from the squad says, "Now I'll have time to study." If he really wanted to make the team, he is

    A. regressing
    B. repressing
    C. projecting
    D. rationalizing

16. Which one of the following reactions is generally instigated by frustration?

    A. Tolerance
    B. Aggression
    C. Identification
    D. Avoidance

17. A patient asserts, "I can't stand the agony I suffer when I go against my mother's wishes." The therapist replies, "You really like to punish that momma inside of you for your dependency, don't you?" This response can be viewed as an example of

    A. reassurance
    B. interpretation
    C. support
    D. reflection of feeling

18. A shy young first-grade boy becomes extremely attached to his teacher. He brings her presents, asks her to help him with his clothing a great deal, and wants to sit near her all the time. He is MOST likely manifesting the mental mechanism of

    A. introjection
    B. sublimation
    C. reaction-formation
    D. transference

19. When Billy was told he could not have a cookie, he lay down on the floor and pounded it with his fists. This could be an example of

    A. repression
    B. inhibition
    C. overcompensation
    D. regression

20. Habit formations in children such biting nails, picking at sores, masturbating, etc. are generally the result of

    A. poor parental supervision and training
    B. local irritations
    C. impaired general health
    D. emotional tensions

21. The attention span of a young child

    A. is not related to his mental ability
    B. can be increased if he has a high I.Q.
    C. cannot be changed before the child learns to read
    D. can be increased if the child is interested in what he is doing

22. Most young children need

    A. few media of expression
    B. to engage in independent planning
    C. many concrete experiences
    D. generalized explanations

23. The person with whom it is MOST important for a five-year-old child to have a good adjustment is

    A. father
    B. mother
    C. teacher
    D. sibling

24. At five, the normal, average child is able to play BEST

    A. alone
    B. in a large group
    C. with one other child somewhat older than himself
    D. in a small group of five or six children

25. Good education for five-year-old children stresses the importance of

   A. learning to sit still and wait for a turn
   B. opportunities to develop skill in crafts
   C. opportunities to explore and experiment
   D. learning to walk with a partner in line

26. Motor activities figure MOST importantly in a young child's intellectual enterprises because, through them, he

   A. learns how to meet new situations successfully
   B. acquires concepts of size, shape, balance, proportion
   C. learns how to live happily with other children
   D. gains confidence in himself as a person

27. Children can BEST be helped to make good choices through

   A. play with peers
   B. many experiences in making choices
   C. absorbing the teacher's sense of values
   D. imitating other children older than they

28. The timid, shy child who hesitates to join in activities and use of materials

   A. should be left alone
   B. should be praised for the work he does by himself
   C. should be drawn into the group and encouraged to participate as often as possible
   D. should have his mother come to his class to visit so that he will have a feeling of security

29. To understand the emotional life of the adolescent, it is MOST important to

   A. appraise the adolescent's emotions in the light of our own experience
   B. take into account the many forces, apparent as well as hidden, that operate in his life
   C. overlook impulsive behavior without apparent motive
   D. draw up a scholastic profile

30. The youngster who says, "I got an A in mathematics, but the teacher gave me a D in reading," is manifesting behavior which may be termed

   A. identification   B. projection
   C. regression   D. repression

31. Of the following comments which might be made by a teacher to a boy who has just misbehaved, the one likely to be MOST effective in correcting the behavior is:

   A. You are a bad boy who likes to misbehave.
   B. You are a silly boy and don't know how to behave.
   C. You are a poor, foolish boy who will get in trouble.
   D. You are a good boy but you made a mistake.

32. The personality development of young children is hampered MOST by
    A. the lack of good schools manned by adequately educated teachers
    B. dissension in the family
    C. the lack of love and affection
    D. failure in school I

33. It has been found that the gap between ability and achievement is generally SMALLEST in the
    A. gifted pupil
    B. dull pupil
    C. average pupil
    D. pupil of high socio-economic background

34. Extreme deviations in motor, adaptive, or language expression or personal-social behavior are
    A. a definite indication that a child is subnormal
    B. cause for alarm on the part of parent and teacher
    C. an indication of a temporary maladjustment
    D. reasons for seeking the advice of a specialist

35. Children's groups about the age of two typically show
    A. much cooperation
    B. sex segregation
    C. parallel activity
    D. all of these

36. Play and reading interests of boys and girls will be found to be MOST different at the age of
    A. three years
    B. six years
    C. ten years
    D. twelve years

37. As children in groups with very limited environments, such as canal-boat dwellers, "hollow-folk," etc., grow older, their I.Q. is found to
    A. increase
    B. increase greatly
    C. stay the same
    D. decrease

38. Transfer from one subject to another or to life situations will be increased if
    A. techniques and applications are emphasized
    B. the first subject is very difficult
    C. a good deal of drill is given in the first subject
    D. the situations seem quite different

39. A contemporary book by Sheldon and Eleanor Glueck reports their findings of a careful research study of juvenile delinquents. They state that
    A. most of their delinquents showed anti-social behavior beginning with their sixth year
    B. most of their delinquents did not show anti-social behavior until after their eleventh year
    C. the delinquents showed more physical defects than non-delinquents
    D. prediction tables can help to detect potential delinquents

40. Finger sucking in early childhood has long been a subject of discussion among psychiatrists. The one of the following statements which is GENERALLY accepted as true is that

    A. finger sucking denotes pending neuroses and the parents need psychiatric consultation
    B. finger sucking is a normal activity of early childhood and should not be interfered with
    C. finger sucking alters the child's facial contours and should be heavily discouraged
    D. finger sucking by a child over nine months old is due to emotional upset and needs treatment

40.____

KEY (CORRECT ANSWERS)

1. B	11. D	21. D	31. D
2. A	12. B	22. C	32. C
3. A	13. C	23. B	33. B
4. B	14. A	24. D	34. D
5. A	15. D	25. C	35. C
6. D	16. B	26. B	36. D
7. D	17. B	27. B	37. D
8. B	18. D	28. C	38. A
9. C	19. D	29. B	39. D
10. B	20. D	30. B	40. B

EXAMINATION SECTION
TEST 1

DIRECTIONS: Each question or incomplete statement is followed by several suggested answers or completions. Select the one that BEST answers the question or completes the statement. *PRINT THE LETTER OF THE CORRECT ANSWER IN THE SPACE AT THE RIGHT.*

1. The psychologist whose name is MOST often associated with the theory that the experience of birth has a profound influence on personality development and that an individual who has a slow, prolonged birth is likely to have a personality which fights, struggles and plunges is

    A. Horney
    B. Freud
    C. Sullivan
    D. Rank

2. Which of the following is the MOST correct statement concerning puberty and physical maturity?

    A. Boys and girls who experience early puberty will achieve physical maturity and cease growing later than will the late maturers.
    B. Boys and girls who experience early puberty will achieve physical maturity and cease growing sooner than will the late maturers.
    C. Boys and girls who experience early puberty will achieve physical maturity and cease growing at approximately the same time as the late maturers.
    D. None of the above

3. The MOST prominent difficulties of the middle years of childhood revolve around

    A. relations with peer groups
    B. parent-child relationships
    C. schooling and the ability to learn
    D. physical development

4. In the normal population, the range of achievement of children of the same age in grades 5 and 6 is approximately from

    A. 1 to 2 years
    B. 2 to 4 years
    C. 3 to 5 years
    D. 5 to 8 years

5. The MOST accurate statement concerning anxiety, of the following, is that anxiety is

    A. needed for the socialization process
    B. not needed for the socialization process
    C. less produced by "mental" punishment than by physical punishment
    D. of negligible effect in producing neurosis

6. Of the following, the area of greatest similarity among children is in their

    A. inherited traits
    B. rates of development
    C. sequences of development
    D. patterns of growth dimensions

2 (#1)

7. Of the following, which is the MOST significant factor in determining the choice of friends among children between the ages of six and ten?

   A. Mutual interests
   B. Similar personality traits
   C. Conveniently close location
   D. Social and economic standing of parents

8. Lewin, in defining his structural concepts of psychology, represented them

   A. topologically
   B. metrically
   C. geometrically
   D. orthographically

9. As part of the socialization process, the phenomenon of ambivalence is at its highest intensity during the

   A. toddler years
   B. preschool years
   C. early school years
   D. intermediate school years

10. The child's need to be a "goody-goody" and his willingness to conform are MOST frequently observed during the

    A. phallic period
    B. latency period
    C. prepubertal period
    D. adolescent period

11. Joe Flirp is a great health education teacher, to a large extent, because the boys model themselves after him. The foregoing illustrates the psychological mechanism of

    A. sublimation
    B. displacement
    C. regression
    D. identification

12. "You're much too authoritarian," said the principal to the teacher. "And I won't stand for that in my school." The principal is demonstrating the psychological mechanism of

    A. sublimation
    B. conversion
    C. projection
    D. identification

13. Margaret Snorble, unhappy because of her lack of friendship, devoted all her energy to studying. She became the number one student in her grade. Margaret is demonstrating the psychological mechanism of

    A. sublimation
    B. conversion
    C. introjection
    D. fantasy

14. Ben was ill now and then. However, each time after a short rest, he quickly became well. This tendency or process is known as

    A. redintegration
    B. regression
    C. homeostasis
    D. somatistation

15. Joanie asked for apple pie and was told that there was none left. "Oh, well," said she, "give me peach pie. I like it better anyway." Joanie is demonstrating the psychological mechanism of

    A. regression
    B. displacement
    C. rationalization
    D. sublimation

16. The principal had just left after telling Miss Jones she had to improve the quality of her lesson plans. Tears came to her eyes; she stamped her foot several times, pounded on the desk and then broke into uncontrolled sobbing. Miss Jones' behavior is an example of the psychological mechanism of

    A. introjection
    B. projection
    C. sublimation
    D. regression

17. Of the following statements concerning praise and punishment, which is LEAST in accord with modern psychological principles?

    A. When a child is bad, spank him.
    B. When a child is bad, say, "If you're not good, I won't love you any more."
    C. When a child is good, give him something to show your approval.
    D. When a child is good, say, "That's O.K. Let's try to do better next time."

18. Which one of the following is NOT characteristic of the development of a group?

    A. Emergence of collective goals
    B. Solidification of individual roles within the group structure
    C. Growth of group norms for behavior
    D. Development of a group atmosphere or social climate

19. The status of an individual in a group is determined, for the MOST part, by

    A. the possession of those qualities the group deems important
    B. his socio-economic level
    C. his status in other groups of which he is a member
    D. the amount of time and energy he is willing to devote to the purposes of the group

20. In comparison with other members of a group, the leader tends to

    A. hold himself in higher esteem
    B. be less spontaneous
    C. be more desirous of being of service to others
    D. be more willing to accept a low level of performance from members of the group

21. The individual who emerges as the leader of a group is usually

    A. the person who, in the judgment of the group, can best meet the demands of the particular problem
    B. superior to the other members of the group in a wide variety of abilities
    C. chosen on the basis of personal qualities rather than ability
    D. the same person, no matter in what activities the group participates

22. The degree of cohesiveness which has been established in a group is MOST likely to be lowered by

    A. unfavorable evaluation of the group by outsiders
    B. favorable evaluation of the group by outsiders
    C. decreasing the amount of interaction in the group
    D. increasing the degree of interaction in the group

23. Research has shown that neighborhood gangs tend to be more cohesive than groups of the same age functioning as clubs in more formal youth agencies. This would suggest that

   A. the club is potentially longer-lived than the gang
   B. young people join clubs only if they are not accepted by the gang
   C. clubs will not be able to function adequately in a given neighborhood until some way is found to destroy gangs already in existence
   D. the activities of the gang meet the needs of its members better than those of the club program do

24. Studies of the cohesiveness of small groups have indicated that the more cohesive a group, the

   A. more willing will the group be to defend itself against external criticism
   B. less likely is it that the group will permit internal disagreement with its objective or goals
   C. less perceptive is the group of its own solidarity
   D. more susceptible is the group to disruption caused by loss of a leader

25. According to Sullivan, anxiety serves as a defense against the danger of

   A. conditioned fears
   B. self-discovery
   C. destructive people on the outside
   D. interpersonal destructiveness

26. The system of classifying people into those who move towards, against, and away from people was devised by

   A. Alexander   B. Fromm
   C. Fenichel   D. Horney

27. Scientific investigators generally agree that the development of human behavior begins

   A. at the time of conception
   B. during the prenatal period
   C. at birth
   D. at the time of initial social interaction

28. Of the following, the MOST frequent reason why two 11-year old boys stop "being friends" is

   A. lack of agreement concerning activities to be undertaken
   B. lack of recent contact
   C. a clash of personalities
   D. parental disapproval

29. Of the following, the MOST important determinant of leadership in pre-adolescent children is the child's

   A. self-confidence   B. sex
   C. physical attractiveness D. socio-economic status

30. Of the following, the one MOST likely to be associated with poor emotional development in a sixth-grade girl is

    A. lack of interest in boys
    B. striving for perfection in all her school work
    C. desire to please her parents in everything she does
    D. a strong interest in arithmetic, with only passive interest in other school subjects

31. The author of FOUNDATIONS OF READING INSTRUCTION is

    A. Paul Witty   B. Emmett A. Betts
    C. David H. Russell   D. Helen M. Robinson

32. The Dolch 220-word basic vocabulary consists of words that

    A. are most commonly used in fifteen basic readers on first and second grade levels
    B. are most commonly used in compositions by primary-grade children
    C. must be recognized as "sight words" because they do not follow regular phonetic principles
    D. make up fifty percent of reading matter used in the elementary schools

33. The MOST rapid rate of growth among children between the ages of 2 and 8 is found at age

    A. 2   B. 4   C. 6   D. 8

34. Studies of the relationship between sex and reading disability of elementary school pupils generally reveal that among pupils with reading disabilities the number of

    A. girls exceeds the number of boys
    B. boys and girls is about equal
    C. boys is slightly greater than the number of girls
    D. boys is about 3 times the number of girls

35. Research reports agree that the reading interests of groups of children

    A. begin to be different for boys and girls during the primary grades
    B. change consistently as children grow older
    C. center on animal stories during pre-adolescent years
    D. show no difference between boys and girls until junion high school years

36. The MOST accurate statement to make regarding the cause of reading disability is that research shows that most reading difficulties are primarily due to

    A. low intelligence
    B. familial discord
    C. insufficient motivation to read
    D. a complex of interrelated factors

37. Fernald's name is associated with a teaching procedure by which a child learns words by means of a

    A. look-and-say technique   B. visual motor approach
    C. tracing-and-writing procedure   D. letter sound blending approach

38. A diagnostic report of a child's reading states that he has no word analysis techniques. This diagnosis is equivalent to saying that he

   A. has a poor meaningful vocabulary
   B. cannot understand what he reads
   C. cannot sound out words
   D. cannot adjust his rate

39. Where mixed dominance is identified as a possible causal factor for a child who makes many reversal errors, it would be BEST for the teacher to

   A. stress left to right direction in reading
   B. change the child's hand preference
   C. change the child's eye preference
   D. stress an oral approach in reading

40. The mother of a first-grade child is concerned about her child's reading. It appears that the child can read only the words in her primer, but cannot sound out any words not in her book. Of the following, the BEST explanation to the mother would be that

   A. it is all right because the children are not taught phonics today
   B. it is all right because the child will learn to sound words
   C. it is serious and the child will get special help soon
   D. it is all right since children are taught to read whole words first, then the sounds

41. As a means of changing the current behavior pattern of an adolescent, which of the following forces will generally prove to be MOST potent? Disapproval of the behavior pattern by

   A. the adolescent's parents
   B. his classroom teacher
   C. a group of his peers
   D. an adult he admires

42. Of the following, the characteristic that is MOST important in determining an individual's status in a group of pre-adolescent girls is her

   A. school achievement
   B. socio-economic status
   C. ability to make friends
   D. intelligence

43. If the results of studies of boys' clubs are applicable to the school situation, one may expect the greatest amount of aggressive behavior to be noted in classes where the classroom climate may be described as

   A. permissive
   B. laissez-faire
   C. democratic
   D. autocratic

44. Which of the following authors would you be LEAST likely to recommend for information about child care?

   A. Sidonie Gruenberg
   B. Jean Piaget
   C. Ernest Harms
   D. Benjamin Spock

45. Of the following, which one is NOT an authority in reading?

    A. Gates
    B. Russell
    C. Harris
    D. Bullis

46. Studies have shown that the ratio of reading disability among boys as compared to girls is:

    A. 4 to 1   B. 3 to 1   C. 2 to 1   D. equal

47. Which of the following terms refers to the maintenance of stability in the physiological functioning of the organism?

    A. functional autonomy
    B. canalization
    C. homeostasis
    D. maturation

48. A recent comprehensive survey of child-rearing patterns in America found mothers of the working class when compared in their toilet-training practices with mothers of the middle class to be

    A. more permissive
    B. more indifferent
    C. more severe
    D. more accepting

49. Studies of the relationship of body build and character traits have in general been found to be

    A. positively correlated
    B. negatively correlated
    C. statistically significantly correlated
    D. inconclusive

50. The theory that psychical compensation for a feeling of physical or social inferiority is responsible for the development of a psychoneurosis is attributed to

    A. Adler
    B. Horney
    C. Freud
    D. Sullivan

KEY (CORRECT ANSWERS)

1. D	11. D	21. A	31. B	41. C
2. B	12. C	22. C	32. D	42. C
3. C	13. A	23. D	33. A	43. D
4. D	14. C	24. A	34. D	44. B
5. A	15. C	25. B	35. B	45. D
6. C	16. D	26. D	36. D	46. B
7. C	17. B	27. B	37. C	47. C
8. A	18. B	28. B	38. C	48. C
9. B	19. A	29. A	39. A	49. D
10. B	20. A	30. B	40. D	50. A

TEST 2

DIRECTIONS: Each question or incomplete statement is followed by several suggested answers or completions. Select the one that BEST answers the question or completes the statement. *PRINT THE LETTER OF THE CORRECT ANSWER IN THE SPACE AT THE RIGHT.*

1. Of the following, the MOST important consideration in distinguishing anxiety from fear is the

    A. intensity of the emotion
    B. extent of relation to subjective as distinguished from objective conditions
    C. actuality of danger
    D. strength of the personality organization of the one who is affected

    1.____

2. Wishes of children of elementary school age deal mainly with

    A. improvement of their own inner strength, character, or intelligence
    B. improvement of their personal appearance
    C. possessions, pleasant experiences, privileges, opportunities for enjoyment
    D. exploitation of family relationships

    2.____

3. The psychological climate of the home which influences adjustment of the child is MOST closely related to the

    A. number of children in the home
    B. educational level of the parents
    C. occupational level of the father
    D. attitudes of the parents

    3.____

4. With reference to emotional stability, intellectually gifted children as a group compared to average children are

    A. generally inferior
    B. the same
    C. generally superior
    D. unpredictably related

    4.____

5. Piaget distinguishes between two kinds of thought, logical and autistic. It is his thesis that the child's way of thinking is

    A. basically autistic
    B. either logical or autistic
    C. basically logical
    D. situated between the logical and the autistic

    5.____

6. According to research findings, the MOST effective way to help a child deal with a specific fear, such as a fear of dogs, is to

    A. have the parents and others who are close to the child set an example of fearlessness
    B. explain matters to him in terms he can understand readily
    C. help him by degrees to come actively and directly to grips with the situation
    D. try to effect "positive reconditioning" by presenting the feared stimulus with an attractive one

    6.____

7. A fundamental principle of the psychoanalytic school which has been accepted by most schools of psychology is the

   A. development of the collective unconscious
   B. theory of the existence of a dynamic unconscious
   C. development of an oedipus complex situation
   D. relationship between early psychosexual development and later adult behavior

8. In comparing the rate of biological growth for boys and girls between the ages of 5-7 and 7-10, the latter period shows

   A. a slightly more accelerated rate than the former
   B. a slightly less accelerated rate than the former
   C. a markedly more accelerated rate than the former
   D. a rate equal to the former period

9. The concept of "stages" in describing human development is LEAST applicable to

   A. Freud's psychoanalytic theory
   B. Piaget's cognitive theory
   C. Skinner's behavior theory
   D. Erikson's personality theory

10. The principal effect of nursery school attendance is upon the child's

    A. social development
    B. intellectual development
    C. perceptual development
    D. motor development

11. Which of the following terms is MOST clearly associated with stubborn reading disability?

    A. Apraxia   B. Dysplasia   C. Dyslexia   D. Aphasia

12. The boy who is encouraged or required to be more independent at an earlier age tends to develop a(n)

    A. low threshold for frustration
    B. inability to work well with others
    C. reluctance to accept adult authority
    D. strong need to achieve

13. Pioneering studies in eliminating children's fears were conducted by Mary Cover Jones. The methods used, which are consistent with present-day learning theory, included all but ONE of the following:

    A. Direct conditioning
    B. Social imitation
    C. Feeding responses
    D. Systematic desensitization

14. In contrast to upward mobile adolescents, downward mobile adolescents are

    A. less ambivalent in self-concept
    B. less interested in job security
    C. more confident in social relationships
    D. more dependent on their parents

15. In which of the following situations would a classroom atmosphere of competitiveness be LEAST detrimental to the cultivation of interpersonal relationships? Classmates are

   A. unfamiliar with one another, but equal in abilities
   B. familiar with one another and equal in abilities
   C. unfamiliar with one another and greatly disparate in abilities
   D. familiar with one another and greatly disparate in abilities

16. On group intelligence tests, Cyril Burt found the highest correlations between

   A. identical twins reared apart
   B. siblings reared together
   C. parents and own children living together
   D. identical twins reared together

17. An adolescent boy would like to have a girlfriend. As an example of sublimation, he might

   A. proclaim himself a "woman-hater"
   B. withdraw from all interpersonal relationships
   C. convince himself that girls are really crazy about him
   D. begin to write romantic poetry

18. Jim studies all night before an examination in an attempt to learn the entire course. This is an example of

   A. distributed practice
   B. massed practice
   C. practice effect
   D. spread of effect

19. The best-controlled studies of the influence of genetic factors on human behavior are found in investigations of

   A. newborn babies
   B. identical twins
   C. fraternal twins
   D. siblings

20. Terman's follow-up studies on a group of gifted children as compared to children of average intelligence revealed them to have

   A. better adjustment as shown on personality and character tests
   B. greater physical problems
   C. lower incomes
   D. more uneven academic achievement

21. Which one of the following is the MOST important determinant of leadership among preadolescent boys?

   A. Intellectual ability
   B. Physical size and strength
   C. Popularity with girls
   D. Sensitivity to the needs of others

22. Billy wants to be admired, but he is too clumsy to achieve this goal through sports. Therefore, although not a bright pupil, he studies long hours and earns very high grades. This may be cited as an example of

    A. compensation
    B. projection
    C. rationalization
    D. reaction formation

23. Of the following, the MOST important factor making for the development of friendship among young children is

    A. similarity in interests
    B. similarity in social class
    C. geographic proximity
    D. friendship among parents

24. Harlow's work on mothering in monkeys suggests that the affective bond between the infant and the mother is based on

    A. feeding
    B. grooming
    C. tactile contact
    D. primitive vocalization

25. The CORRECT order of Piaget's developmental stages is

    A. concrete operations, preoperational, sensorimotor, formal operational
    B. concrete operations, sensorimotor, preoperational, formal operational
    C. sensorimotor, concrete operations, preoperational, formal operational
    D. sensorimotor, preoperational, concrete operations, formal operational

26. Piaget's process which states that children invent increasingly more and better schemata for adapting to their environment is known as

    A. assimilation
    B. equilibrium
    C. accommodation
    D. conservation

27. Which of the following is NOT considered by Erikson to be a developmental task of adolescence?

    A. Development of a sense of shared identity with another
    B. Development of sexual identity
    C. Ability to see one's life in perspective
    D. Experimentation with different roles

28. A six-year-old child who is able to solve a conservation problem would be classified under which of the following stages described by Piaget?

    A. Sensorimotor
    B. Formal operations
    C. Preoperational
    D. Concrete operations

29. During adolescence, girls *generally* surpass boys in

    A. scientific ability
    B. mathematical ability
    C. ability to perform verbal tasks
    D. gross motor skills

30. The CORRECT order of Freud's stages of psychosexual development is:

   A. Oral, latency, anal, phallic, genital
   B. Oral, anal, phallic, latency, genital
   C. Phallic, oral, anal, latency, genital
   D. Latency, oral, genital, anal, phallic

31. According to Erikson, a MAJOR developmental conflict a child faces in the elementary school age period is the conflict between

   A. initiative and guilt
   B. identity and identity diffusion
   C. industry and inferiority
   D. trust and mistrust

32. According to Piaget, in the preoperational stage children

   A. begin to classify and order activities internally
   B. begin to integrate sensory and motor activities
   C. gain the ability to think logically about a problem
   D. are unable to transcend the here and now and are dependent on immediate perception

33. A pupil is able to reason simultaneously about whole and part and is able to classify according to two or three properties. According to Piaget, the pupil is in the _____ stage.

   A. sensory-motor
   B. formal operations
   C. preoperational
   D. concrete operations

34. According to Kohlberg, moral development proceeds through a sequence of stages that are

   A. dependent on the individual's personality and the way in which society reacts to that personality
   B. strongly influenced by individual differences in educational experience and religious training
   C. characterized by increasing symmetry, conventionality, and objectivity
   D. universal and invariant from one culture to another

35. The technique in which a particular form or sequence of behavior is established by reinforcing successively closer approximations to that behavior is called

   A. discriminative responding
   B. shaping
   C. classical conditioning
   D. fading

36. The HIGHEST need in Maslow's hierarchy of human needs is

   A. safety
   B. love
   C. self-actualization
   D. integration

37. According to Piaget, a child's thinking becomes completely general and capable of dealing with the hypothetical during the _____ stage.

    A. sensorimotor
    B. concrete operations
    C. preoperational
    D. formal operations

38. MOST child development specialists believe that a child's peer groups begin to replace the family as a socializing agent

    A. after the age of 5 or 6
    B. between the age of 2 or 3
    C. near the beginning of adolescence
    D. toward the end of adolescence

39. According to Erik Erikson, a key developmental task for the early elementary school years involves

    A. establishing a personal identity
    B. building confidence, resourcefulness, and enthusiasm
    C. surviving a psychosocial moratorium
    D. handling developmental discontinuity

40. Peter maintains that "everyone else in my class thinks I'm a crook." The mechanism of adjustment Peter is probably utilizing is usually referred to as

    A. projection
    B. rationalization
    C. compensation
    D. identification

41. Of the following, the BEST means of helping a child develop tolerance for tension is to

    A. protect the child from experiencing frustration
    B. make the child face reality through frequent experience of failure
    C. make sure that the child is uniformly successful
    D. help the child achieve some success and face some failure

42. Phil always develops a headache when he is called upon to complete a difficult task. Phil's headache is a(n)

    A. hysteroid reaction
    B. compensatory reaction
    C. reaction formation
    D. paranoid reaction

43. Which of the following is characteristic of the person who overcompensates?

    A. Projection
    B. Repression
    C. Self-repudiation
    D. Rationalization

44. A child who has been rejected by his parents tries to "show off" at every opportunity. Such a child is usually

    A. unaware of the nature of his frustration
    B. not capable of reacting more effectively
    C. reacting objectively to his stress situation
    D. deliberately trying to show his parents his need for affection

45. CHILD-CENTERED GROUP GUIDANCE OF PARENTS as described by Slavson deals with   45.____

    A. the understanding of the behavior and specific acts
    B. of children and ways of dealing with them appropriately
    C. free-associative catharsis which uncovers anxiety-inducing memories, acts and situations
    D. diminution of guilt on the part of the parents
    E. intellectually recognizing and emotionally accepting latent, covert and repressed impulses and strivings in children

46. Which of the following statements BEST expresses the central theme in Bruno Bettelheim's book, LOVE IS NOT ENOUGH? The disturbed child needs to identify with a person who   46.____

    A. accepts his feelings
    B. clearly structures his environment
    C. permits regression
    D. is maternal and "giving"

47. The leisure time activities of the typical pre-adolescent boys' group are mainly given over to   47.____

    A. a succession of activities suited to a changing number of players
    B. games governed by a highly organized series of rules
    C. aimless circulation over a relatively large area looking for something to do
    D. just "hanging around with the boys"

48. The normal age range of reading ability between the best and the poorest reader in a typical sixth grade is about   48.____

    A. 2 years   B. 3 years
    C. 5 years   D. 7 years

49. Of the following books, the one NOT written by A.T. Jersild is   49.____

    A. IN SEARCH OF SELF
    B. CHILDREN'S FEARS
    C. LOVE IS NOT ENOUGH
    D. WHEN TEACHERS FACE THEMSELVES

50. Studies in child development at Yale University were done primarily under the direction of   50.____

    A. Lawrence K. Frank   B. Samuel R. Slavson
    C. Arnold Gesell   D. Albert Deutsch

KEY (CORRECT ANSWERS)

1. B	11. C	21. B	31. C	41. D
2. C	12. D	22. A	32. A	42. A
3. D	13. D	23. C	33. B	43. C
4. C	14. D	24. C	34. B	44. A
5. D	15. B	25. D	35. B	45. A
6. C	16. D	26. B	36. C	46. A
7. B	17. D	27. C	37. D	47. A
8. B	18. B	28. D	38. D	48. D
9. C	19. B	29. C	39. A	49. C
10. A	20. A	30. B	40. A	50. C

EXAMINATION SECTION
TEST 1

DIRECTIONS: Each question or incomplete statement is followed by several suggested answers or completions. Select the one that BEST answers the question or completes the statement. *PRINT THE LETTER OF THE CORRECT ANSWER IN THE SPACE AT THE RIGHT.*

1. The founder of the kindergarten idea and the kindergarten was 1.____
   - A. Pestalozzi
   - B. Froebel
   - C. Comenius
   - D. Rousseau

2. A leader in the field of the nongraded primary school is 2.____
   - A. John Goodlad
   - B. John Dewey
   - C. Donald Durell
   - D. Jack Kough

3. In Lancasterian schools, 3.____
   - A. a part or all of the teaching was done by the more advanced pupils
   - B. education for citizenship played an important role
   - C. a relaxed attitude prevailed
   - D. children were not graded

4. All of the following are authors of well-known children's books EXCEPT 4.____
   - A. Lois Lenski
   - B. Vladimir Nabokov
   - C. Marjorie Flack
   - D. May Hill Arbuthnot

5. Left to right directional movement in reading 5.____
   - A. must be taught
   - B. is natural to children
   - C. is common to all cultures
   - D. has no connection with the reading process

6. Of an incoming first grader, a teacher may reasonably expect to find that 6.____
   - A. he expresses his thoughts in complete simple sentences
   - B. his dialogue consists of several ideas which are connected by *and* or *and then*
   - C. he develops concepts inductively through comparatives such as *taller* and superlatives such as *earliest*
   - D. he conveys information through the use of casual connections such as *because* or *in order that*

7. If a child who has been assigned to a second-grade class in September is at the pre-primer level in her reading, the MOST fundamental policy should be to 7.____
   - A. have this child keep pace with the bulk of the class in the reader
   - B. determine the nature of the child's handicap as the basis for remediation
   - C. reassign the child to the same pre-primer until she has registered her mastery of the text
   - D. help the child catch up to the others through flash card drill using Dolch cards

8. The rate and pattern of early motor development of children depend MAINLY upon

   A. maturation
   B. training
   C. experience
   D. acculturation

9. Of the following, the physical activity which is LEAST suitable for kindergarten pupils is

   A. climbing a jungle gym
   B. running a relay race
   C. playing shadow tag
   D. doing a duck waddle

10. In seeking to direct children's activities toward goals, the teacher of early childhood classes must take into account children's developing capacities and should note that the capacity which is likely to emerge last is the capacity to

    A. persist and persevere in a self-adopted task
    B. relate things by analyzing a general class into its sub-classes
    C. go ahead on his own, once he knows what to do and how to do it
    D. organize his thoughts into a simple sequence

11. In maintaining the classroom, kindergarten pupils may be expected to help in all of the following activities EXCEPT

    A. adjusting windows
    B. taking care of plants and animals
    C. scrubbing tables
    D. mopping the floor

12. Evidence is accumulating to the effect that the preschool years are

    A. a period during which all pupils learn at the same rate
    B. a period when very little intellectual growth takes place
    C. not unlike any other age level with respect to intellectual growth
    D. an optimum period for rapid intellectual growth

13. In accordance with our knowledge of the growth characteristics of children in the lower grades, all of the following may be used as basic guidelines in conducting early childhood classes EXCEPT

    A. separating boys and girls during free-play time
    B. planning a variety of activities for each day
    C. planning classroom play with a definite aim
    D. utilizing concrete experiences wherever possible to teach concepts

14. Of the following statements dealing with establishing a desirable classroom atmosphere, the one which would be approved by MOST educational authorities is:

    A. It is wise to let no act of misbehavior go unpunished
    B. There are times when a teacher should deal with behavior itself, rather than the causes of that behavior

C. A teacher who genuinely loves her pupils and shows them this love will, as a result of this single factor, rarely have discipline problems
D. A teacher can develop good relationships with the pupils if she leads them to look upon her as their *pal*

15. Appropriate social attitudes, such as living harmoniously in class with one's classmates, are BEST taught in the early grades of school in

    A. situations as they arise, casually and incidentally, during the course of the school year
    B. situations for which the teacher makes deliberate plans, and in which she will praise children who exhibit cooperative behavior
    C. conjunction with all intellectual learnings as they occur in mathematics and language arts
    D. isolation from intellectual learnings, which would only be distracting elements with respect to the goal of harmonious relationships among school children

16. Building with blocks is an effective tool for developing each of the following EXCEPT

    A. a sense of balance and design
    B. manual skill
    C. observation and imagination
    D. a sense of color

17. Of the following statements regarding the philosophy of the social studies curriculum, the one with the LEAST validity is that

    A. skills and research techniques should be developed sequentially
    B. learning activities should aim at conceptualization
    C. the accumulation of data rather than the teaching of concepts should be emphasized
    D. unit procedures of instruction should be encouraged

18. In a unit in the first grade on the interdependence of communities, the LEAST appropriate fact among the following to stress is that

    A. the food we eat is grown or produced in other places
    B. we buy our food in stores
    C. many forms of transportation bring food to the city
    D. the foods we eat contain *the basic seven*

19. A first-grade teacher plans to introduce *counting by groups*. The LEAST appropriate first step would be to

    A. observe the methods the children use as they count
    B. ask all the children if they can count in a way other than by ones
    C. ask the children if they can count by ones
    D. line the class up in pairs and have the class repeat after her as she counts off each pair cumulatively as 2, 4, 6, 8, etc.

20. All of the following concepts are suitable for pre-kindergarten children EXCEPT

    A. one-half of the contents of a container
    B. number line direction
    C. number in sets of five objects
    D. clockwise direction

21. The MAIN purpose of guiding children in the use of tools and materials in the early childhood stage is to

    A. train them in manual dexterity as an end in itself
    B. hasten the development of children's fine muscles
    C. repeat the embryonic stages of development through which the vertebrates have evolved
    D. expose children to a variety of ways of using their senses and hands

22. Concerning the teaching of art, the statement among the following that is LEAST acceptable is:

    A. The teacher accepts whatever the child does, and feels it is good because the child did it
    B. The teacher provides skillful guidance and encouragement all along the way
    C. The teacher leads the child to originate and solve his problems and to think for himself
    D. Success in teaching art depends more on the teacher's interest, resourcefulness, and planning than on her ability to draw or paint

23. Of the following phases of the art program, the one MOST effective as a guidance technique is

    A. block building   B. painting
    C. puppetry   D. working with paper

24. The LEAST important criterion for selection of rote songs for Kg-2 is that the

    A. songs be short, melodious, rhythmic
    B. range of the song corresponds to the range of the children's voices
    C. songs be greatly varied in topics
    D. songs provide repetition of words and musical phrases

25. In developing the science topic, *How do we know it is windy today?*, a pre-kindergarten teacher takes the children outdoors on a warm but somewhat windy day. She tells the children, *Think about what you see the wind doing.* A few moments later, the class returns to the room, and the teacher lists pictorially the children's statements of what they saw the wind do.
    In this activity, the MOST serious lack in the teacher's approach is her failure to

    A. provide a variety of motor-sensory experiences
    B. individualize her approach
    C. encourage non-verbal children
    D. present a problem for solution

KEY (CORRECT ANSWERS)

1. B
2. A
3. A
4. B
5. A

6. A
7. B
8. A
9. B
10. B

11. A
12. D
13. A
14. B
15. B

16. D
17. C
18. D
19. D
20. C

21. D
22. A
23. C
24. C
25. A

TEST 2

DIRECTIONS: Each question or incomplete statement is followed by several suggested answers or completions. Select the one that BEST answers the question or completes the statement. *PRINT THE LETTER OF THE CORRECT ANSWER IN THE SPACE AT THE RIGHT.*

1. The child's need for love and security is satisfied through each of the following EXCEPT 1.____

   A. praise for work well done
   B. praise for genuine effort
   C. freedom to express himself whenever and however he wishes
   D. encouragement when he is slow to learn or to understand

2. All of the following have written books on cognition EXCEPT 2.____

   A. Albert Harris
   B. Arthur Jonas
   C. Jean Piaget
   D. David Russell

3. Of the following concepts basic to the development of the language arts program, the MOST important is that 3.____

   A. language instruction be based on the child's social experience
   B. many and varied materials be used to stimulate pupil expression
   C. pupil participation be encouraged by a warm, friendly environment
   D. language experiences be planned to help children to interpret, classify, and generalize

4. The MOST important factor in a reading readiness program is 4.____

   A. good oral communication
   B. recognition of differences in sounds
   C. understanding of sequence
   D. enjoyment of rhyme and rhythm

5. To introduce the type of book which does NOT tell a story, the teacher would probably select 5.____

   A. MAKE WAY FOR DUCKLINGS - McCloskey
   B. WILD AND TAME ANIMALS - Ipcar
   C. ASK MR. BEAR - Flack
   D. GROWL BEAR - Austin

6. The stories about the *devilish and incorrigible* little girl Madeline were written by 6.____

   A. Ludwig Bemelmans
   B. Dr. Seuss
   C. Wanda Gag
   D. Roger Duvoisin

7. All of the following are considered to be advantages of story-telling as opposed to story-reading EXCEPT: 7.____

   A. Story-telling requires a greater degree of familiarity with the story
   B. Story-telling enables the teacher to see as well as sense the reactions of children
   C. The story-teller may substitute synonyms when necessary
   D. The story-teller may add or omit incidents in the story

8. All of the following help to improve children's listening habits EXCEPT

   A. repetition of answers by the teacher to assure every child an opportunity to hear
   B. listening for errors or contradictions in oral reports
   C. preparation of pupil questions on the basis of discussions held in class
   D. frequent reading aloud by the teacher with the children answering questions on the content of the reading

9. Of the following trends in the organization of early childhood classes, the MOST recent is

   A. heterogeneous grouping
   B. the self-contained classroom
   C. the non-graded primary school
   D. homogeneous grouping

10. Of the following expectations of pre-kindergarten children, the MOST unreasonable is to ask the child to

    A. prepare and serve snacks to his classmates
    B. feed and care for a classroom pet
    C. refer to the clock to know when it is clean-up time
    D. scrub a table after a finger-painting activity

11. The educational movements, known as the infant school and the monitorial system, which influenced education in the United States during the 19th century originated in

    A. Germany   B. England   C. France   D. Russia

12. Of the following immediate measures for stopping individual misbehavior, the MOST sound pedagogically is to

    A. stand the child outside the classroom door
    B. focus your glance on him until he stops
    C. stop the lesson and scold him
    D. isolate him

13. If a teacher receives a long, rambling note from a parent complaining of prejudicial treatment to her child in class, the BEST policy for her to follow is to

    A. ignore the letter
    B. refer the parent to the guidance counselor

14. Of the following values of an anecdotal record, the MOST important is that it

    A. includes the interpretations of the teacher-observer
    B. need not be written regularly
    C. brings into focus the child's pattern of behavior
    D. records the most conspicuous incidents of a child's, behavior

15. Of the following map and globe skills, the MOST appropriate for development in the pre-kindergarten is

    A. becoming familiar with map symbols
    B. learning to make map plans

C. learning names of cardinal directions
D. orienting one's directions

16. The LEAST effective way of making a child aware of the form and rhythm of music is by

    A. encouraging him to respond with body movements
    B. developing a feeling for accent through clapping
    C. providing mimetic play experiences while listening to music
    D. affording him a large number of listening experiences

17. Although coloring books are a common means by which children satisfy their art activities, it is BEST if the teacher

    A. encourages their use
    B. discourages their use as they inhibit creativity
    C. uses them as busy work
    D. creates her own outline drawings

18. In teaching clay modeling, it is BEST if the teacher encourages the child to _____ method.

    A. discover his own   B. use the lump
    C. use the slab   D. use the coil

19. When children wish to use a hammer and nails during construction activities, it is MOST advisable for the teacher to

    A. discourage the activity as it is dangerous
    B. nail the construction
    C. supply only glue
    D. show the children how to use the tools

20. Of the following reasons why young children may scribble, the MOST usual is that scribbling is

    A. symbolic of disorganized thinking
    B. a stage of growth in drawing
    C. an indication of a child with a low I.Q.
    D. poor artistic ability

21. The paper which children generally use to paint on is called

    A. manila   B. newsprint
    C. construction   D. oak-tag

22. Of the following ways to teach kindergarten children the concept that *a magnet picks up things which have iron,* the BEST is to

    A. tell them
    B. let them play with toys with magnets in them
    C. let them discover it for themselves by experimentation
    D. use magnetic bulletin boards

23. Of the following activities, the one LEAST desirable in teaching kindergarten children to use mathematical concepts is

   A. setting the table for the number of boys and girls present
   B. counting crayons by twos
   C. blockbuilding to see size and shape relationships
   D. buying milk and crackers to learn about money

24. In order to individualize the teaching of mathematics in the first grade, the teacher should do all of the following EXCEPT

   A. have flexible grouping
   B. help the child make discoveries for himself
   C. develop various mathematical concepts through experiences
   D. have the child memorize addition and subtraction facts

25. Of the following procedures to be followed when taking a class on a trip, the one of LEAST value is

   A. a responsible child should be assigned to a troublesome child as a buddy
   B. children should not be permitted to purchase anything in subway stations
   C. children should wear name tags
   D. an attempt should be made to use first or last subway cars so that it will be easier to supervise the children

KEY (CORRECT ANSWERS)

1. C
2. A
3. C
4. A
5. B

6. A
7. A
8. A
9. C
10. C

11. B
12. B
13. D
14. C
15. D

16. D
17. B
18. A
19. D
20. B

21. B
22. C
23. B
24. D
25. D

TEST 3

DIRECTIONS: Each question or incomplete statement is followed by several suggested answers or completions. Select the one that BEST answers the question or completes the statement. *PRINT THE LETTER OF THE CORRECT ANSWER IN THE SPACE AT THE RIGHT.*

1. All of the following standardized tests contain tests of reading skills EXCEPT the

    A. Pintner-Cunningham Primary Test
    B. Iowa Every Pupil Test of Basic Skills
    C. Stanford Achievement Test
    D. Metropolitan Achievement Test

2. All of the following aspects of the Initial Teaching Alphabet method of teaching beginning reading are true EXCEPT the fact that:

    A. Each character has only one sound value
    B. The difference between upper case and lower case is eliminated
    C. This approach makes writing as well as reading easier for some children
    D. Children seem to experience marked difficulty in making the transition to traditional reading material

3. Among the requisites of a successful program to develop creative expression, the item of LEAST importance is

    A. experience with literature suited to interests and needs of children
    B. preparation in spelling and sentence structure
    C. flexibility and freedom from pressure
    D. wholesome social climate in classroom among peers

4. Of the following statements about reading readiness, the one of LEAST importance is the idea that

    A. practice to improve keenness of visual and auditory perception is usually necessary
    B. children must show a spontaneous desire to begin reading before they are taught to read
    C. the left to right progression requires more emphasis with some children than with others
    D. practically every aspect of a well-rounded kindergarten program has some value in building readiness for reading

5. Of the following types of poetry used in the early childhood program, the one of LEAST importance is

    A. counting rhymes   B. lyric poems
    C. free verse   D. narrative poems

6. The FIRST printed words that a child learns to read are generally introduced in context and are developed

    A. by phonetic analysis   B. as sight words
    C. by structural analysis   D. by contextual clues

7. All of the following have published well-known lists of children's vocabularies useful in the teaching of reading EXCEPT

   A. Arthur Jersild
   B. Edward Dolch
   C. Arthur Gates
   D. Clarence Stone

8. When a test measures what it purports to measure, it

   A. has reliability
   B. is objective
   C. is standardized
   D. has validity

9. *The formulation of generalizations drawn from experience and the dealing with abstractions* may be given as a definition of the mental activity known as

   A. sensation
   B. perception
   C. imagination
   D. reasoning

10. A second-grade class is given standardized tests in reading and arithmetic. If the medians of both tests are practically identical, the correlation between the achievement of individual pupils in the class is

    A. high
    B. low
    C. average
    D. undetermined

11. A recent trend in the organization of the elementary school is

    A. classification according to standardized testing
    B. the non-graded primary
    C. the self-contained classroom
    D. homogeneous grouping

12. All of the following aspects of kindergarten routines are considered worthwhile EXCEPT:

    A. All routines should be carefully planned and established
    B. Routines teach children to follow directions
    C. All routines should be listed on a chart to help children remember them
    D. Some routines can be matters of general school policy

13. A child in a teacher's class suddenly becomes ill. He doubles up in pain, turns pale, complains of severe abdominal pain, and says he feels faint.
    Of the following things, the one that the teacher should do FIRST is to

    A. send the child to the school nurse, accompanied by another child
    B. call the parent and tell her to come to school
    C. consult the health card to help determine how serious this attack is
    D. send for the nearest supervisor and get his assistance

14. In considering educational programs for the disadvantaged child, all of the following are generally accepted EXCEPT:

    A. The school and its staff are key elements in preventing and overcoming educational retardation
    B. There are strengths in the lifestyle of the disadvantaged that can be capitalized on in building an educational program
    C. Early experiential deprivation has no effect on cognitive and perceptual development

D. Training and retraining in the implementation and modification of the curriculum should be ongoing

15. Several stories that help teach young children good manners were written by   15.____

    A. Munro Leaf   B. Dr. Suess
    C. Eleanor Farjeon   D. P.L. Travers

16. That it is wiser to join forces to beat a common enemy than to fight at home was the decision resolved upon by two characters in   16.____

    A. BILL AND BLAZE - C.W. Anderson
    B. FINDER'S KEEPERS - Will and Nicolas
    C. THE FAST SOONER HOUND - Arna Bontemps and Jack Conroy
    D. BUTTONS - Tom Robinson

17. POET LAUREATE OF CHILDHOOD is MOST often associated with   17.____

    A. Robert Louis Stevenson   B. Kate Greenaway
    C. Rachel Field   D. Amy Lowell

18. All of the following titles are matched correctly with their author EXCEPT   18.____

    A. MILLIONS OF CATS - Wanda Gag
    B. THE STORY ABOUT PING - Marjorie Flack
    C. MADELINE - Margaret Wise Brown
    D. THE STORY OF BABAR, THE LITTLE ELEPHANT - Jean de Brunhoff

19. In teaching map skills in the first grade, it is LEAST appropriate to use   19.____

    A. blocks to make a map of the school block
    B. the sandbox to reconstruct a trip to the boiler room
    C. a road map to trace the trip to the zoo
    D. clay to depict the construction site visited on a trip

20. All of the following factors affect seasonal changes in weather EXCEPT the   20.____

    A. slant of the sun's rays as they strike the earth
    B. rotation of the earth on its axis
    C. revolution of the earth around the sun
    D. tilt of the earth's axis

21. It is UNREASONABLE to expect first-grade pupils to be able to   21.____

    A. select dominoes and name the number of spots on each part
    B. write numerals on prepared worksheets
    C. estimate the numerical value of a group of coins
    D. find a subset within a set

22. All of the following mathematical activities are suitable for pre-kindergarten children EXCEPT   22.____

    A. pouring liquids into differently shaped containers
    B. finding a place to sit at the table for a snack
    C. placing books in a vertical alignment
    D. measuring ingredients for baking cookies

23. Of the following statements regarding mathematical learnings, the one with the LEAST validity is:

    Children

    A. develop their mathematical ideas best when they can use materials constructively
    B. who can work and play independently are more likely to learn mathematics easier
    C. must be able to use mathematical sentences and terms before they can absorb mathematical ideas
    D. who are able to be comfortable with the teacher have less difficulty in developing mathematical ideas

24. Of the following statements regarding art experiences for young children, the one with the LEAST validity is:

    A. Creative expression should be encouraged
    B. A variety of materials should be accessible
    C. Challenging experiences to stimulate ideas should always be individualized
    D. Manipulation of materials is to be expected

25. In AMERICA, the line following *Author of liberty* is

    A. Thy name I love
    B. To Thee we sing
    C. Of Thee we sing
    D. Of thee I sing

KEY (CORRECT ANSWERS)

1. A
2. D
3. B
4. B
5. C

6. B
7. A
8. D
9. D
10. D

11. B
12. C
13. D
14. C
15. A

16. B
17. A
18. C
19. C
20. B

21. C
22. D
23. C
24. C
25. B

TEST 4

DIRECTIONS: Each question or incomplete statement is followed by several suggested answers or completions. Select the one that BEST answers the question or completes the statement. *PRINT THE LETTER OF THE CORRECT ANSWER IN THE SPACE AT THE RIGHT.*

1. One concept that is NOT true in considering individualized reading is that

   A. reading is an active, aggressive thinking process, a complex and individualized experience which contributes to a child's living
   B. individualized reading is not so much a method as a different organization of time and materials
   C. individualized reading obviates the need for having a controlled vocabulary in early reading instruction
   D. the development of reading skills is an important aspect of individualized reading, although the approach does not attempt to organize their development in prescribed sequence

2. Dr. Martin Deutsch is known for his

   A. book YOUNG CHILDREN'S THINKING
   B. work with the Educational Testing Service
   C. connection with the Institute for Developmental Studies
   D. book THE CULTURALLY DEPRIVED CHILD

3. Of the following educational leaders, the one MOST closely associated with the origin of the kindergarten is

   A. Francis Petrarch   B. Friedrich Froebel
   C. Johann Pestalozzi   D. Herbert Spencer

4. When a parent comes to a teacher for help with a problem involving her child, the MOST fruitful way, of the following, for the teacher to end the interview is to

   A. assure the parent that the teacher will find a satisfactory solution
   B. thank the parent, and say that, now that the teacher is aware of the problem, she will deal with it the very next time it arises
   C. agree with the parent on a definite, cooperative course of action
   D. assure the parent that, if the problem becomes serious enough, she will bring it to the attention of the school guidance counselor

5. Of the following uses of testing, the LEAST desirable is to

   A. discover pupils' learning difficulties
   B. verify the placement of pupils in groups or grades
   C. measure the progress of individuals or of the class
   D. enable parents to compare the achievement of their children with that of other children in the class

6. Most authorities would agree that deprived children tend to come to school with all of the following handicaps EXCEPT that they

   A. have a poorer self-image than middle-class children have
   B. have inadequate training in auditory discrimination

C. are generally less independent in caring for themselves than middle-class children are
D. do not adequately understand the need for deferring gratification

7. All of these statements about the Initial Teaching Alphabet (I.T.A.), a medium for teaching beginning reading, are correct EXCEPT:

   A. It is an alphabet with more than 26 characters
   B. It is based on the fact that English is a phonetic language
   C. A book printed in I.T.A. has a different appearance from one printed in traditional orthography
   D. Children learning I.T.A. usually make the transition to traditional orthography with little difficulty

8. All of the following are appropriate procedures in the first lessons in the teaching of penmanship EXCEPT: The

   A. paper is properly placed on the desk
   B. children should be taught good habits of posture
   C. children should write in ink
   D. children should be motivated to write well

9. In planning activities for very young children, all of the following are important EXCEPT

   A. planning blocks of time of varied length
   B. alternating active and quiet activities
   C. allowing flexibility to meet children's immediate needs and interests
   D. arranging at least one period every day when the children can practice writing their names

10. All of the following are correct statements about teaching young children EXCEPT:

    A. Young children should not be required to memorize poems
    B. The teacher can sometimes read a story to only one or two children while the others are working at something else
    C. Teachers should refrain from *making up* stories to tell the children since there are so many fine children's books available
    D. It is best if stories are short

11. In the social studies program in the first grade, the LEAST effective source of learning would be

    A. a picture history of the United States
    B. a child's interview with his father about his work
    C. celebration of national holidays
    D. a class visit to the neighborhood firehouses

12. The metal parts of a pupil's desk may affect experiments he performs which involve

    A. a compass   B. a dry cell
    C. static electricity D. spring scales

13. Among the following, the planned experience in a center of interest on pets that is likely to teach the MOST science is a   13.____

    A. lecture about the care of a turtle
    B. story about a turtle
    C. filmstrip about the care of pets
    D. turtle cared for in the classroom

14. Even a very young child can discover that air exerts pressure through   14.____

    A. observing the air he blows into a plastic bag lift a notebook
    B. listening to the teacher read a science story, ALL ABOUT AIR
    C. watching the weather vane
    D. looking at pictures of air pumps

15. In testing for automatic response to basic mathematical facts, it is GOOD practice to   15.____

    A. test only those children who, it is believed, have automatic response to the facts
    B. test the whole class at one time
    C. test those children who it is believed have no automatic response to the facts
    D. allow children plenty of time to think through to the answers

16. Children in the second grade learn the concept of taking away 2 from numbers   16.____

    A. by copying the subtraction examples on the board
    B. by reversing the order of the numbers
    C. by finding the missing numeral
    D. through experience situations using representative material

17. In teaching basic facts, such as 7 plus 7, the procedure which is LEAST effective is to   17.____

    A. have children count out the sum on their tens frames
    B. relate to the double, 6 and 6
    C. relate to 10 (7+3) + 3
    D. relate to the double, 7 and 7

18. All of the following are musical concepts to be developed in early childhood EXCEPT   18.____

    A. melodic direction
    B. major and minor modes
    C. variations in tonal volume
    D. tempo

19. An orchestral instrument in the woodwind family is the   19.____

    A. viola   B. French horn
    C. tuba   D. English horn

20. The following melodies all have three beats to a measure EXCEPT   20.____

    A. AMERICA   B. SKATERS' WALTZ
    C. SHOO FLY   D. ON TOP OF OLD SMOKEY

21. Of the following, the procedure MOST likely to result in development of children's art expression is	21._____

   A. directed learning of specific techniques
   B. exploration and use of materials
   C. practice in using one medium
   D. familiarity with great works of art

22. Of the following, the dance NOT specifically designated as a basic dance for an early childhood grade is	22._____

   A. CHIMES OF DUNKIRK   B. PUTTJENTER
   C. HOPP MOR ANNIKA   D. OH, SUSANNA

23. Of the following, the one that can be used to reinforce the concept of *left* and *right* is	23._____

   A. LOOBY LOO   B. SALLY GO ROUND THE SUN
   C. SKIP TO MY LOU   D. RIG A JIG, JIG

24. Meaningful expression through art in early childhood grades is likely to be inhibited by	24._____

   A. fingerpainting with one color
   B. cutting out ready-printed patterns
   C. having the children's painting exhibited in the classroom
   D. making a collage

25. If the teacher insists on realistic representation in painting in pre-kindergarten classes, she will	25._____

   A. inhibit the child with a highly developed tactile sense
   B. encourage all children to produce better drawings
   C. produce students who are excellent draftsmen
   D. encourage enthusiasm for the art lesson

KEY (CORRECT ANSWERS)

1.	C	11.	A
2.	C	12.	A
3.	B	13.	D
4.	C	14.	A
5.	D	15.	A
6.	C	16.	D
7.	B	17.	A
8.	C	18.	B
9.	D	19.	D
10.	C	20.	C

21. B
22. B
23. A
24. B
25. A

EXAMINATION SECTION
TEST 1

DIRECTIONS: Each question or incomplete statement is followed by several suggested answers or completions. Select the one that BEST answers the question or completes the statement. *PRINT THE LETTER OF THE CORRECT ANSWER IN THE SPACE AT THE RIGHT.*

1. In pre-kindergarten groups, the paraprofessionals should participate in all of the following EXCEPT

    A. reporting to parents about children's behavior
    B. assisting at parent workshops
    C. cooperating in the planning and preparation of the day's activities
    D. assisting with the clean-up routines

2. In connection with planning for teaching a kindergarten class, all of the following statements are true EXCEPT that

    A. effective planning for kindergarten teaching starts with long-range goals
    B. specific short-range plans should be realistic and appropriate for the specific children involved
    C. the extent of detail in planning depends largely on the personality and experience of the teacher
    D. a plan for teaching once made should not be departed from

3. Of the following statements relating to the importance of children's discovering new ideas and new relationships for themselves, the one which is INCORRECT is:

    A. The name of Piaget has been associated with this method of learning
    B. The child comes to some understanding of his environment through his own efforts
    C. This method does not allow for the giving of direct instructions
    D. Organized information may be supplied directly for the child's use

4. The arithmetic mean of a set of reading scores is calculated by

    A. dividing the sum of all the scores by the number of scores
    B. adding the sum of all the scores to the number of scores
    C. multiplying by their average the scores occurring most frequently
    D. none of these methods

5. De facto school segregation refers to school segregation which results from

    A. federal education laws
    B. rulings of the State Commissioner of Education
    C. housing patterns
    D. state laws

6. In setting up classroom routines and safety procedures, the teacher should be guided by the principle that in these areas

    A. the teacher should never ask for pupils' suggestions
    B. generally the interests of an individual must be subordinated to those of the group

C. the interests of the individual are supreme
D. the needs of the entire school are paramount, without regard to the children in any one class

7. When kindergarten children ask questions about matters dealing with sex and the origin of life, the teacher should deal with such questions by

   A. tactfully evading the questions until the children are older
   B. answering frankly and truthfully to satisfy the children's curiosity
   C. referring the children to experts
   D. ignoring them completely

8. Knowing only the highest and lowest obtained scores on a test makes it possible to compute which one of the following?

   A. Standard deviation
   B. Range of scores
   C. Semi-interquartile range
   D. Average deviation

9. If a parent, during an interview with her son's teacher, finds fault with the colleague who taught her boy the previous year, the teacher should do which one of the following?

   A. Listen until the mother has finished and then begin discussing the boy's work
   B. Refer the mother to the principal
   C. Defend her colleague and then point out the boy's strengths and weaknesses
   D. Interrupt her politely and ask her to discuss with you the boy's present progress

10. Of the following statements regarding procedures to be used by the teacher when dealing with an ill child, the one which is INCORRECT is:

    A. Call the parent and send the child home immediately
    B. Send the child to the school nurse with an adult escort
    C. Write a medical referral slip
    D. Notify the supervisor if the nurse is not available

11. With regard to parent-teacher conferences, the LEAST acceptable of the following statements is:
    The

    A. teacher should select no more than one or two aspects of the child's problem for consideration during a single conference
    B. parent should be encouraged to talk; the teacher's listening should be passive
    C. teacher should indicate at the beginning of the conference how much time is alloted to it
    D. teacher should summarize briefly at the conclusion of the conference the points dealt with

12. Of the following, the educational thinker who is BEST known for emphasizing the use of pictures as visual aids to learning is

    A. John Amos Comenius   B. Friedrich Froebel
    C. John Locke   D. William C. Bagley

13. In a court decision, Federal Judge J. Skelly Wright extended the Supreme Court's decision prohibiting *de jure* school segregation to include *de facto* segregation in the city of   13.____

    A. New York
    B. Washington, D.C.
    C. Atlanta
    D. Chicago

14. If a first-grade pupil who is active on the playground refuses to participate in classroom activities and cries when asked to do so, his teacher should   14.____

    A. encourage him gradually, on the assumption that he is afraid
    B. insist that he participate, on the assumption that he is stubborn
    C. recommend that he stay at home until he is more mature
    D. none of the above

15. The author and book paired INCORRECTLY below are: 15.____

    A. Montessori - THE CULTURALLY DEPRIVED CHILD
    B. Passow - EDUCATION IN DEPRESSED AREAS
    C. Bruner - PROCESS OF EDUCATION
    D. James - TALKS TO TEACHERS

16. The artist Ernest H. Shepard is the celebrated illustrator of all of the following EXCEPT   16.____

    A. WINNIE THE POOH
    B. THE WIND IN THE WILLOWS
    C. PETER RABBIT
    D. NOW WE ARE SIX

17. A character who is determined to keep his promise, no matter what circumstances befall, is to be found in Dr. Seuss' story   17.____

    A. HORTON HATCHES THE EGG
    B. THIDWICK, THE BIGHEARTED MOOSE
    C. YERTLE THE TURTLE
    D. BARTHOLOMEW AND THE OOBLECK

18. All of the following popular books have Black children, attractively pictured, as major characters EXCEPT   18.____

    A. Ezra Jack Keats' THE SNOWY DAY
    B. Selina Chonz's A BELL FOR URSLI
    C. Lorraine & Jerrold Beims's TWO IS A TEAM
    D. Marguerite d'Angeli's BRIGHT APRIL

19. A husband-and-wife team recognized as outstanding authorities on Mother Goose and other nursery rhymes includes   19.____

    A. Ingri and Edgar d'Aulaire
    B. Maud and Miska Petersham
    C. Berta and Elmer Hader
    D. Peter and Iona Opie

20. A character finds a book and carries it around all the time, in the hope of looking wise, even though unable to read, in   20.____

    A. Marjorie Flack's THE STORY ABOUT PING
    B. Don Freeman's DANDELION
    C. Lydia Freeman's PET OF THE MET
    D. Roger du Voisin's PETUNIA

21. The story of a little boy's anguish in his determined efforts to obtain his own library card is told in

   A. Beverly Cleary's HENRY HUGGINS
   B. Leo Politi's LITTLE LEO
   C. Eleanor Estes' RUFUS M.
   D. Dorothy Rowe's RABBIT LANTERN

22. The concepts of *little, middle-sized,* and *big* are developed in which one of the following stories?

   A. THREE LITTLE PIGS
   B. AMELIA BEDELIA
   C. THREE BILLY GOATS GRUFF
   D. HENNY-PENNY AND CHICKEN LITTLE

23. An account of a little girl who lived in a mole's house is found in the fairy tale entitled

   A. THE OLD HOUSE
   B. THE SNOW QUEEN
   C. THUMBELINA
   D. THE LITTLE MATCH GIRL

24. Margaret Wise Brown was the author of a popular series about a little dog called

   A. Angus   B. Ribsy   C. Muffin   D. Blaze

25. *NO, no, no, and again no! I promised my Good Fairy to become a well-conducted boy, and I will keep my word* is a declaration of good intentions uttered in

   A. Hans A. Rey's CURIOUS GEORGE
   B. C. Collodi's PINOCCHIO
   C. Hardie Gramatky's LITTLE TOOT
   D. Elsa Beskow's PELLE'S NEW SUIT

26. All of the following are correct statements about kindergarten methods and materials EXCEPT:

   A. *Playing house* helps children to interact
   B. The block collection should consist of blocks in many different sizes and shapes
   C. Simple tools, but now saws, should be used at the workbench
   D. Children may dip their fingers into paint and then move their fingers on paper

27. In planning for a good language-arts activity in the kindergarten, the LEAST valuable of the following is to

   A. arrange the furniture so that children sit in a cozy circle
   B. plan the lesson very carefully in advance
   C. have the more verbal children sit together
   D. arrange to have attractive manipulative and illustrative materials at hand

28. The LEAST valuable of the following ways for a child to follow up the teacher's reading of a story to the class is to

   A. read it aloud to the other children
   B. re-enact parts of the story dramatically
   C. tell the class of similar experiences he has had
   D. make a hand puppet representing a character in the story and with it dramatize the story

29. Of the following experiences, the one that would be LEAST appropriate for a kindergarten program is

   A. looking at alphabet picture books
   B. singing alphabet rhymes
   C. feeling felt and sandpaper letters
   D. tracing letters with a pencil

30. Which of the following may NOT be considered one of the current approaches to teaching beginning reading?

   A. The Initial Teaching Alphabet
   B. *Hooked On Phonics*
   C. Senesh materials
   D. The *language experience* method

31. Of the following physical characteristics of the pre-kindergarten child, the one which is INCORRECT is that he

   A. begins to develop small muscle control
   B. is susceptible to communicable diseases
   C. is usually nearsighted
   D. needs frequent rest

32. When treating a child for a puncture wound, a teacher may do all of the following EXCEPT

   A. apply iodine to sterilize the wound
   B. apply tincture of green soap to cleanse the wound
   C. wash the wound with cold water
   D. cover the wound with a sterile gauze pad

33. The part of the eye responsible for controlling the amount of light which enters the eyeball is the

   A. cornea   B. retina   C. lens   D. iris

34. In attempting to develop awareness of pitch in young children, the teacher may have pupils match various notes she plays on the piano with sounds they make on

   A. triangles
   B. bells on sticks
   C. cymbals
   D. melody bells

35. All of the following kinds of vocal music are correctly paired EXCEPT

   A. round - descant
   B. chantey - work song
   C. plain song - chant
   D. unison - counterpoint

36. Numbering the bars of a flat xylophone from 1 to 8 beginning with the longest one at her left, the teacher strikes the bars numbered 3-2-1-2-3-3-3. She expects the children correctly to identify the melody as the first phrase of

   A. HOME ON THE RANGE
   B. MARY HAD A LITTLE LAMB
   C. THE MUFFIN MAN
   D. BLUEBIRD

37. All of the following statements about the music program are generally true EXCEPT: 37._____

    A. Children in kindergarten can make their own percussion instruments
    B. Rhythm instruments should be available to pre-kindergarten children during free play
    C. JENNIE JENKINS is a song that can be used for reinforcing concepts of colors
    D. String orchestras are usually organized in the kindergarten

38. Of the following practices, when teaching a song with a record, the MOST educationally sound is to 38._____

    A. have the children say the words
    B. provide for rhythmic response
    C. select a song that does not contain much repetition
    D. play the record as loudly as possible

39. The following instruments are all suitable for use in an average first-grade class EXCEPT 39._____

    A. tambourine   B. bells
    C. triangle   D. recorder

40. To ask a child engaged in an art activity, *What is it?* 40._____

    A. may engender confusion and uncertainty
    B. shows that the teacher is interested
    C. helps the child to clarify his thoughts
    D. suggests that the pupil may not have responded to the teacher's directions

41. Beginning finger painting with preschool children would involve all of the following EXCEPT 41._____

    A. the use of one color selected by the child himself
    B. the use of glossy paper
    C. the free choice of many colors from jars placed on each desk
    D. painting at available tables

42. Of the following, the LEAST sound practice, educationally, is for the kindergarten teacher to 42._____

    A. provide exposure to and discussion of attractive pictures and illustrations
    B. establish routines for the putting away of materials
    C. provide well-cut stencils for the children to trace
    D. let children paint with water on the chalkboard

43. Of the following, the MOST important thing the careful study of all of a child's art experiences could possibly show would be that the 43._____

    A. child was introduced to many media
    B. child was skillfully motivated
    C. art experiences had promoted the child's creative and mental growth
    D. teacher's corrections on the child's art work had made his drawing more recognizable

44. The author of ART AS EXPERIENCE who saw education as *the continuing re-creation of experience* was

    A. Erich Fromm
    B. Henry Barnard
    C. John Dewey
    D. Horace Mann

45. Choose the statement LEAST appropriate to clay experiences in early childhood classes.

    A. Each child should have a lump of clay the size of a small grapefruit.
    B. The child should be permitted to experiment with the manipulation of clay.
    C. The teacher should praise non-realistic forms that result from good handling of clay.
    D. The teacher should urge the children to strive for realism in their work.

46. In order to help children learn to tell wind direction, the teacher can construct with them a simple

    A. hygrometer
    B. wind vane
    C. aneroid barometer
    D. bar magnet compass

47. All of the following can be grown from bulbs EXCEPT

    A. amaryllis
    B. hyacinth
    C. narcissus
    D. marigold

48. In introducing scientific concepts to early childhood classes, the LEAST acceptable technique is to

    A. hear the children express scientific principles read to them by their parents
    B. provide simple, home-made demonstrations of scientific principles
    C. encourage pupil observation and discussion
    D. show a filmstrip depicting ideas in concrete, clear fashion

49. Which one of the following statements about the area of science is NOT acceptable to a teacher of early childhood classes?

    A. Demonstration by the teacher should follow a study of appropriate texts.
    B. The science program should give children an understanding of the influence of science on modern living.
    C. Science is both a content area and a method of learning.
    D. Characteristics that distinguish the scientifically minded person can be developed in young children.

50. Games in which children dramatize *off* and *on*, *up* and *down*, *small* and *large* can be used in a first-grade class CHIEFLY to

    A. develop concepts and a vocabulary for mathematics
    B. release pupils' tensions
    C. provide large muscle activity
    D. develop manuscript writing

KEY (CORRECT ANSWERS)

1. A	11. B	21. C	31. C	41. C
2. D	12. A	22. C	32. A	42. C
3. C	13. B	23. C	33. D	43. C
4. A	14. A	24. C	34. D	44. C
5. C	15. A	25. B	35. D	45. D
6. B	16. C	26. C	36. B	46. B
7. B	17. A	27. C	37. D	47. D
8. B	18. B	28. A	38. B	48. A
9. D	19. D	29. D	39. D	49. A
10. A	20. D	30. C	40. A	50. A

TEST 2

DIRECTIONS: Each question or incomplete statement is followed by several suggested answers or completions. Select the one that BEST answers the question or completes the statement. *PRINT THE LETTER OF THE CORRECT ANSWER IN THE SPACE AT THE RIGHT.*

1. MOST educators believe that the prime factor which determines the quality of learning in early childhood classes is

    A. the quality of experiences the children engage in
    B. the selection of materials
    C. a sympathetic teacher
    D. an appropriate classroom climate

    1._____

2. A parent should do all of the following to prepare a pre-school child for reading EXCEPT to

    A. re-use and pronounce carefully words that the child mispronounces
    B. call his attention to signs or labels in stores, railroad stations, etc.
    C. help him to *spell out* words that he does not seem to recognize
    D. help him to play with alphabet blocks so that he begins to recognize letters

    2._____

3. Of the following procedures, the one with which the teacher should be LEAST concerned on the first day she meets her class in September is

    A. being certain that pupils learn something new about which they can tell their parents
    B. establishing routines for the daily functioning of the class
    C. consulting previous records of children, if they are available
    D. arranging for the giving of a standardized reading test so that she may group pupils accurately

    3._____

4. Each of the following is matched with his contribution to education EXCEPT

    A. Horace Mann - practical interest in public education
    B. William Holmes McGuffey - compilation of material for reading texts reflecting the political, religious, and moral issues of the 19th century
    C. John Locke - stress on habit formation
    D. William H. Kilpatrick - emphasis on the prestige of erudition

    4._____

5. Your supervisor asks you to select the principle underlying play activities which you consider most important for discussion with your class mothers who have remarked that your children have too much play.
    Which of the following would be MOST helpful in this situation?
    Play activities

    A. are carefully planned with definite purposes in mind
    B. are a limited part of the day's program
    C. afford relaxation for the children
    D. present opportunities for small group and individual instruction with children other than those in the play group

    5._____

6. All of the following are true of effective questioning during a lesson EXCEPT that

   A. questions may serve a variety of purposes
   B. key questions should be written down in advance by inexperienced teachers
   C. questions should be directed only to volunteers, to avoid embarrassment
   D. questions should be posed just once to insure attention

7. As Miss Jones, the kindergarten teacher, passes the blocks area, Johnny asks her to *go for a ride on the bus* with him.
   The MOST acceptable reaction for her would be to

   A. spend the next ten minutes riding on his *bus*
   B. say that she is very busy, but will ride later
   C. perch briefly on *a seat on the bus*
   D. suggest that one of the other children should be his passenger

8. If a parent asks how she may help her five-year-old child to prepare for reading, the POOREST suggestion that a teacher might give is to

   A. read aloud to him
   B. take him on trips
   C. teach him the alphabet
   D. engage him in conversation frequently

9. All of the following names are associated with standardized reading tests EXCEPT

   A. Gates
   B. Gray
   C. Pintner-Cunningham
   D. Durrell-Sullivan

10. All of the following are associated with Pestalozzi EXCEPT

    A. Leonard and Gertrude
    B. The Evening Hour with a Hermit
    C. Neuhof
    D. Emile

11. In planning a schedule for the day in kindergarten, the teacher should do all of the following EXCEPT

    A. provide for rest periods
    B. allow time for children to *clean up*
    C. guide children into using various centers of interest
    D. set a specific unvarying time for shifting from each activity to the next

12. All of the following are desirable elements of an expressional writing lesson EXCEPT

    A. a multi-sensory approach to motivating for writing
    B. strong emphasis on correct usage and punctuation
    C. discussion prior to writing
    D. stress on precise use of words to express meaning

13. Handwriting instruction in the primary grades places LEAST emphasis upon the

    A. amenities of note-writing
    B. development of the mechanics of writing

C. speed of writing
D. relationship of writing to experiences

14. All of the following statements about reading are generally true EXCEPT: 14._____

    A. Listening-comprehension skills are related to reading-comprehension skills
    B. Writing should precede reading
    C. Activities should develop motivation for reading
    D. Teachers' manuals suggest many worthwhile activities

15. All of the following statements about the use of experience charts as an effective bridge between the spoken and the written word are true EXCEPT: 15._____

    A. Children with meager vocabularies cannot contribute
    B. The charts are used to reinforce reading skills
    C. Standards of readability must be maintained
    D. The children learn to select pertinent ideas for recording

16. Of the following, the LEAST appropriate activity for early childhood classes learning the alphabet is   16._____

    A. observing the letters on the alphabet chart
    B. using felt and sandpaper letters
    C. writing the alphabet for homework
    D. recognizing letters in alphabet picture books

17. Of the following animated cartoon characters used by Walt Disney, the one which was NOT his own creation is   17._____

    A. Mickey Mouse   B. Dumbo
    C. Snow White   D. The Singing Whale

18. Limericks, Jumblies, and the BOOK OF NONSENSE recall the author-artist who also wrote   18._____

    A. THE POBBLE WHO HAS NO TOES
    B. JABBERWOCKY
    C. THE PURPLE COW
    D. THE LITTLE MAN WHO WASN'T THERE

19. Mulock's LITTLE LAME PRINCE describes how the prince learned about the world by means of his use of   19._____

    A. a swallow who was his friend
    B. wise old advisers
    C. a magic flying coat
    D. a magic crystal ball

20. Curious George in the series by H.A. Rey is a(n)   20._____

    A. little boy   B. monkey
    C. elephant   D. goat

21. A cat swallows an ogre who had changed himself into a mouse and then gives the ogre's head to the Lord Marquis of Carabas in   21._____

    A. THE FIRE CAT
    B. MILLIONS OF CATS
    C. PUSS IN BOOTS
    D. THE CAT WHO WENT TO HEAVEN

22. Both WINNIE THE POOH and DICK WHITTINGTON AND HIS CAT take place in   22._____

    A. Paris   B. London
    C. Dublin   D. New Orleans

23. Of the following, the one who is NOT an author of folk or fairy tales for children is   23._____

    A. Herbert Zim   B. Claire Huchet Bishop
    C. Beatrix Potter   D. Margery Bianco

24. A princess is made to laugh in the story of   24._____

    A. THE GOLDEN GOOSE   B. THE MUSICIANS OF BREMEN
    C. THE THREE BROTHERS   D. THE SNOW CHILD

25. All of the following collaborators are noted for their work in children's literature EXCEPT   25._____

    A. Richard and Florence Atwater
    B. Maud and Miska Petersham
    C. Mary and Daniel Beard
    D. Ann and Paul Rand

26. The central character of Roger Duvoisin's series of books about Petunia is a   26._____

    A. goat   B. pig   C. goose   D. donkey

27. In the teaching of social studies to a first-grade class, the practice which is LEAST acceptable is   27._____

    A. emphasis on activities suggested in workbooks
    B. relation of content to pupils' experiences
    C. relation of activities to a holiday at the appropriate time
    D. conducting informal discussions about work done by parents

28. Of the following attempts of a teacher to smooth the transition of children who have come to her kindergarten class from prekindergarten, the one LEAST to be recommended is   28._____

    A. making a careful study of the children's prekindergarten records
    B. encouraging parents to attend workshops
    C. planning lessons on familiar stories
    D. having reading activities take the place of play

29. All of the following statements about neighborhood field trips are generally true EXCEPT: 29._____

    A. They can provide meaningful science learnings
    B. They are a resource near at hand for pupil discovery
    C. No planning is needed for a neighborhood walk
    D. The effects of natural forces may be seen

30. Among the following, the LEAST appropriate activity for a second-grade class studying about animals is to

   A. ask the zoo to provide a speaker with live pets
   B. invite a local veterinarian to address the class
   C. encourage the children to bring in caterpillars
   D. test the children on their ability to identify birds most likely to be found in the city

31. All of the following are suitable pets for the classroom terrarium EXCEPT _____ snakes.

   A. milk   B. coral   C. garter   D. grass

32. All of the following are useful procedures in building kindergarten science experiences EXCEPT

   A. caring for plants
   B. observing weather and how it affects children
   C. caring for fish
   D. building models of cars and airplanes

33. Of the following, the key signature which has 3 flats is

   A. B flat major   B. G minor
   C. E flat major   D. D minor

34. The musical term *adagio* means

   A. in running tempo   B. with animation
   C. slowly, leisurely   D. faster

35. Of the following, the MOST educationally valid reason for having young children sing in a variety of classroom situations is to

   A. build readiness for part-singing
   B. help the unresponsive child find his singing voice
   C. build readiness for choral speaking
   D. help the child learn words to songs

36. When the teacher calls attention to the sound of a *honk* from an automobile horn, her main purpose is likely to be to develop

   A. pitch consciousness   B. rhythmic response
   C. conversational singing   D. tone production

37. The minor key relative to A^b major is _____ minor.

   A. F sharp   B. E flat   C. E   D. F

38. Children's art activities are USUALLY most self-satisfying when they are derived from

   A. their own experiences and interests
   B. exercises in art textbooks and bulletins
   C. the teacher's wide experience
   D. models exhibited on classroom bulletin boards

39. When looking at a young child's scrawled drawing, a teacher should

   A. try to identify the subject matter
   B. say, *Tell me about it*
   C. reprimand the child for being messy
   D. show the child how the drawing should look

40. During an art activity, while the children are working, the teacher's main concern should be to

   A. use the time mainly to catch up on clerical work
   B. keep a watchful eye for any discipline problems that might arise
   C. walk around the room to make certain that all the children are working
   D. watch for children who may need guidance so that she may give help and encouragement

41. An activity INAPPROPRIATE as an early childhood art experience is

   A. woodworking
   B. modelling in papier mache
   C. block building
   D. metalcraft

42. Of the following, the one which is an indispensable part of every lesson in cut-paper design is having

   A. individual or group evaluation at the end
   B. prepared designs for all pupils
   C. a large supply of construction paper
   D. crepe paper and heavy cardboard

43. Of the following, the art activity that will give the prekindergarten child MOST satisfaction in the exercise of his limited motor control is to

   A. weave on a cardboard loom
   B. trace around and cut out a specific object
   C. crayon within the limits of an outlined shape
   D. manipulate prepared dough or clay

44. In general, young children are MOST readily attracted by

   A. rhythmic line
   B. bright color
   C. strongly silhouetted shapes
   D. related three-dimensional forms

45. All of the following are acceptable procedures in the development of meaning in mathematics in the first grade EXCEPT

   A. postponing mathematics instruction until pupils can read
   B. leading children to discover number relationships before expecting memorization
   C. providing experiences to build understanding
   D. using beads on a frame to represent numbers

46. A check of the environmental and safety factors of the classroom should be made as part of 46.____

    A. spring and fall health days
    B. the daily health observation
    C. a weekly safety survey
    D. the teacher's term plan

47. A kindergarten teacher plays the piano. Her children turn and jump up and down; some waddle, then walk in a disconnected way. 47.____
    The MOST likely explanation for this is:

    A. This teacher has a disorderly room
    B. The children are bringing a free interpretation of movement to music
    C. The children are merely having fun
    D. This is a class for the handicapped

48. A single circle is the basic formation for each of the following song plays EXCEPT 48.____

    A. BLUEBIRD   B. LET YOUR FEET GO TAP
    C. LOOBY LOO   D. GAY MUSICIAN

49. A child with a hearing defect should be referred to an 49.____

    A. oculist   B. orthopedist
    C. otologist   D. orthodontist

50. Of the following health procedures, the INCORRECT one is to 50.____

    A. weigh children with shoes and jackets on
    B. mark a line 20 feet from the chart for the Snellen eye test
    C. recommend that children visit a dentist at least once a year
    D. administer first aid to a child who is bleeding

KEY (CORRECT ANSWERS)

1. A	11. D	21. C	31. B	41. D
2. C	12. B	22. B	32. D	42. A
3. D	13. C	23. A	33. C	43. D
4. D	14. B	24. A	34. C	44. B
5. A	15. A	25. C	35. B	45. A
6. C	16. C	26. C	36. A	46. B
7. C	17. C	27. A	37. D	47. B
8. C	18. A	28. D	38. A	48. B
9. C	19. C	29. C	39. B	49. C
10. D	20. B	30. D	40. D	50. A

EXAMINATION SECTION
TEST 1

DIRECTIONS: Each question or incomplete statement is followed by several suggested nswers or completions. Select the one that BEST answers the question or ompletes the statement. *PRINT THE LETTER OF THE CORRECT NSWER IN THE SPACE AT THE RIGHT.*

1. Of the following, the BEST procedure for the kindergarten teacher to develop pupil concepts of working together in the home is by

    A. encouraging dramatic play in the playhouse
    B. decorating the room with attractive pictures of home life
    C. reading stories of the home life of great people
    D. having the pupils tell stories of life in their own homes

    1.____

2. Of the following, the CHIEF value of blockbuilding for young children lies in the

    A. enjoyment derived from it
    B. use of large muscles
    C. provision for self-expression as well as an outlet for pent-up feelings
    D. provision for a group experience

    2.____

3. Of the following, the MOST useful concept for the teacher concerning the kindergarten child's number sense is that it is

    A. well developed when he enters kindergarten
    B. limited to concepts under 5
    C. developed by counting to 20
    D. ready for development through functional number experience

    3.____

4. Of the following, the BEST way for the kindergarten to provide worthwhile socializing experiences is by

    A. separating children who are already interested in each other
    B. emphasizing daily routines
    C. giving the children daily opportunities for sharing and planning
    D. having a flexible program

    4.____

5. In order to BEST fulfill the objectives of a kindergarten program, the physical arrangement of the room should be set up in order to provide for

    A. ease in teaching the entire class as a group
    B. maximum child self-help with the quiet play area separated from the noisy area
    C. elimination of movement of furniture
    D. independent work on the part of the children

    5.____

6. The kindergarten room should supply at least one piece of apparatus which encourages active play because

    A. small children need an opportunity to exercise big muscles
    B. such an apparatus affords a chance for dramatic play
    C. the home cannot always provide for it
    D. many children can use it at the same time

    6.____

7. The composer who is known as the *March King* is 7.____

   A. John P. Sousa B. Irving Berlin
   C. George Gershwin D. Walter Damrosch

8. Of the following, the one which is MOST apt to develop rhythm in a child MOST naturally is 8.____

   A. a rhythm band B. interpretive melodies
   C. singing D. bodily action

9. Of the following, the unit BEST suited to kindergarten children is 9.____

   A. children of other lands B. Eskimos
   C. community helpers D. a shoe store

10. When some children in the kindergarten group display little interest in the use of finger-paints and easel paints, of the following, the BEST procedure is to 10.____

    A. make them use them occasionally
    B. dismiss them from the group whenever these materials are being used
    C. encourage them to experiment and gradually gain confidence in the use of these materials
    D. allow them to play housekeeping, puzzles, etc. when others are painting

11. In the kindergarten when children are using clay, of the following, the BEST procedure for the teacher to follow is to 11.____

    A. provide models for copying
    B. tell the children what to make
    C. encourage them to make good models so that they can take them home
    D. emphasize the fact that *we are having lots of fun*

12. Of the following, the MAIN reason for including finger-painting in the activities of the kindergarten child is that 12.____

    A. they enjoy the feeling of the paint
    B. they use the paint enthusiastically and enjoy the colors
    C. it quickly frees inhibited children for greater spontaneity
    D. they learn how to clean up carefully

13. Of the following, the GREATEST factor in the motor development of a five year old child is 13.____

    A. steady practice B. mental ability
    C. maturation D. home environment

14. In rhythm activity with children of kindergarten age, of the following, the stress should be placed on 14.____

    A. perfection of rhythm B. large free movements
    C. discipline D. exact interpretation

15. Dramatization of songs and stories on the kindergarten level should be 15.____

    A. used as an informal means of teaching music
    B. rehearsed and performed by talented children

C. free and informal so as to bring the content into a close relation to child life
D. a finished performance

16. Of the following, the CHIEF reason for affording young children a chance to work and play in small groups is that

    A. a basis for the understanding of future family relationships is developed
    B. the opportunity for learning to live cooperatively is at the maximum
    C. they can get better results with things they make
    D. there are fewer opportunities for the development of anti-social behavior

17. Of the following, the MAIN reason for encouraging puppetry in the kindergarten is that the child can

    A. use functionally the materials he has been experimenting with
    B. have some concrete accomplishment to show his mother
    C. play alone effectively when he arrives at home
    D. develop creative ability, self-expression, and muscular skills

18. The music of AMERICA is the same as that of

    A. RULE BRITANNIA
    B. GOD SAVE THE KING
    C. POMP AND CIRCUMSTANCE
    D. ONWARD, CHRISTIAN SOLDIERS

19. Of the following, the character that does NOT appear in PETER AND THE WOLF is a

    A. duck   B. dog   C. cat   D. grandfather

20. GOD BLESS AMERICA was written by

    A. Cole Porter
    B. Jerome Kern
    C. Irving Berlin
    D. Frank Loesser

21. Of the following, the PRINCIPAL reason for including *trips* in the kindergarten program is the

    A. need for showing children how to behave outside the classroom
    B. importance of limiting experiences to those things with which young children are already familiar
    C. need to break up the routine of everyday work
    D. importance of giving children contacts with first-hand sources of information

22. Of the following, the MOST appropriate kindergarten first excursion into the environment would be a

    A. ride in the subway
    B. trip to a farm
    C. walk around the block
    D. visit to a museum

23. Of the following, the independence of action displayed by a child of kindergarten age is MOST likely to be a(n)

    A. indication of emotional disturbance
    B. way of avoiding difficulties
    C. sign of growth
    D. assertion of inadequacy

4 (#1)

24. Of the following, the LEAST important task for the kindergarten teacher to attempt during the first days of the playground season is to

   A. be a substitute mother
   B. help the children meet new situations
   C. soothe any fears the children may have
   D. allay uncertainties

25. Of the following, the CHIEF reason why a jungle gym is NOT considered a suitable type of equipment for the kindergarten room is that it

   A. is dangerous
   B. attracts children away from other activities
   C. requires too much supervision
   D. takes up too much room

26. Of the following, the CHIEF reason for providing centers of play interest for children in the kindergarten is to

   A. give all the children an opportunity to work and play one and in groups
   B. take care of those children who are not interested in work areas
   C. permit them to play continuously with things they like
   D. teach them the value of personal and public property

27. Of the following, the MOST valid statement regarding the participation in play by the teacher in the kindergarten is that it

   A. is always accepted by the children
   B. usually evokes resentment
   C. must be used with discrimination
   D. is planned to introduce new content into the play

28. Jessie Wilcox Smith is BEST known for her pictures of

   A. flowers   B. houses   C. animals   D. children

29. Of the following, the MOST important health habit to establish in kindergarten is

   A. the use of paper towels
   B. drinking plenty of water
   C. keeping all objects but food away from the mouth
   D. the use of a handkerchief

30. Of the following, the story which is MOST apt to stress the idea of obedience is

   A. CINDERELLA
   B. THE TALE OF PETER RABBIT
   C. MISTRESS MARY, QUITE CONTRARY
   D. EPAMINANDOS

31. Of the following, the one which is a technique used in ceramics is

   A. fresco   B. dry point   C. bas-relief   D. applique

32. Of the following, the MOST satisfying nature experience for children of kindergarten age is

   A. the planting of seeds
   B. friendly contact with animals
   C. the arranging of flowers
   D. experiments such as putting water out of doors to freeze

33. In ceramics, the process of wedging the clay is done to

   A. make it pliable
   B. make it dry rapidly
   C. remove the air bubbles
   D. make it more moist

34. Of the following pairs of colors, the one which represents the warm colors is

   A. yellow and orange
   B. green and violet
   C. black and white
   D. blue and purple

35. Of the following, the pair that does NOT represent complementary colors is

   A. blue-orange
   B. yellow-violet
   C. red-green
   D. gray-white

36. John James Audubon is BEST known for his paintings of

   A. southern wild flowers
   B. birds of America
   C. Eskimo life
   D. views of the Hudson

37. Of the following, the material BEST suited for use in making school posters is

   A. opaque tempera paint
   B. oil paint
   C. transparent water color
   D. colored chalk

38. SUMMERTIME is an excerpt from

   A. PORGY AND BESS
   B. NAUGHTY MARIETTA
   C. THE RED MILL
   D. THE WIZARD OF OZ

39. Of the following, the type of song that children of kindergarten age sing with the MOST nthusiasm is the one which

   A. is tuneful
   B. contains the words which they know
   C. has dramatic qualities
   D. tells of familiar things

40. Of the following patriotic songs, the one which is considered BEST for use with children of kindergarten age is

   A. AMERICA
   B. STAR SPANGLED BANNER
   C. AMERICA THE BEAUTIFUL
   D. GOD BLESS AMERICA

41. Of the following, the BEST reason for having children sing songs in the kindergarten is

   A. to provide voice training
   B. to teach them the words of songs
   C. to develop the quality of tone
   D. for their enjoyment

42. Of the following, the MAJOR reason for selecting songs used in the kindergarten is their

    A. interesting accompaniment
    B. appeal to children
    C. appeal to the teacher
    D. story content

43. Of the following, the one which is NOT a tag game is

    A. three deep
    B. drop the handkerchief
    C. Charley over the Water
    D. Newcomb

44. Of the following, the GREATEST benefits from art education for young children will be produced by having them

    A. copy paintings
    B. experiment with art materials
    C. draw with a pencil
    D. draw figures with charcoal

45. Of the following methods, the teacher can BEST encourage the kindergarten child to use rawing as a means of expression by

    A. suggesting what to draw
    B. showing the child how to draw
    C. encouraging the child in his own efforts
    D. having group discussions about his finished work

46. Of the following, the material which provides the GREATEST opportunity for manipulation is

    A. construction paper
    B. blocks
    C. pegs
    D. self-hardening clay

47. Of the following, the MOST practical material for a kindergarten child to use in making puppets is

    A. plastic wood
    B. cardboard
    C. paper maché
    D. cloth

48. Of the following, the type of play that allows for the LEAST free use of the imagination is _____ play

    A. sand   B. water   C. block   D. toy

49. Of the following, the MOST important element to stress during the game period is

    A. rules of the game
    B. a joyous play spirit
    C. winning the game
    D. physical development

50. Of the following, the type of brush MOST suitable for use by children in tempera painting is a _____ brush.

    A. hard horsehair
    B. small red sable
    C. soft camel's hair
    D. large bristle

KEY (CORRECT ANSWERS)

1. A	11. D	21. D	31. C	41. D
2. C	12. C	22. C	32. B	42. B
3. D	13. C	23. C	33. C	43. D
4. C	14. B	24. A	34. A	44. B
5. B	15. C	25. D	35. D	45. C
6. A	16. B	26. A	36. B	46. B
7. A	17. D	27. C	37. A	47. B
8. A	18. B	28. D	38. A	48. D
9. C	19. B	29. D	39. B	49. B
10. C	20. C	30. B	40. D	50. D

TEST 2

DIRECTIONS: Each question or incomplete statement is followed by several suggested answers or completions Select the one that BEST answers the question or completes the statement. *PRINT THE LETTER OF THE CORRECT NSWER IN THE SPACE AT THE RIGHT.*

1. Of the following, the MOST important reason for providing properly supervised and well-quipped playgrounds in every community is that

   A. mothers need a place to leave children in order that they may have some free time
   B. children feel secure in a playground
   C. children are safe when they are properly supervised
   D. group play and recreation are important in the achievement of democracy in living

2. Of the following, the name MOST closely associated with the field of early childhood education is

   A. Patty Hill   B. G. Stanley Hall
   C. S.D. Porteus   D. Alfred Binet

3. In planning play experiences for kindergarten children, of the following, the teacher should

   A. be chiefly concerned with equipment
   B. be sure every child has a toy to use
   C. consider the need for balancing quiet and active play
   D. provide group leaders for each activity

4. LOOBY LOO is a

   A. team game   B. song play   C. stunt   D. relay

5. WALTZ OF THE FLOWERS is from

   A. HANSEL AND GRETEL   B. PETER AND THE WOLF
   C. CARNIVAL OF THE ANIMALS   D. NUTCRACKER SUITE

6. THE STAR SPANGLED BANNER is written in _____ time.

   A. 4/4   B. 3/4   C. 2/4   D. 6/8

7. In planning the routine of the day, of the following, the kindergarten teacher should strive MOST for

   A. variety of activity   B. proper timing of activity
   C. orderliness   D. accomplishment

8. In teaching art to the kindergarten child, of the following, the BEST procedure for the teacher to follow is to

   A. set up attainable standards of accomplishment
   B. allow the pupil to express his imaginary world freely
   C. guide the child to create work which looks finished
   D. direct the child's choice of color, form, and design

9. Of the following, the CHIEF reason for using song plays in the kindergarten is to   9.____

   A. teach the children how to play together
   B. teach the children how to sing
   C. teach the children how to dance
   D. enrich the children's rhythmic experiences

10. When kindergarten children are dramatizing a favorite story, of the following, the teacher should   10.____

    A. have a large group as the audience and several children performing
    B. have numerous and elaborate costumes and properties to stimulate ideas
    C. relate the story in detail as the performance is in action
    D. attempt to include all or most of the children in the dramatization

11. Of the following, the ESSENTIAL factor in putting on a play in the kindergarten is that   11.____

    A. there be an audience situation
    B. there be scenery
    C. there be costuming
    D. the play be improvised by the children

12. Andrew Lang is famous in children's literature as the   12.____

    A. author of such English folk tales as DICK WHITTINGTON and JACK THE GIANT KILLER
    B. compiler and editor of THE BLUE FAIRY BOOK
    C. collector of Black folk tales and songs
    D. editor of a book of Indian folk tales

13. A prototype for nonsense poems and for popular songs based on nonsense lines is a poem by Lewis Carroll.
    The title is   13.____

    A. HOW DOTH THE LITTLE CROCODILE
    B. THE BAKER'S TALE
    C. JABBERWOCKY
    D. SLUMBER TIME

14. The HERE AND NOW STORY BOOK containing realistic stories about everyday happenings in children's lives was written by   14.____

    A. Andrew Lang   B. Lynd Ward
    C. Lucy Mitchell Sprague   D. Emilie Poulsson

15. The combination of colors that will produce green is   15.____

    A. yellow and red   B. blue and yellow
    C. red and blue   D. orange and blue

16. Of the following, the BEST way for the teacher to introduce a new song to a kindergarten group is to   16.____

    A. have the children repeat the words
    B. have them sing the song
    C. have them practice the difficult parts
    D. sing the song to the children

17. Of the following, the PRIMARY objective in teaching songs to children of kindergarten age is to

   A. stimulate the children to sing for pleasure
   B. develop a sense of tone
   C. enrich the child's musical knowledge
   D. arouse inherent musical ability

18. Of the following, the type of story that is BEST suited for the kindergarten child is one that is

   A. realistic
   B. a fairy tale
   C. a folk tale
   D. a fable

19. Of the following rhymes, the one in which no reference is made to animals is

   A. SEE SAW MARGERY DAW
   B. TOM, TOM, THE PIPER'S SON
   C. DING DONG BELL
   D. HICKORY, DICKORY DOCK

20. Plasticine is the term PROPERLY associated with

   A. ceramic clay
   B. oil base clay
   C. self-hardening clay
   D. plaster of paris

21. Which of the following is the SOUNDEST educational principle underlying the selection of music for kindergarten rhythms?
    The music should

   A. be easily recognized by children as a run, a skip, or a march
   B. always be simple and uniformly interpreted by the children
   C. be introduced by telling the children what the music *tells us to do*
   D. lend itself to many different interpretations

22. Of the following, the INCORRECT association is:

   A. THE TALE OF PETER RABBIT - Rose Fyleman
   B. ANGUS, THE CAT - Marjorie Flack
   C. SNIPP, SNAPP, SNURR AND THE RED SHOES - Maj. Lindman
   D. GOOPS AND HOW TO BE THEM - Gelett Burgess

23. The poem THE OWL AND THE PUSSY CAT was written by

   A. Lewis Carroll
   B. Robert Louis Stevenson
   C. Edward Lear
   D. W.S. Gilbert

24. The poet who wrote UNDER THE TREE, a volume of poems for children based on nature and life in the country, is

   A. Elizabeth Madox Roberts
   B. Lois Lenski
   C. Rose Fyleman
   D. Walter de la Mare

25. The fairy story THE HAPPY PRINCE was written by

   A. Charles Kingsley
   B. Oscar Wilde
   C. Howard Pyle
   D. Hans Christian Andersen

26. The fact books for children, MANNERS CAN BE FUN and SAFETY CAN BE FUN, were written and illustrated by
    A. Paul Lawrence Dunbar
    B. Munro Leaf
    C. Grant Wood
    D. Maud and Miska Petersham

27. What kind of musical instrument is the clarinet?
    A. String   B. Woodwind   C. Percussion   D. Brass

28. Of the following, the PRIMARY purpose of art activities for the young child is to
    A. help him to express his thoughts clearly and purposefully
    B. train him in the proper blending of colors and pigments
    C. give him a release for his feelings and emotions
    D. teach him to create artistically

29. In attempting to help a child who has difficulty working or playing with a group, of the following, the BEST procedure to follow is to
    A. remove him from the group and place him with younger children
    B. condition the child to a large group as quickly as possible
    C. encourage him to work with one other child and gradually add others to the group
    D. place the child in a different activity with another teacher

30. Of the following, the experiences which a five year old appears MOST interested in are
    A. past experiences
    B. immediate experiences
    C. future experiences
    D. experiences of others

31. Of the following, the MOST natural way to introduce dramatic experiences in kindergarten is through
    A. story telling
    B. painting
    C. block play
    D. rhythms

32. Of the following, the one who BEST represents an outstanding modern poet for little children is
    A. Hilda Conkling
    B. Marjorie Flack
    C. A.A. Milne
    D. R.L. Stevenson

33. Of the following, the reason behind MOST questions asked by a kindergarten child is to
    A. get attention
    B. be annoying
    C. express curiosity
    D. evade issues

34. Of the following, the PRIME reason for the teacher's singing for the children when teaching a song is to
    A. entertain the class
    B. get practice in singing
    C. focus the children's attention on listening
    D. try out the song on the class

35. Music plays an important part in the kindergarten child's life.
    Of the following, the musical experience which makes the GREATEST impression on the young child is

    A. piano selections
    B. victrola records
    C. the teacher's own singing
    D. the children's orchestra

36. Of the following, the BEST incentive for encouraging further interest in an activity such as painting among kindergarten children is

    A. comparison of their work with a model
    B. praise and approval of adults
    C. awarding of a prize for achievement
    D. asking the child to show the painting and tell the story behind it to the class

37. Of the following stories, the one in which Troll is an important character is

    A. THE THREE PIGS
    B. BLOWAWAY HATS
    C. SNOW WHITE AND THE SEVEN DWARFS
    D. THREE BILLY GOATS GRUFF

38. Of the following, the MOST important aspect of the work of the kindergarten teacher is the development of the children's

    A. truthfulness and honesty
    B. obedience and self-control
    C. muscle tone
    D. good health habits

39. EDUCATION IN THE KINDERGARTEN was written by

    A. Foster and Headley   B. Rugg
    C. Storm   D. Stevens

40. Of the following, the CHIEF educational value to small children of a Mother Goose rhyme lies in its

    A. simple verse form   B. rhythm
    C. humor   D. expression of folk-ways

41. Of the following, the MOST important aspect of dramatic play in the kindergarten lies in the

    A. opportunity it affords for expression
    B. practice children get in dramatizing stories
    C. pleasure children feel in acting out the story
    D. training the pupils get in speaking in sentences

42. Of the following, the type of story considered BEST to read or tell to foreign-born children is one that is

    A. quiet and soothing   B. long and rhythmic
    C. short and repetitious   D. full of action and ideas

43. In introducing block building as an activity in the kindergarten, of the following, the BEST method is to

    A. allow only boys to participate
    B. permit only one child at a time to work under the teacher's direct supervision
    C. plan activities for groups of three or more children at a time
    D. organize small groups but permit children to work as individuals if they wish

44. Of the following, the PRIMARY purpose in using marionettes in the kindergarten program is to

    A. establish better class spirit
    B. correct a behavior problem
    C. stimulate oral expression and dramatic play
    D. develop skill in handwork

45. Of the following, the MOST important reason for including toy telephone in the housekeeping area of the kindergarten is that

    A. children learn numbers through dial activities
    B. proper telephone speech can be learned
    C. conversations often provide insights regarding the children
    D. children will be less likely to overuse real telephones at home

46. Of the following, the statement which BEST describes the child of kindergarten age is that he

    A. is adept at projecting himself into other places and times
    B. is incapable of any flights of imagination
    C. seldom questions anything in his physical environment
    D. is bound to the here and now by his stage of organic development, as well as by his limited experience

47. Percussion instruments are used in the kindergarten CHIEFLY as a means of

    A. developing rhythmical control of the body
    B. teaching children to keep time
    C. providing an opportunity for fun
    D. helping children to learn to play as a group

48. Of the following, the BEST procedure to follow in handling a timid child who hesitates to join in the activities of the kindergarten is to

    A. leave him alone
    B. praise him for the work he does by himself
    C. draw him into the group and encourage him to participate as often as possible
    D. have his mother accompany him to the class so that he will have a feeling of security

49. What kind of song is THREE BLIND MICE?

    A. Folk song   B. Art song
    C. Round   D. Patriotic song

50. Of the following, the PRIME reason why spools are useful for manual activities in the kindergarten is that they   50.____
    A. are waste material
    B. may be obtained in various sizes and shapes
    C. may be easily painted
    D. are good to use as wheels

KEY (CORRECT ANSWERS)

1. D	11. D	21. D	31. D	41. A
2. A	12. B	22. A	32. C	42. C
3. C	13. C	23. C	33. C	43. D
4. B	14. C	24. A	34. C	44. C
5. D	15. B	25. B	35. D	45. C
6. B	16. D	26. B	36. B	46. D
7. A	17. A	27. B	37. D	47. A
8. B	18. A	28. C	38. D	48. C
9. D	19. A	29. C	39. A	49. C
10. D	20. C	30. B	40. B	50. B

TEST 3

DIRECTIONS: Each question or incomplete statement is followed by several suggested answers or completions. Select the one that BEST answers the question or completes the statement. *PRINT THE LETTER OF THE CORRECT ANSWER IN THE SPACE AT THE RIGHT.*

1. In selecting a story for children of kindergarten age, the teacher should look PRIMARILY for

    A. colorful descriptive passages
    B. realistic situations within the children's experiences
    C. macabre situations
    D. humorous situations

    1._____

2. Of the following, which description of kindergarten behavior is probably indicative of the MOST serious mental disturbance?

    A. Joe talks loudly very often.
    B. Jim is aggressive and pushes other children when he wants something.
    C. Bill takes other children's crayons and toys once in a while.
    D. Harry sits quietly and almost never talks to others or participates in group activity.

    2._____

3. The findings of recent experiments indicate that initial painting experiences of kindergarten children should be with _____ color(s).

    A. one
    B. two
    C. the three primary
    D. all six

    3._____

4. Left-handedness in a kindergarten child should be

    A. corrected
    B. discussed with the child
    C. accepted without comment
    D. discouraged

    4._____

5. In order for the children to derive the GREATEST value from the game period in kindergarten, of the following, the MOST important procedure to follow is to

    A. insist that the rules of the game be strictly adhered to
    B. organize the games so that the children's enjoyment is maintained at a high peak
    C. impress on the children that they are not to become too excited
    D. provide for maximum competition among the group

    5._____

6. Of the following, the BEST arrangement of books in the kindergarten room is

    A. near the light and where the children can reach them and use them
    B. in a special place where the teacher can get them easily for the children
    C. in a place where they can be displayed attractively but not handled by children
    D. near the teacher's desk

    6._____

7. Of the following, which is the SOUNDEST educational principle concerning the introduction of a new musical instrument to the kindergarten class?

    A. Attention should be focused on the singing tone it will produce.
    B. The teacher should not burden the children with the name of the instrument.
    C. Nothing should be said about it until all the children have experimented with it.
    D. No specific directions should be given by the teacher for its use.

    7._____

8. A kindergarten child derives the MOST benefit from playing instruments when

    A. he can play them in any way he wishes
    B. he has the proper respect for them and handles them with care
    C. they are used in a rhythm band
    D. he is taught how to read notes

9. When kindergarten children have learned to sing a particular song, the BEST way to deal with this learned skill is to

    A. *discontinue* singing this song in class while other similar songs are learned.
    B. *discontinue* singing this song in class while other dissimilar songs are learned
    C. *continue* singing this song often without varying the original interpretation
    D. *continue* singing this song often with opportunities to discover new ways to interpret it

10. Of the following, the suitability of a song for young children depends CHIEFLY on

    A. its technical range within the octave
    B. whether it is listed for school use
    C. its emotional appeal
    D. its adaptability to dramatization

11. Of the following, the poem MOST suitable for children in a kindergarten class is

    A. THERE WAS A CHILD WENT FORTH
    B. WHEN I WAS DOWN BESIDE THE SEA
    C. THE BELLS
    D. WHEN LILACS BLOOMED

12. The housekeeping area in the kindergarten room should receive the careful and frequent observation of the teacher because

    A. the toys will be misused if she is not alert
    B. play sessions show clearly how a child reveals his emotional reactions and hanles his difficulties
    C. the children feel more secure when the teacher watches them and plays with them
    D. it is necessary to be present to maintain good control over the children

13. Of the following, the CHIEF reason for encouraging free dramatic play of a domestic nature among kindergarten children is that

    A. they thoroughly enjoy it
    B. they increase their understanding of family relationships through identification with the roles of adults in their homes
    C. children should know about their home, school, and neighborhood
    D. it is an activity which keeps children occupied purposefully

14. Of the following, the BEST way to develop an interest in and knowledge of family life in kindergarten children is by

    A. stories of family life
    B. dramatic play with dolls, dishes, brooms, etc.
    C. construction and building of houses, stores, trains
    D. purchase and sale of foods, supplies, and clothing

15. Of the following, which is the MOST important characteristic of a good teacher of kindergarten age children?

    A. Insistence upon perfect obedience at all times
    B. Understanding of children's needs and interests
    C. Sympathy with deprived children
    D. Maintenance of high standards of achievement for all children

16. Of the following, the outdoor play activity that is LEAST desirable for young children is

    A. rolling hoops
    B. playing ball
    C. jumping rope
    D. marching

17. Of the following, the PRINCIPAL reason for including climbing, swinging, and jumping in children's physical activities is that these activities are

    A. a challenge to children
    B. nature's way of helping children grow
    C. necessary for developing team spirit
    D. required by law

18. Of the following, the PRIME reason why five year olds are often willing to share their things is that they

    A. seek adult approval
    B. have no interest in possessions
    C. have no use for them
    D. prefer companions to possessions

19. Of the following, the instrument which can be made by children in kindergarten and used successfully as a rhythm instrument is the

    A. violin
    B. zither
    C. drum
    D. penny whistle

20. Blowing across tops of empty bottles of different sizes is an excellent device to

    A. develop lung power
    B. experiment with sound
    C. use in a kindergarten rhythm band
    D. make children conscious of rhythm

21. In dancing, the term *set* refers to a

    A. group of dancers performing as a unit
    B. simple pattern
    C. group waiting for instruction
    D. group waiting for its turn to perform

22. The INCORRECT association of dance and country of origin is

    A. Cshebogar - Russia
    B. Flip - Netherlands
    C. Bleking - Sweden
    D. Rigodon - France

23. Color Tag is a game in which the child who is *It*

   A. has a color pinned on his back
   B. tries to discover which color is pinned on the other child's back
   C. tries to identify missing colors
   D. tries to tag as many children as he can

24. Of the following, the BEST activity which the kindergarten teacher can use for helping the teacher to control children's responses is

   A. formal rhythmic activities
   B. finger painting
   C. block building
   D. dramatic play

25. Of the following, the television performer whose program is of MOST appeal to kindergarten children is

   A. Carol Reed
   B. Jack Paar
   C. Shari Lewis
   D. Perry Como

26. *"She cut off their tails with a carving knife"* is a line from which of the following?

   A. RING AROUND THE ROSIE
   B. THREE BLIND MICE
   C. A WANDERING MINSTREL I
   D. THE SADDEST STORY TOLD

27. Of the following, the relay race MOST suitable for a kindergarten group is the _____ relay.

   A. single file
   B. four corner
   C. shuttle
   D. circle ball

28. The educational purpose of having a teacher encourage kindergarten children to tap various objects is to

   A. relieve tension
   B. test their hearing
   C. experiment with sound
   D. give children exercise

29. Of the following, the MOST suitable type of program for kindergarten children is a(n) _____ program.

   A. experiential
   B. active
   C. highly structured
   D. unstructured

30. The finger play that begins with *"Here are mother's knives and forks"* ends with

   A. *"Here is John and Mable"*
   B. *"Here is the baby's cradle"*
   C. *"Here is good brown bread"*
   D. *"Help her if you're able"*

31. A work bench in the kindergarten should be equipped with all of the following EXCEPT   31._____

    A. a vise
    B. pine wood
    C. a hammer
    D. pinking shears

32. A kindergarten child should NOT be expected to   32._____

    A. identify colors
    B. perform creatively
    C. color in workbooks
    D. know the names of his classmates

33. Of the following, the one that BEST describes the *polka* is   33._____

    A. brush-slide-brush-brush
    B. hop, step-close step
    C. step - hop step-hop - hop, hop, hop
    D. walk - walk-hop, hop, hop

34. The song FIVE LITTLE CHICKADEES refers to five small   34._____

    A. hens   B. chicks   C. birds   D. children

35. Of the following, the CHIEF reason why young children should rest after vigorous play is that   35._____

    A. fatigue develops quickly
    B. they are not capable of vigorous play
    C. they need sedentary activities more than vigorous play
    D. the teacher needs a rest too

36. House play in the kindergarten is MOST valuable because of the opportunity it affords the child   36._____

    A. to play with toys
    B. for leadership
    C. for self-expression
    D. to learn how to clean up

37. The author of MAKE WAY FOR DUCKLINGS also wrote   37._____

    A. BAHOUSHKA
    B. LITTLE RED AUTO
    C. THE BIGGEST BEAR
    D. BLUEBERRIES FOR SAL

38. Of the following, the INCORRECT association of dance and country is   38._____

    A. Children's Polka - Germany
    B. Shoemakers Dance - Norway
    C. Chimes of Dunkirk - England
    D. Circassian Circle - U.S.

39. In square dancing the term *Honor your lady* means the boy faces   39._____

    A. the girl and promenades
    B. his partner and curtsies
    C. his corner and bows
    D. the girl and bows

40. In square dancing, *Do-si-do your partner* is CORRECTLY associated with

    A. passing one's partner
    B. weaving in and out of the circle
    C. bowing to one's neighbors
    D. balancing one's partner

41. Of the following, the pair that is INCORRECTLY associated is

    A. England - THE GALLANT SHOP
    B. United States - BINGO
    C. Netherlands - GAY MUSICIAN
    D. Czechoslovakia - ANNIE GOES TO THE CABBAGE FIELD

42. Of the following types of instruments, the ones which are BASIC for a kindergarten rhythm band are the _____ instruments.

    A. rhythmic   B. melodic
    C. plucking   D. rubbing

43. In treating a victim of nosebleed, of the following, the LEAST effective procedure is to

    A. have the victim lie down immediately
    B. press the nostrils firmly together
    C. apply a large, cold, wet cloth to the nose
    D. pack the nose gently with gauze

44. Of the following, the appropriate first aid treatment for an abrasive wound of the hand which does NOT bleed freely is to

    A. paint the wounded area with iodine or other antiseptic
    B. apply a sterile gauze dressing and bandage it in place
    C. wash the wound with soap and water
    D. tape a cotton swab over the wound

45. The MOST important factor to be considered in early education and one which affects all others is

    A. truthfulness   B. obedience
    C. oral English   D. health

46. The BEST time for manual work in the kindergarten is

    A. early in the day's session
    B. just before the children go home
    C. after the rest period
    D. before the lunch period

47. The teacher's FIRST concern during an excursion should be

    A. safety   B. destination   C. interest   D. outcomes

48. In order to appeal to the young child, a poem must contain, as its MOST important essential,

    A. beautiful language   B. familiar vocabulary
    C. a riddle   D. a simple rhyme scheme

49. In planning a program for the day, health is BEST safeguarded by 49._____

   A. multiple activity
   B. mid-morning lunch
   C. alternating active and quiet periods
   D. outdoor activity

50. FRERE JACQUE is a 50._____

   A. game B. part song C. round D. chorale

KEY (CORRECT ANSWERS)

1. B	11. B	21. A	31. D	41. C
2. D	12. B	22. A	32. C	42. A
3. A	13. B	23. B	33. B	43. A
4. C	14. B	24. A	34. C	44. B
5. B	15. D	25. C	35. A	45. D
6. A	16. D	26. B	36. C	46. A
7. A	17. B	27. A	37. D	47. A
8. B	18. A	28. C	38. C	48. B
9. D	19. C	29. A	39. D	49. C
10. C	20. B	30. A	40. A	50. C

EXAMINATION SECTION
TEST 1

DIRECTIONS: Each question or incomplete statement is followed by several suggested answers or completions. Select the one that BEST answers the question or completes the statement. *PRINT THE LETTER OF THE CORRECT ANSWER IN THE SPACE AT THE RIGHT.*

1. All of the following statements are true of the singing game THE MUFFIN MAN, EXCEPT:

    A. One or more players may stand inside a circle formed by the other participants
    B. Players in the center choose partners from the circle
    C. Drury Lane is mentioned
    D. Verses are sung only by the players in the outer circle

2. It is important for a teacher to find out what the children in her group know about various topics so that these topics can be

    A. omitted from the curriculum
    B. taken as important teaching objectives
    C. used as a familiar starting point
    D. considered adequately understood without further instruction

3. Of the following, the PRIMARY value in telling stories to young children is that

    A. entertainment is provided
    B. socializing objectives may be met
    C. thought is aroused
    D. interest in and background for reading is developed

4. In music, the dot placed over or under a note

    A. doubles the value of the note
    B. adds half value of the note
    C. indicates staccato
    D. indicates accents

5. Of the following singing games, the one that appeals MOST to little boys is

    A. FARMER IN THE DELL   B. A-TISKET A-TASKET
    C. HUNTING   D. KEEP MOVING

6. Of the following, the CORRECT characteristics of I SPY is that it is a game

    A. that requires physical activity
    B. of hide and seek
    C. of guessing
    D. that permits only a limited number of contestants

7. For a four-year-old child, the events of the present are _____ those of the _____.

    A. less vivid than; past
    B. less vivid than; future
    C. more vivid than; past or future
    D. as vivid as; past or future

8. The term *O'Leary* is MOST correctly associated with a 8.__

   A. game that requires the use of a small rubber or tennis ball
   B. form of Tag
   C. guessing game
   D. word game

9. A child is MOST likely to understand and accept simple standards of conduct which a teacher attempts to teach if 9.__

   A. his failure to meet these standards is met with careful explanations and consistent disciplinary measures
   B. the standards are taught as rules to be followed whether they are understood or not
   C. he is made to feel guilty and ashamed whenever he fails to meet the standards
   D. the teacher attributes the standards to some authority figure such as a policeman or the principal

10. DOWN YOU GO is a game properly classified as a(n) 10.__

    A. word game
    B. active game
    C. game essentially for young children
    D. team game

11. The one of the following which is NOT a running and chasing game is 11.__

    A. THREE DEEP   B. WHO IS IT?
    C. FOLLOW THE LEADER   D. DROP THE BLOCK

12. Of the following, the MOST positive method for the teacher to use in helping the child who is a *show-off* is to 12.__

    A. give him opportunities to play important roles in the classroom
    B. exclude him from any leadership role
    C. place him in situations that will lead to class ridicule
    D. ignore him completely

13. Of the following, the BEST method of helping the shy child to achieve greater participation in class activities is to 13.__

    A. allow him to work and play alone as long as he wishes
    B. guide him into small group activities by easy stages
    C. assign him to an occasional leadership role in circle games
    D. discuss the situation with the child's parents in conference

14. All of the following are recommended techniques in story telling EXCEPT: 14.__

    A. *Catch* phrases should be memorized by the story teller
    B. Encourage listeners frequently to answer questions such as *What do you think happened next?*
    C. A low-pitched voice has an effect that is pleasing and is conducive to controlling the group
    D. Occasional brief explanations are necessary and advisable, even though this results in interruption

15. All of the following statements are true of the game CHARLEY OVER THE WATER EXCEPT:

    A. It is popular only with small children
    B. It is a form of *tag*
    C. Singing and marching are involved
    D. Teams line up on lines facing one another

16. All of the following are true of the singing game THE MULBERRY BUSH EXCEPT:

    A. Each player spins around rapidly on the singing of *So early in the morning*
    B. Action indicated by the lines is given in pantomine by half the participants
    C. The game starts with contestants forming a circle with clasped hands
    D. Days of the week are mentioned in the verse

17. Knowledge of a child's background and capacity is MOST valuable to the kindergarten teacher for use in

    A. reporting to parents about the child
    B. completing school records about the child
    C. planning learning experiences for the child
    D. providing for his safety

18. Of the following, the MOST comprehensive purpose of rhythms in the kindergarten is to

    A. develop the body
    B. teach various kinds of time
    C. teach dancing
    D. provide a means of expression

19. Of the following, the MOST desirable outcome of a child's experience with play materials is growth in ability to

    A. follow directions
    B. express his own ideas and feelings
    C. organize and manipulate the materials
    D. appreciate the cost of the materials

20. In music, the term applied to a broken chord is

    A. cadenza   B. arpeggio   C. discord   D. tremolo

21. For children who have poor ability in matching tones, of the following, the BEST thing for the teacher to do is to

    A. sing to the children
    B. give practice in tone matching
    C. let children listen to victrola records of good singing
    D. pay no attention to it

22. Of the following, the music of TURKEY IN THE STRAW is BEST suited for

    A. marching
    B. waltzing
    C. skipping
    D. clog dancing

23. THE MARCH OF THE TOYS is from
    A. BABES IN TOYLAND   B. BAMBI
    C. SNOW WHITE   D. DUMBO

24. ROW, ROW, ROW YOUR BOAT is a
    A. game   B. part song   C. round   D. chorale

25. The song LITTLE DAVID, PLAY ON YOUR HARP is a
    A. round   B. spiritual   C. madrigal   D. ballad

26. The PRIMARY objective of organizing spontaneous dramatization by six-year-olds is to provide opportunities for the children to
    A. work in groups
    B. learn correct grammar
    C. express ideas and feelings
    D. release tension and hostility

27. Of the following, the MOST important value young children derive from poetry is that they
    A. gain new ideas from the content of the poem
    B. gain understanding of familiar experiences
    C. experience the beauty of language
    D. improve their listening habits

28. All of the following are true of the game MOTHER, MOTHER, THE POT BOILS OVER EXCEPT:
    A. Twenty to forty players may play this game simultaneously
    B. This is a traditional dramatic game suitable for young children
    C. A *witch* plays a part in this game
    D. This game involves running

29. ROCK THE CRADLE, CHASE THE FOX, CALLING IN, and BEGGING are
    A. terms applied to rope jumping
    B. the names of word games
    C. forms of Tag
    D. quiet games

30. Of the following, the game which is MOST suitable for primary grade children is
    A. SQUIRREL IN THE TREES   B. POISON
    C. NEWCOMB   D. STICK BALL

31. Most often children acquire their racial and religious prejudices from
    A. direct contact with members of other races and religions
    B. derogatory comments in books and newspapers
    C. social contact with prejudicial adults
    D. independent efforts to understand other people

32. The *symphony* in which toy instruments are used was written by   32.____

    A. Handel   B. Haydn   C. Mozart   D. Schumann

33. When a child shows an unusually large number of nervous symptoms (e.g., nailbiting, head scratching, knuckle cracking, etc.), it is USUALLY considered as symptomatic evidence of   33.____

    A. low intelligence   B. ill health
    C. cerebral dominance   D. psychological disturbance

34. Threat to a child's self-esteem will USUALLY produce   34.____

    A. anxiety   B. depression
    C. compensation   D. repression

35. All of the following are Aesop's Fables EXCEPT   35.____

    A. THE WIND AND THE SUN   B. THE FISHERMAN AND HIS WIFE
    C. THE DOG AND THE BONE   D. THE MAID AND THE MILK CAN

36. Humorous, realistic stories of American children and adolescents have been written by   36.____

    A. James B. Cabell   B. Stephen Crane
    C. Theodore Dreiser   D. Booth Tarkington

37. The MOST appropriate characteristic of stories for young children, of the following, is   37.____

    A. a simple plot   B. fantastic situations
    C. long, unusual words   D. heroes and villains

38. The character of the little girl called THUMBELINA was created by   38.____

    A. Milne   B. Lindsay   C. Grimm   D. Andersen

39. Of the following authors, the one who has written simple little stories of the small child's everyday activities in which emphasis is placed on the way things feel, look, and sound to the very young child is   39.____

    A. Elizabeth Enright   B. Dorothy P. Lathrop
    C. Monica Shannon   D. Lucy Sprague Mitchell

40. Sensitive and effective adaptations of folk tales have been made by   40.____

    A. Virginia Burton   B. Wanda Gag
    C. Dr. Seuss   D. Lois Lenski

41. The character Peter Pan was created by   41.____

    A. Sir Arthur W. Pinero   B. Sir James M. Barrie
    C. A.A. Milne   D. Lord Byron

42. Of the following Mother Goose rhymes, the one which young children would MOST enjoy dramatizing is   42.____

    A. OLD WOMAN WHO LIVED IN THE SHOE
    B. DING DONG BELL
    C. JACK BE NIMBLE
    D. LITTLE JACK HORNER

43. EDUCATION IN THE KINDERGARTEN was written by

   A. Foster and Headley
   B. Rugg
   C. Storm
   D. Stevens

44. The author of THE TALE OF PETER RABBIT is

   A. Maude Lindsay
   B. Beatrix Potter
   C. Kate Douglas Wiggin
   D. Margery Clark

45. The author of HERE AND NOW STORY BOOKS is

   A. Kate Douglas Wiggin
   B. Alice Thorne
   C. Sara Cone Bryant
   D. Lucy Sprague Mitchell

46. Of the following, the art material that is MOST suitable for elementary school early grades is

   A. a drawing pencil
   B. transparent water color
   C. opaque water color
   D. oil paints

47. Each year the Children's Library Association of the American Library Association awards a prize to the author of the *most distinguished contribution to American literature for children.*
    This award is called the

   A. Pulitzer Prize
   B. John Newberry Medal
   C. Eugene Field Prize
   D. Julia Ellsworth Ford Award

48. One of the earliest and finest examples of poetry written about the child's world of play and imagination and written for the child's pleasure rather than his instruction is

   A. RHYMES FOR THE NURSERY
   B. A CHILD'S GARDEN OF VERSES
   C. POEMS FOR LITTLE PEOPLE
   D. A BAG OF SONGS FOR BOYS AND GIRLS

49. In all of the following stories for children, the villain or villainess meets a violent death EXCEPT in

   A. HANSEL AND GRETEL
   B. CINDERELLA
   C. ALI BABA AND THE FORTY THIEVES
   D. THE THREE LITTLE PIGS

50. Of the following, the MOST suitable material for use in stringing puppets is

   A. black fish line
   B. shoemaker's thread
   C. heavy cord
   D. sewing cotton

KEY (CORRECT ANSWERS)

1. D	11. B	21. B	31. C	41. B
2. C	12. A	22. D	32. B	42. C
3. D	13. B	23. A	33. D	43. A
4. C	14. B	24. C	34. A	44. B
5. C	15. D	25. B	35. B	45. D
6. C	16. B	26. C	36. D	46. C
7. C	17. C	27. C	37. A	47. B
8. A	18. D	28. A	38. D	48. B
9. A	19. B	29. A	39. D	49. B
10. A	20. B	30. A	40. B	50. A

TEST 2

DIRECTIONS: Each question or incomplete statement is followed by several suggested answers or completions. Select the one that BEST answers the question or completes the statement. *PRINT THE LETTER OF THE CORRECT ANSWER IN THE SPACE AT THE RIGHT.*

1. A teacher is preparing a talk for a group of parents of primary children on the topic of HELPING YOUR CHILD.
   Which one of the following ideas should she attempt to drive home MOST forcefully?

   A. Ask your child each day what and how he did in school
   B. Take a genuine interest in the information the child volunteers about school activities
   C. Impress upon your child the need to do better than the other children in his class
   D. Supervise the child's home assignments, insisting on correct work, neatly prepared

2. When a kindergarten child brings home a painting he has made, parents should be encouraged to

   A. point out the imperfections in it
   B. be as noncommittal as possible about it
   C. praise it and display it
   D. ask him to tell them what it represents

3. The MAJOR curricular significance of a visit to the Post Office by kindergarten children lies in the fact that they learn

   A. the location of the Post Office
   B. how to mail their own cards
   C. to regard the Post Office as a source of public information
   D. to recognize the uniform of a postman

4. Of the following devices, the one which offers the MOST effective means of producing the *choo-choo* effect of a steam locomotive in a rhythm band is

   A. rhythm sticks   B. maracas
   C. sand blocks   D. cymbals

5. The 4th step in a major scale is called

   A. la   B. fa   C. re   D. ti

6. All of the following are valid concerning story telling EXCEPT:

   A. Small children who cannot read like stories about themselves and events familiar to them
   B. Fairy tales should be introduced to children at an early age, before they can read
   C. Older children enjoy advanced folk tales and hero tales
   D. Humor and nonsense should not be omitted from children's selections

7. Of the following, the one which is a fundamental aim of kindergarten education is the

   A. total development of the individual
   B. inculcation of knowledges needed in living
   C. development of physical skills
   D. full utilization of the play instinct

8. Of the following, the factor which is MOST important in bringing about the close relationship that is necessary between school and home is

   A. a modern school building
   B. an *open door* policy on the part of the principal of the school
   C. an upper middle class group of parents
   D. appropriate attitudes on the part of teachers in the school

9. Flicka, Ricka, and Dicka in the Maj Lindman books are

   A. three girls
   B. three dogs
   C. three kittens
   D. a girl and 2 boys

10. The minuet is a dance written in _____ measure.

    A. 2/4   B. 4/4   C. 6/8   D. 3/4

11. Parents should react to a child's questions about birth and sex differences by

    A. forbidding the child to think of such matters
    B. explaining to the child that only adults may know about such matters
    C. telling the child that these will be discussed in school at the right time
    D. helping the child to understand these matters insofar as his maturity permits

12. In THE PIED PIPER OF HAMELIN, the word *pied* refers to the

    A. piper's multicolored clothing
    B. kind of pipe he played upon
    C. piper's peculiar fascination for children
    D. piper's love of mince pies

13. In PETER AND THE WOLF, the theme that identifies the Cat is played by a(n)

    A. oboe   B. trombone   C. clarinet   D. trumpet

14. The Trapp Family was a well-known

    A. choral group
    B. string ensemble
    C. jazz orchestra
    D. swing band

15. In THE STAR-SPANGLED BANNER, the phrase following the words of the third line, *Whose broad stripes and bright stars,* is *through the perilous* _____.

    A. night   B. flight   C. fight   D. light

16. Of the following, the MOST functional way to teach children to cross the street properly and independently is to

    A. invite the policeman to talk to the class
    B. discuss the many accidents that happen to careless children
    C. sing safety songs
    D. *act out* crossing the street in the classroom with lights

17. Of the following, the BEST way to introduce the library to kindergarten children is to   17.____

    A. act out a *Visit to the Library* during dramatic playtime
    B. have the librarian come and tell them a story
    C. visit the neighborhood library and meet the librarian
    D. show a short filmstrip to them on the library and discuss it in class

18. BABAR, the hero of a children's song, is a(n)   18.____

    A. elephant who does much traveling
    B. bear who spends his life in a zoo
    C. jet black horse
    D. sheep-like lion

19. Of the following, the MOST effective method of encouraging kindergarten children to make puppets for dramatic play is to   19.____

    A. have a display of puppets in the play center of the classroom to stimulate interest
    B. tell the children about puppets
    C. show them pictures of puppets
    D. ask them to ask their parents about puppets and recommend a good puppet show

20. Of the following types of outdoor equipment, the one which will be MOST creatively challenging to children of kindergarten age is   20.____

    A. swings and teeter-totters
    B. shuffle boards and jungle gyms
    C. doll carriages and wheelbarrows
    D. wooden crates and hollow blocks

21. A guessing game suitable for developing auditory acuity is   21.____

    A. What color is missing?   B. The Hunt
    C. Follow What Leader?   D. Who is it?

22. A perennial favorite of all ages is Kipling's   22.____

    A. ADVENTURES OF BROWNIES   B. WONDER CLOCK
    C. JUST-SO STORIES   D. THE BRAVE TIN SOLDIER

23. Of the following activities, the one which is LEAST appropriate for kindergarten children is   23.____

    A. swings and jungle gym
    B. simple competitive games, such as kickball
    C. circle games, such as Looby Lou
    D. catching balls and bean bags

24. In selecting toys for five and six year olds, it is MOST important to provide   24.____

    A. sturdy, well-made commercial toys
    B. housekeeping toys for girls and mechanical toys for boys
    C. toys that can be used in a variety of ways
    D. toys that require adult help for proper use

25. Of the following, which is the educationally SOUNDEST description of the teacher's role in relation to the play activity of children?
She

    A. provides space and materials for the activity
    B. organizes the activity and then withdraws when it is in full swing
    C. supervises the selection and use of materials needed for the activity
    D. uses the activity to enrich the experiences of the children

25.____

26. The teacher should observe the children in the play corner to see that they

    A. use the materials without wasting them
    B. carry out the assignments given them
    C. cooperate with one another no matter what they do
    D. work harmoniously and safely with each other

26.____

27. The EARLIEST aesthetic experiences of the young child are likely to occur in play with

    A. blocks and paints
    B. games and toys
    C. swings, see-saws, and sliding ponds
    D. kitchen and household utensils

27.____

28. The teacher can BEST help the overaggressive child in a kindergarten group by

    A. excluding him from the group as soon as he becomes overaggressive
    B. keeping him near her at all times
    C. pointing out the trouble his overaggressiveness causes
    D. providing an outlet for him through vigorous play

28.____

29. A child who has fainted should be

    A. propped up on a pillow or head rest
    B. laid flat and kept quiet
    C. given a warm drink
    D. aroused as soon as possible

29.____

30. Of the following well-known fairy tales, the one that was NOT written by Hans Christian Andersen is

    A. THE EMPEROR'S NEW CLOTHES
    B. BEAUTY AND THE BEAST
    C. THE UGLY DUCKLING
    D. THE CONSTANT TIN SOLDIER

30.____

31. Of the following, the dramatic play period should be designed PRIMARILY to enable a kindergarten child to

    A. extend his experience
    B. enter into group relationships
    C. carry out a predetermined plan
    D. have an adventure

31.____

32. The tempo of POP GOES THE WEASEL is   32.____

    A. 6/8   B. 2/4   C. 3/8   D. 4/4

33. An outstanding composer of kindergarten music is   33.____

    A. Stephen Foster   B. Satis Coleman
    C. Arthur Sullivan   D. J.L. Molloy

34. Of the following games, the one MOST suitable for kindergarten children is   34.____

    A. Jackstraws
    B. Jolly is the Miller
    C. Legos
    D. Annie Goes to the Cabbage Field

35. In music, R.H. stands for   35.____

    A. retard here   B. right hand
    C. rest and hold   D. repeat heavily

36. Of the following, the SOUNDEST educational reason why rhythm instruments should be within reach of the kindergarten child is that he can   36.____

    A. experiment with them on an individual basis
    B. reach an instrument readily when it is time for the rhythm band to perform
    C. select his own instrument
    D. learn to replace the instrument easily

37. Of the following, the PRIMARY reason why walking boards are included in the kindergarten equipment inventory is that   37.____

    A. they provide exercise for the children
    B. the children enjoy them
    C. they help children develop muscular coordination and balance
    D. they are safer than other pieces of equipment

38. In order to prevent hardening, modeling clay should be stored in   38.____

    A. covered earthenware crocks
    B. tin cans accompanied by a slice of apple
    C. galvanized containers to prevent electrolytic action
    D. wet cloths to prevent evaporation

39. Of the following reasons why sand might be used in a kindergarten, the one which is MOST important is that it   39.____

    A. attracts the dull child with only limited abilities
    B. is relatively inexpensive
    C. presents a minor housekeeping problem
    D. affords sensory satisfactions to the child

40. Water color painting is a particularly satisfying experience to kindergarten children because they can 40._____

    A. develop their latent artistic talents
    B. feel free to paint large masses and shapes without restrictions
    C. learn to paint and develop a taste for painting
    D. learn to put on an apron before painting

41. A hurdy gurdy is a 41._____

    A. stringed instrument   B. hand organ
    C. player piano   D. concertina

42. Of the following, the material BEST suited for kindergarten sewing activities is 42._____

    A. raffia   B. wool
    C. reed   D. embroidery cotton

43. For BEST results, powdered tempera paints are usually mixed with 43._____

    A. linseed oil   B. turpentine
    C. water   D. fixative

44. Of the following, the one which is a reed instrument is the 44._____

    A. French horn   B. piccolo
    C. flute   D. clarinet

45. A soundly democratic home is BEST described as one in which the children 45._____

    A. have as much influence on decisions as the parents do
    B. are allowed to make all decisions as the parents do
    C. accept the decisions made by their parents
    D. express their desires freely about matters that must be decided

46. In the children's song, THE MUFFIN MAN, we are told that the muffin man lives in 46._____

    A. the house at the end of the lane
    B. a house without a window pane
    C. Drury Lane
    D. baker's lane

47. In teaching a simple song to a group of 6-year-old children, a teacher does all of the following things. 47._____
    Which is the POOREST procedure?

    A. Repeating the song several times
    B. Encouraging all the children to sing the song
    C. Presenting both the words and melody the first day
    D. Teaching one line of the song at a time

48. Which of these phonograph records would be MOST useful in kindergarten? 48._____

    A. THE SNOW GOOSE   B. CINDERELLA
    C. LITTLE INDIAN DRUM   D. PETER CHURCHMOUSE

49. SINGING TIME was written by

    A. Patty Hill
    B. Neidlinger
    C. Kathleen Malone
    D. Coleman and Thorn

50. Of the following, the one which is NOT a percussion instrument is the

    A. drum
    B. xylophone
    C. double-bass
    D. cymbal

KEY (CORRECT ANSWERS)

1. B	11. D	21. D	31. B	41. B
2. C	12. A	22. C	32. A	42. B
3. B	13. C	23. B	33. B	43. C
4. C	14. A	24. C	34. C	44. D
5. B	15. C	25. D	35. B	45. D
6. B	16. D	26. D	36. A	46. C
7. A	17. C	27. A	37. C	47. D
8. D	18. A	28. D	38. A	48. C
9. A	19. A	29. B	39. D	49. D
10. D	20. D	30. B	40. B	50. C

EXAMINATION SECTION
TEST 1

DIRECTIONS: Each question or incomplete statement is followed by several suggested answers or completions. Select the one that BEST answers the question or completes the statement. *PRINT THE LETTER OF THE CORRECT ANSWER IN THE SPACE AT THE RIGHT.*

1. A person preparing for the field of elementary school teaching will come across the words *mixed dominance* when studying methods of teaching

    A. mathematics
    B. reading
    C. music
    D. creative writing

    1.____

2. Of the following, the program which is designed to give pre-kindergarten children some school experience is entitled

    A. Higher Horizons
    B. Early Identification Program
    C. Pre-School Study Centers
    D. Operation Head Start

    2.____

3. All of the following educators are matched correctly with the institutions they primarily served EXCEPT

    A. Benjamin Willis - Harvard School of Education
    B. John Fischer - Teachers College
    C. James Allen - New York State Education Department
    D. Francis Keppel - Department of Health, Education, and Welfare

    3.____

4. Of the following, the pairing which is INCORRECT is

    A. The Initial Teaching Alphabet - Sir James Pitman
    B. study of precocious readers - Dolores Durkin
    C. study of the disadvantaged child - Martin Deutsch
    D. revival of the Montessori method - Omar K. Moore

    4.____

5. YOUTH IN THE GHETTO is a publication of

    A. The Educational Policies Commission
    B. Harlem Youth Opportunities, Unlimited
    C. The Great Cities School Program
    D. The New York State Education Department

    5.____

6. Of the following, the MOST accurate statement about the growth of mental ability is that it

    A. is rapid during the pre-school years and then slows down sharply
    B. is rapid during the pre-school and early school years
    C. starts slowly but accelerates quickly when children enter school
    D. is more and more rapid as children progress through elementary and secondary schools

    6.____

7. If a parent objects to a teacher's use of television in the classroom, indicating that all the children have more than enough TV at home, the BEST of the following actions for the teacher to take would be to

   A. refer her to the principal
   B. tell her that TV is a new trend
   C. ask her to curtail her child's home viewing of TV
   D. invite her to see a class TV lesson

8. All of the following questions might well be used to put a parent at her ease during a parent-teacher interview EXCEPT:

   A. Do you have time to read to John?
   B. Does John like to help you at home?
   C. Why do you let John cling to you?
   D. What special things do you want us to know about John?

9. The BEST way of reporting to his parents a first-grade child's progress in school is by means of a(n)

   A. leaflet-type report card in which the child is rated Satisfactory or Unsatisfactory in the various curriculum areas
   B. checklist which indicates the child's growth in social behavior and work habits
   C. report card which contains anecdotal comments on the child's growth but no specific ratings
   D. individual parent-teacher conference

10. All of the following statements relating to mental hygiene are correct EXCEPT:

    A. When a disturbed child is given help, progress often is occurring when the behavior of the child seems to indicate regression.
    B. Symptoms can be eliminated while the causes of undesirable behavior remain.
    C. Praise may frequently affect a child adversely.
    D. Children feel more secure when limits are clearly set.

11. All of the following safety precautions should be taken by a teacher when on a trip with a class EXCEPT:

    A. Arrange the class in two's with the slow-moving children at the head of the line
    B. When crossing a street with the class, go to the rear of the line to see that all the children get across safely
    C. Avoid the first and last cars of a subway train
    D. Have identification tags or cards for the children to wear or carry on the trip

12. If a first grade child refuses to accompany the class to the gym for a game period, the teacher should, after trying to persuade the child to come along, BEST do which one of the following?

    A. Take the class to the gym and wait for the child to follow.
    B. Cancel the game period and send for the child's mother to discuss how to handle this situation should it ever occur again.
    C. Send a note to her supervisor and wait in the room with her class until he arrives.
    D. Take her class to the gym, start the game period, and then return to her room to talk to the child.

13. To see experience charts in their proper relationship to the whole primary program, it is important to understand all of the following EXCEPT that

    A. the curriculum must provide meaningful first-hand experiences
    B. records of experiences can take pictorial as well as written form
    C. records of experiences afford opportunities for building the self-image of children
    D. all class experiences must be recorded for review of learnings

14. If a first grade teacher finds that in a number of instances money which the children brought to school to purchase cookies has *disappeared*, her BEST course of action among the following is to

    A. discontinue the selling of cookies
    B. advise the parents of the situation and inform them that children bring money to school at their own risk
    C. tell the children to give her any money they have with them when they enter the room in the morning and that she will return it to them when the time comes to purchase cookies
    D. tell the children that when they bring money to school, they are to place it on their desks so that they can keep it in view at all times

15. During the first few months of the school year, the first grade teacher is usually BEST advised to emphasize which one of the following kinds of reading approaches?

    A. Experiential   B. Corrective
    C. Phonic   D. Basal

16. The Bank Street Readers were developed specifically to meet the needs of _____ children.

    A. mentally retarded   B. bilingual
    C. rural   D. urban

17. If a kindergarten teacher finds that one of her children is able to read a first grade reader, her BEST course of action usually is to

    A. keep the child in kindergarten but give him many opportunities to read a variety of books
    B. send the child to the office with a note asking the principal to check the child's reading ability to determine whether or not he should be in the first grade
    C. discuss the situation with the first grade teachers to see if one of them would be willing to have the child join her class for a daily reading lesson
    D. ask the child's mother to see the principal about putting the child in the first grade

18. Inconsistent with the current philosophy of teaching English as a second language is the precept that the teacher should do which one of the following?

    A. Capitalize upon experience in which there is a need for speaking English.
    B. Plan activities demanding the use of English.
    C. Schedule practices on necessary vocabulary prior to the experience.
    D. Key experiences for helping children acquire English to the regular curriculum of the class.

19. Auditory discrimination refers to all of the following EXCEPT the ability to

    A. sustain attention to sound
    B. note differences in the volume of sound
    C. distinguish changes in the pitch of sound
    D. note differences in the rhythm of sound

20. A left-handed child in the second grade makes many reversals and directional errors in writing.
    The teacher should do all of the following EXCEPT have the child

    A. begin to write at the left-hand side of the paper
    B. usually write from memory rather than from copy
    C. referred to the Bureau of Child Guidance
    D. practice words in which reversals occur

21. Going on trips is a vital part of the social studies curriculum.
    All of the following statements about trips in the early childhood grades are true EXCEPT:

    A. The same trip may be taken more than once.
    B. The teacher should plan with the children what they will look for on the trip.
    C. No planning by the teacher is needed for a walk around the school block.
    D. The teacher should be familiar with the area to be visited and the route to be taken.

22. All of the following statements about basal readers are generally true EXCEPT:

    A. It is undesirable to permit children to keep their basal readers in their desks.
    B. It is desirable to set up the goal of having children cover all pages in their basal reader as the end-point objective of a semester's work.
    C. As a rule, a basal reader's content is built with a controlled vocabulary repeated with studied regularity.
    D. Stories may be read out of order for special purposes or to develop specific skills.

23. All of the following statements regarding the teaching of mathematics in early childhood education are generally accepted by authorities EXCEPT:

    A. The systematic teaching of mathematical processes begins in the kindergarten
    B. Mathematics is taught by the teacher in a definite sequence
    C. Each mathematics topic is developed through the four developmental levels
    D. Non-numerical concepts involve making comparisons

24. Of the following activities through which children in grades Kg-2 should be helped to acquire an orientation to the universe, the one LEAST appropriate is

    A. studying cloud formations
    B. discussing how gravity helps us
    C. tracing shadows at different times of the day
    D. observing the sun in relation to nearby structures

25. Of the following science experiences, the one LEAST desirable for a first grade class is the

    A. teacher shows the class pictures of an experiment done by her last year's class
    B. teacher encourages children to bring in seeds which they plant in milk containers
    C. children discuss the weather and then dictate a weather experience chart to the teacher
    D. children care for a rabbit which the teacher has brought to school

26. If a student in your class has a running nose, blotchy skin, and a temperature elevation, he is MOST likely suffering from

    A. diphtheria   B. mumps
    C. measles   D. acne

27. Which of the following characteristics of a ball would cause a kindergarten teacher to reject it as UNSUITABLE for her children?
    It is

    A. caught with a rudimentary clasping motion
    B. light enough to be thrown with a limited forearm motion
    C. a standard size handball
    D. medium-sized, brightly colored rubber

28. Of the following ballets, the one that might appeal to children because of its setting in a doll shop is

    A. GISELLE   B. COPPELIA
    C. SLEEPING BEAUTY   D. SWAN LAKE

29. The teacher should bear in mind that the PRIMARY responsibility for the health of the child rests with the

    A. school medical office   B. school principal
    C. parent   D. teacher

30. Lorraine and Jerrold Beim's TWO IS A TEAM has for its main characters

    A. two small boys, one Black, one white
    B. twin sisters who are often mistaken for each other
    C. two brothers who are in the same class in school
    D. a sister and brother who help each other out of trouble

31. Eleanor Frances Lattimore's stories about Little Pear concern themselves with

    A. an Indian girl's life on a reservation
    B. a puppy's adventures in a big city
    C. the experiences of a child in kindergarten
    D. a mischievous Chinese boy

32. H.A. Rey is the author of a popular series of stories about a monkey called

    A. LITTLE LEO   B. SCRAPPY
    C. CURIOUS GEORGE   D. FRIENDLY FRANK

33. The surprise ending of Marjorie Flack's ASK MR. BEAR consists of

    A. a new den for Mr. and Mrs. Bear and their cubs
    B. how Bear Mountain got its name
    C. a party cake baked in the shape of a bear
    D. the great big bear hug a little boy gives his mother

34. The story of WHERE THE WILD THINGS ARE, winner of a Caldecott medal, is about

    A. a child's adventures in the jungle
    B. exotic fauna and flora
    C. a little boy's dream of monsters
    D. a zoo

35. Of the following, the one who is NOT an author of fairy tales for children is

    A. Henry James
    B. Oscar Wilde
    C. Hans Christian Andersen
    D. Charles Perrault

36. All of the following were written by Eugene Field EXCEPT

    A. WYNKEN, BLYNKEN, AND NOD
    B. THE SUGAR-PLUM TREE
    C. THE DUEL
    D. HALFWAY DOWN

37. In the poem AND TO THINK THAT I SAW IT ON MULBERRY STREET by Dr. Seuss, the little boy on the way to school sees a(n)

    A. organ grinder
    B. clown
    C. horse and wagon
    D. crane

38. THE LAND OF COUNTERPANE is one of the poems in

    A. Stevenson's A CHILD'S GARDEN OF VERSES
    B. Field's POEMS OF CHILDHOOD
    C. Milne's WHEN WE WERE VERY YOUNG
    D. Unknown - MOTHER GOOSE

39. *"Little playmate, dance with me"* is sung to the music of

    A. HANSEL AND GRETEL
    B. JUMP JIM JO
    C. I WANT TO BE A FARMER
    D. SLEEPING PRINCESS

40. On a piano, G flat is the same as

    A. C sharp   B. F sharp   C. A sharp   D. A flat

41. THE MUFFIN MAN about whom young children like to sing lives in

    A. Limerick Town
    B. Berkeley Square
    C. Old New York
    D. Drury Lane

42. A song which uses only the first three notes of the scale, both up and down (123 and 321), is

    A. GO TELL AUNT RHODIE
    B. HOT CROSS BUNS
    C. OATS, PEAS, BEANS
    D. TWINKLE, TWINKLE

43. The symbol *pp* in a musical selection indicates that the selection should be played very

   A. fast B. slowly C. loudly D. softly

44. In music, to modulate means to

   A. play in a key other than the original
   B. play with dynamics
   C. use a mute
   D. go from one key to another by a chord progression

45. To help the child sing in tune, the teacher should do any of the following EXCEPT

   A. have the children imitate a train whistle
   B. ask the child not to sing
   C. ask the child to sing phrases from a familiar song
   D. call the roll in song

46. In fingerpainting, it is MOST important to allow young children to

   A. work on wet paper
   B. mix colors on the paper
   C. use as many colors as they wish
   D. depict people and objects rather than abstractions

47. Young children are introduced to painting with tempera color through the use of

   A. one brush and two colors
   B. one brush and one color
   C. two brushes and two colors
   D. one brush and the mixing of one color with another

48. Of the following ways of cleaning up after an art activity, the MOST desirable practice is to

   A. require each child to clean up the place where he has worked
   B. go about the classroom using a sponge to clean up
   C. save time by waiting until the end of the day to clean up
   D. appoint monitors to clean up for their classmates

49. When there is limited room to store art work in the classroom, all of the following are advisable EXCEPT to

   A. put the work on display in the classroom
   B. throw the work away immediately
   C. allow the children to take the work home
   D. ask for permission to display the work in a corridor

50. Of the following, the MOST educationally valid reason for careful planning of an art program for young children is that, without guidance, they might

   A. attempt things beyond their mental and manual development
   B. experiment with various materials
   C. waste material
   D. be unable to represent things accurately

KEY (CORRECT ANSWERS)

1. B	11. B	21. C	31. D	41. D
2. D	12. C	22. B	32. C	42. B
3. C	13. D	23. A	33. D	43. D
4. D	14. C	24. B	34. C	44. D
5. B	15. A	25. A	35. A	45. B
6. D	16. D	26. C	36. D	46. A
7. B	17. A	27. C	37. C	47. B
8. C	18. C	28. B	38. A	48. A
9. D	19. A	29. C	39. A	49. B
10. C	20. B	30. A	40. B	50. A

TEST 2

DIRECTIONS: Each question or incomplete statement is followed by several suggested answers or completions. Select the one that BEST answers the question or completes the statement. *PRINT THE LETTER OF THE CORRECT ANSWER IN THE SPACE AT THE RIGHT.*

1. Of the following tests, the one that measures ability in phonics is

    A. Kuhlmann-Anderson
    B. New York Reading Readiness
    C. Roswell-Chall
    D. Metropolitan Primary

2. Of the following, the BEST procedure for the teacher to follow with a child who comes to kindergarten already reading is to

    A. give the child help in moving to the next sequential level of reading growth
    B. explain to the child that he must wait until first grade for reading instruction
    C. give him daily instruction in a readiness book
    D. permit this child to select all the stories to be read to the class

3. An outstanding analysis of American culture which has frequently been cited as predicting the civil rights *revolution* is

    A. THE AMERICAN DEMOCRACY - Harold Laski
    B. DEMOCRACY IN AMERICA - Alexis de Tocqueville
    C. AN AMERICAN DILEMMA - Gunnar Myrdal
    D. PUBLIC EDUCATION AND THE STRUCTURE OF AMERICAN SOCIETY - James Bryant Conant.

4. Of the following, the LEAST acceptable purpose of a home visit by a teacher is to

    A. foster parent-teacher relations
    B. provide the teacher with a clearer understanding of the child's background
    C. help the teacher understand factors in the home that are helping or hindering the child's development
    D. provide an opportunity to discuss the child's school behavior

5. If an early childhood teacher notices that the Puerto Rican children in her class cluster together during work-play activities, she should

    A. ask the principal to transfer some of the Puerto Rican children to other classes in the interest of integration
    B. not interfere in any way so as to avoid the charge some parents may make that she is engaging in *social engineering*
    C. quietly attempt to interest some of the Puerto Rican children in participating in activities involving other groups
    D. call a meeting of the Puerto Rican children's mothers and ask for their help

6. All of the following are characteristics of the normal child's mental powers during early childhood EXCEPT that

    A. the capacity for perception is remarkably active
    B. retention and recall are functioning excellently

169

C. logical memory is as well developed as rote memory
D. memory during this period depends upon the child's interests and proper motivation

7. If a teacher notes that a child in her class is coming to school improperly clothed because the family is poor, her BEST course of action is to

   A. refer the matter to the principal
   B. ask the other children in the class to bring in any clothing their families can spare
   C. ask the mothers of other children in her class if they can provide some clothing for this child
   D. ignore the situation to avoid embarrassing the child

8. Which one of the following is NOT identified with the early development of the testing movement in America?

   A. Lawrence K. Frank   B. Lewis Terman
   C. J.M. Rice   D. Edward L. Thorndike

9. If a teacher receives a letter from a private social agency asking for information on a child in her class because the agency is working with the family, the teacher should

   A. supply the information called for
   B. notify the child's parent and get her permission to supply the information
   C. do nothing about the request since private social agencies may misuse this information
   D. turn the letter over to her principal for whatever action he deems advisable

10. When it is necessary to establish a double kindergarten, which one of the following is the MOST desirable procedure?

    A. While one teacher is teaching, the other teacher uses the time for preparation, planning, and clerical work.
    B. Both teachers are actively responsible for all the children throughout the day.
    C. One teacher has to assist the other teacher only during the work-play period.
    D. The principal will decide which teacher will be the assistant teacher throughout the year.

11. If a teacher plans a trip to the local firehouse and finds that two of her children went there last year with another teacher, she should

    A. arrange to have these two children go on another trip with a different class in lieu of this one
    B. make no special arrangements but simply take them along with the rest of the class
    C. ask a supervisor to place them in another class on the day of the trip
    D. suggest to their mothers that they be kept home on the day of the trip since they have already been there and will be bored

12. All of the following statements about habit formation in early childhood are true EXCEPT: 12.____

    A. Guidance in habit formation is unnecessary.
    B. Many important habits are the basis for habits formed later on.
    C. Childhood habits are the basis for habits formed later on.
    D. The child should build adequate and correct habits by trying to do all things as well as he can.

13. All of the following statements regarding the Initial Teaching Alphabet (I.T.A.) in the teaching of reading are true EXCEPT: 13.____

    A. It utilizes the same books now being used in teaching beginning reading.
    B. It requires special orientation of parents since it is so radically different from present methods.
    C. It is predicted upon the sounds of the alphabet rather than on the letters themselves.
    D. When pupils have mastered the basic skills of reading, they stop using the I.T.A. and make the appropriate transition.

14. Which one of the following statements is CORRECT with regard to the establishment of routines in the kindergarten? 14.____

    A. Routines in the kindergarten give evidence that the class is teacher-dominated.
    B. Routines established early in the year leave time for creative activities later.
    C. The children can easily establish their own routines in all areas.
    D. The teacher who establishes routines is an uncreative teacher.

15. In THROUGH THE LOOKING GLASS by Lewis Carroll, the walrus and the carpenter *"wept like anything to see such quantities of"* 15.____

    A. sand   B. stone   C. cheese   D. fruit

16. *"Any fool can despise what he cannot get"* is the lesson to be learned from the fable by Aesop entitled 16.____

    A. THE WOLF AND THE CRANE
    B. THE FOX AND THE GRAPES
    C. THE DOG AND THE SHADOW
    D. THE CAT AND THE MICE

17. In the poem ANIMAL CRACKERS by Christopher Morley, the poet tells of a supper of animal crackers and 17.____

    A. milk   B. cocoa   C. soda pop   D. tea

18. ERMINKA AND THE CRATE OF CHICKENS is a story found in the collection entitled 18.____

    A. THE POPPY SEED CAKES
    B. STARS AND STEEPLES
    C. JATAKA TALES
    D. PICTURE TALES FROM THE RUSSIANS

19. In a fairy tale written by the Grimm Brothers, Rumpelstiltskin is the name of a 19.____

    A. fairy queen
    B. princess
    C. miller
    D. little man

4 (#2)

20. With respect to story telling and reading aloud to young children, the statement among the following that is CORRECT is that

    A. there must be a set time during the school day for story telling
    B. kindergarten children are not mature enough to enjoy accumulative folk tales
    C. listening to stories beyond the children's reading level should have a legitimate place in the early childhood classroom
    D. reading aloud to children decreases their interest in independent reading

21. Of the following, the consonant sound which the average young child is able to articulate before the others is

    A. r   B. b   C. l   D. f

22. Research in the field of language growth of young children indicates that

    A. *only children* tend to surpass in language development children who have siblings
    B. twins generally tend to progress more rapidly in language development than do children of single birth
    C. boys are generally more shy than girls and ask fewer questions
    D. the child who associates more frequently with adults than with other children develops less rapidly in language

23. Of the following, the LEAST useful material upon which the kindergarten teacher may effectively base her social studies program is

    A. songs appropriate to observance of holidays
    B. occupations of members of the children's families
    C. simple textbooks
    D. neighborhood trips

24. Of the following experiences, the one LEAST effective for the development of geographic concepts in kindergarten is

    A. noting changes in seasons and weather
    B. observing the direction of the rising and setting sun
    C. locating such natural features in the neighborhood as a hill, a river, a lake
    D. comparing the size of Europe with the size of the United States from a study of area symbols

25. In making the nose on the *fish* for a magnetic fishing game, the MOST suitable object among the following is a

    A. brass fastener   B. nickel brad
    C. steel clip   D. copper rivet

26. Of the following, the MOST appropriate piece of equipment for a teacher to use to demonstrate the concept that the sun heats the earth is a

    A. magnifying glass   B. candle
    C. filmstrip projector   D. transit

27. Of the following, the BEST way to introduce the meaning of halves to children in the first grade is to

   A. write 1/2 on the board
   B. fold a paper in half
   C. draw a circle on the board and divide it through the center
   D. ask a child to share a piece of construction paper with another child, giving the other child half

27.____

28. Of the following, the EARLIEST step in learning to count is

   A. writing the numerals from 1 to 10
   B. noting one-to-one correspondence
   C. rote counting to 100
   D. counting things verbally by ones

28.____

29. All of the following are from the opera HANSEL AND GRETEL EXCEPT

   A. Brother, come and dance with me
   B. March of the Dwarfs
   C. Suzy, Little Suzy
   D. Children's Prayer

29.____

30. Of the following, the composition which would be LEAST appropriate to introduce the instruments of the orchestra is

   A. CARNIVAL OF ANIMALS
   B. SCENES FROM CHILDHOOD
   C. PETER AND THE WOLF
   D. TUBBY THE TUBA

30.____

31. The teacher may use all of the following instruments to provide a choral accompaniment for singing EXCEPT the

   A. recorder   B. piano   C. autoharp   D. guitar

31.____

32. Of the following, a song that may effectively be used to teach counting is

   A. BLUEBIRD, BLUEBIRD
   B. THIS OLD MAN
   C. BINGO
   D. GO TELL AUNT RHODY

32.____

33. The musical term *adagio* means

   A. with spirit   B. slow   C. fast   D. moderate

33.____

34. In early childhood grades, all of the following are accepted activities EXCEPT

   A. singing rote songs
   B. singing observation songs
   C. part singing
   D. playing rhythm instruments

34.____

35. WHERE IS THUMBKIN? is sung to the tune of

   A. JACK AND JILL
   B. HEY, DIDDLE, DIDDLE
   C. RINGA, RINGA, REIA
   D. FRERE JACQUES

35.____

36. Of the following, the percussion instrument that has definite pitch is the

   A. snare drum
   B. kettle drum
   C. tambourine
   D. bass drum

36.____

37. Of the following compositions, the one MOST aptly described as a *fairy tale for children* is 37.____

	A. THE NUTCRACKER SUITE - Tchaikcvsky
	B. APPALACHIAN SPRING - Copland
	C. GRAND CANYON SUITE - Grofe
	D. SUITE BERGAMASQUE - Debussy

38. The average young child's inability to do art work skillfully is due CHIEFLY to 38.____

	A. lack of muscular coordination
	B. inattention
	C. lack of interest
	D. stubbornness

39. Young children, when they begin to paint with colors, should use 39.____

	A. one color only	B. two colors
	C. black and white	D. any number of colors

40. Of the following, the MOST compatible modeling medium for the young child is 40.____

	A. plasticine	B. plaster of paris
	C. ceramic clay	D. beaten egg white

41. For MOST satisfactory use, a teacher should condition opaque water paint (tempera) to the consistency of 41.____

	A. whipped cream	B. skimmed milk
	C. coffee cream	D. gelatine

42. It is appropriate to send children to the chalkboard to do water painting when they 42.____

	A. know how to handle a brush
	B. need a play activity
	C. deserve a reward
	D. are being introduced to painting

43. The young child often shows distortion in his pictures because he 43.____

	A. emphasizes what is important to him
	B. cannot remember everything
	C. knows very little
	D. tries to hide his real feelings

44. For fingerpainting, kindergarten children may use all of the following papers successfully EXCEPT 44.____

	A. glazed shelf paper	B. butcher paper
	C. magazine covers	D. newspaper

45. To have MAXIMUM educational value, craft activities in the early grades should begin with 45.____

	A. tasks assigned by the teacher for drill or exercise in motor control
	B. the manipulation of the materials and personal experimentation

C. the teaching of techniques that will help the children to select the right tool or medium
D. group block-building, sharing blocks of the Carolyn Pratt type

46. The type of wound MOST likely to result in tetanus is a(n)

   A. incision
   B. abrasion
   C. laceration
   D. puncture

47. Evidence of pediculosis in a child's hair should cause the teacher to

   A. refer the child to the school nurse
   B. call the parent
   C. exclude the child from school
   D. refer the child to the principal

48. Of the following song plays, the one which starts with a double circle is

   A. LOOBY LOO
   B. THE GALLANT SHIP
   C. THE FARMER IN THE FIELD
   D. THE SNAIL

49. All of the following dances are appropriately listed for grades kindergarten - one EXCEPT

   A. CHILDREN'S POLKA
   B. SHOEMAKER'S DANCE
   C. SHOO FLY
   D. JESSIE POLKA

50. All of the following diseases are transmitted by direct contact with an infected person EXCEPT

   A. mumps
   B. malaria
   C. ringworm
   D. tuberculosis

KEY (CORRECT ANSWERS)

1. C	11. B	21. B	31. A	41. C
2. A	12. A	22. A	32. B	42. D
3. C	13. A	23. C	33. B	43. A
4. D	14. B	24. D	34. C	44. D
5. C	15. A	25. C	35. D	45. B
6. C	16. B	26. A	36. B	46. D
7. A	17. B	27. D	37. A	47. A
8. A	18. A	28. B	38. A	48. B
9. D	19. D	29. B	39. A	49. D
10. B	20. C	30. B	40. C	50. B

EXAMINATION SECTION
TEST 1

DIRECTIONS: Each question or incomplete statement is followed by several suggested answers or completions. Select the one that BEST answers the question or completes the statement. *PRINT THE LETTER OF THE CORRECT ANSWER IN THE SPACE AT THE RIGHT.*

1. Of the following, the one which is usually considered to be the technique which is LEAST useful in interviewing parents is

    A. recording all that is said by making accurate notes during the conversation
    B. letting the parent speak freely, especially about any complaint that he may wish to make
    C. telling the parent the child's accomplishments, as well as his deficiencies
    D. ending the interview with plans for further meetings and/or definite action

    1.____

2. All of the following are closely associated with studies of the underprivileged child EXCEPT

    A. Frank Riessman
    B. Carolyn Pratt
    C. Martin P. Deutsch
    D. Kenneth B. Clark

    2.____

3. All of the following are primary developmental tasks of the young child EXCEPT learning

    A. skill in controlling his body
    B. about the world about him
    C. to accept frustrations
    D. to read independently

    3.____

4. The objective of all art experiences in the elementary grades is to

    A. develop the ability to draw realistically
    B. keep children busy with motor activity
    C. secure a uniform standard and type of expression
    D. promote emotional stability, muscular coordination, and originality of expression

    4.____

5. All of the following may correctly be used to rate the behavior of young children EXCEPT the

    A. Winnetka Scale
    B. Fairbanks Scale
    C. Ohio Social Acceptance Scale
    D. Haggerty-Olson-Wickman Rating Schedules

    5.____

6. Research tends to show that all of the following are true of development of language in children of pre-school and elementary school age EXCEPT that

    A. girls tend to be poorer than boys in clarity of enunciation and freedom from speech defects
    B. the number of basic words known increases by several thousands per year
    C. the length of responses tends to increase with the age of the child
    D. the average length of sentences spoken by girls is greater than it is for boys of the same age

    6.____

7. Reading readiness tests are properly used for all of the following purposes EXCEPT to   7.____

   A. indicate need for differentiated instruction and individual guidance
   B. provide a basis for remedial drill to correct the weakness disclosed
   C. indicate the type of program needed for a class
   D. serve as background material for parent conferences

8. Of the following, the BEST statement for inclusion in an anecdotal record of Carl's conduct for a particular morning is   8.____

   A. Carl's behavior was unruly
   B. Carl kicked Vince, who sits in front of him
   C. Carl was aggressive and defiant
   D. Carl gave evidence of emotional disturbance

9. Which of the following situations is MOST clearly indicative of good emotional climate in a class?   9.____

   A. A pupil acts as chairman and asks questions of the class.
   B. A pupil voluntarily asks a question.
   C. The teacher calls upon many pupils to answer questions.
   D. All the pupils in the class raise their hands to answer a question asked by the teacher.

10. Of the following, the BEST definition of *correlation* is   10.____

    A. the ratio between the number of exercises correctly done and the number of exercises attempted
    B. the degree of relationship existing between two or more sets of measures
    C. a standard by which a test or other product is judged or evaluated
    D. the use of equal forms of a standardized test, which yield closely similar scores

11. Which one of the following statements about social relationships is TRUE of most kindergarten children?   11.____
    They

    A. like to play together in groups of not more than four or five children
    B. prefer parallel play, one child near another
    C. seek the esteem of large social groups
    D. choose as leaders those children who have leadership ability

12. A six-year-old child in your first grade class refuses to come to school. Her mother tells you that the child cries and vomits each morning.   12.____
    In such a case, the BEST thing for the teacher to do is to

    A. tell the mother to scold the child every time she does this
    B. tell the mother to bring the child to school every day
    C. tell the parent that the child can be discharged from school since she is under 7 years of age
    D. suggest an appointment with the guidance counselor or refer the parent to a supervisor for help in obtaining guidance service

13. The MOST important value of the classroom use of projective techniques, such as the *wishing well* and autobiography, is to

    A. help teachers understand and guide individual children who need special help
    B. resolve deep emotional conflicts of individual children
    C. provide experiences involving creative activity
    D. train teachers to develop skills in psychiatric therapy

14. Babar, in the children's story by Jean de Brunhoff, is a(n)

    A. monkey   B. bear   C. mongoose   D. elephant

15. The story of HANSEL AND GRETEL is among the tales to be found in a famous collection by

    A. Hans Christian Anderson
    B. Johanna Spyri
    C. Bishop Percy
    D. The Grimm Brothers

16. Animals talk in each of the following children's works EXCEPT

    A. JUNGLE BOOK
    B. WHITE FANG
    C. BLACK BEAUTY
    D. CHICKEN LITTLE

17. All of the following are titles of verses in ALICE'S ADVENTURES IN WONDERLAND EXCEPT

    A. The Owl and the Pussy Cat
    B. The Walrus and the Carpenter
    C. Jabberwocky
    D. Father William

18. Each of the following poems from an anthology of poetry for children is matched with its author EXCEPT

    A. THE JUMBLIES - Walter de la Mare
    B. THE SWING - Robert Louis Stevenson
    C. THE FIDDLER OF DOONEY - William Butler Yeats
    D. THE FALLING STAR - Sara Teasdale

19. Felix Salten's BAMBI is a story about a

    A. deer   B. cow   C. rabbit   D. mouse

20. Peter Pan saves Tinker Bell's life by

    A. asking the audience if they believe in fairies
    B. rescuing her from the crocodile
    C. applying artificial respiration after dragging her from the water
    D. slaying Captain Hook, the pirate

21. If a group of children in a first grade class do not seem to be ready to learn to read, the teacher should

    A. postpone reading instruction for the rest of the class until this group is ready to join them
    B. plan experiences for this group which are prerequisites to success and satisfaction in reading

C. ask her supervisor to place this group in another class for part of the school day while she teaches the remainder of the class
D. start the formal reading program with them anyway, lest they fall too far behind

22. *Enumeration, Description,* and *Interpretation* are terms used to refer to

    A. levels on which children relate experiences they have had
    B. methods used to introduce a new story in a basal reader
    C. levels of dramatic play
    D. levels on which children read pictures

23. In the early childhood program, letter writing

    A. is usually done cooperatively with the teacher doing the recording
    B. is usually done by individual children provided the emphasis is on form rather than content
    C. should be avoided since it is not part of the curriculum
    D. should be undertaken only by those children able to write independently

24. All of the following are characteristic of the teaching of manuscript writing EXCEPT that

    A. letters are taught in the order in which they appear in the alphabet
    B. if a child experiences difficulty in making a particular letter, the teacher teaches the component parts of that letter
    C. the teacher must show the children the correct position for writing
    D. the letters are written vertically rather than slanted

25. All of the following statements regarding language arts in early childhood education are true EXCEPT:

    A. If a number of children wander away while the teacher is reading a story, it may be that they have had too many sedentary activities that day
    B. Storytelling—as opposed to story reading—should be undertaken only when the teacher feels she is unable to read the story with sufficient dramatic expression to maintain the children's interest
    C. Listening to rhythmic poetry affords much enjoyment to young children
    D. The line between fantasy and reality is generally not sharply defined in the mind of the four-year-old child

26. When children in Grades 1 and 2 are reproducing a piece of writing, the teacher should do all of the following EXCEPT

    A. provide the children with pens
    B. observe the children for fatigue
    C. prepare a perfect copy for the class
    D. proofread the completed copy with the children

27. Among the following, the MOST recent trend in the development of primary reading materials is the inclusion of

    A. more illustrations and fewer new words
    B. illustrations reflecting the pluralistic nature of our society
    C. words designed to enrich vocabulary
    D. vocabulary lists for self-checking

28. All of the following statements regarding language arts in early childhood education are true EXCEPT:

    A. In written expression, content takes precedence over form
    B. Primary grade children, even first graders, are capable of much creativity in oral expression
    C. The classroom atmosphere is of prime importance in the development of language
    D. A child who is experiencing considerable difficulty in learning to read should be taught to write first

29. In a sensibly organized democratic classroom in the early grades (Kg-2), the one practice of the following which may be UNWISE is to

    A. treat each pupil with respect
    B. avoid all teacher domination
    C. maintain an atmosphere of security for children
    D. plan work in which pupils may participate in group activities

30. Among the following, the MOST practical way to provide social studies reading materials for developmentally disabled readers is to

    A. arrange for a workshop with several colleagues
    B. read stories to the class
    C. rewrite the text in simple language
    D. adhere strictly to mainstream curriculum

31. Of the following plants, the one which is a member of the grass family is

    A. asparagus   B. onion   C. rye   D. lettuce

32. Cuttings of all of the following plants may be forced to produce flowers in the early spring under classroom conditions EXCEPT

    A. hemlock   B. cherry
    C. forsythia   D. pussy willow

33. All of the following plants are often found growing on school lawns or nearby lots EXCEPT

    A. dandelion   B. broad leaf plantain
    C. ragweed   D. sagittaria

34. All of the following principles are basic to planning for mathematical growth in the early childhood grades EXCEPT:

    A. Mathematics is taught in a definite sequence, from the first grade on
    B. Each mathematics topic is developed by beginning with a first-hand experience
    C. The teacher avoids overlapping among the four developmental levels
    D. Mathematics is an abstract science requiring that even young children do mathematical thinking

35. Willard C. Olson's emphasis on self-selection and pacing has had an especially strong influence on proponents of

    A. meaningful mathematics   B. programmed instruction
    C. individualized reading   D. free choice of art media

36. Of the following, the representative material LEAST likely to provide for a thinking-out of meaningful mathematical relationships is

    A. pennies
    B. beads strung on a lace
    C. posters
    D. plastic discs

37. All of the following *song plays* utilize a circle formation EXCEPT

    A. THE FARMER
    B. A-HUNTING WE WILL GO
    C. THREE BLIND MICE
    D. PAW PAW PATCH

38. All of the following are games played without equipment and are appropriate for primary grades EXCEPT

    A. SKIP TAG
    B. LINE ZIG-ZAG
    C. HOUND AND RABBIT
    D. FLOWERS AND WINDS

39. In administering first aid to a child in school, it is now permissible for a teacher to

    A. give aspirins for a headache
    B. clean a minor wound with tap water and plain soap
    C. give liquids to an unconscious person
    D. use the fingers as a probe to dislodge foreign matter in the throat

40. An entry of *deciduous teeth* on the child's health record card refers to

    A. decayed teeth
    B. dentures
    C. baby teeth
    D. crooked teeth

41. On the piano keyboard, the note immediately to the left of middle *C* is

    A. B flat
    B. B natural
    C. C sharp
    D. D flat

42. A CHILDREN'S OVERTURE by Roger Quilter interest children MOSTLY because in it they discover

    A. quiet melodies
    B. opportunities for rhythmic response
    C. familiar instruments
    D. familiar songs they have already learned

43. The number of accented beats in each full measure of a march written in 6/8 tempo, such as Sousa's WASHINGTON POST MARCH, is

    A. 2
    B. 4
    C. 6
    D. 8

44. Of the following, the statement NOT in harmony with the music program for the early childhood years is:

    A. The teacher who lacks confidence in her singing may use records
    B. Children should master the words of every song taught
    C. Teachers should encourage original rhythmic responses
    D. Attitudes are more important than skills

45. All of the following are objectives of primary grade teaching in music EXCEPT to have the children

    A. develop pitch consciousness
    B. recognize instruments of the orchestra as string, woodwind, percussion, or brass
    C. play simple percussion instruments
    D. recognize variations in accent and beat in 2/4 or 3/4 time

46. Satisfying safe experiences in block printing for young children may be achieved by using which one of the following instead of linoleum?

    A. Commercial rubber stamps
    B. Balsa wood
    C. Self-hardening clay
    D. Potatoes

47. In teaching fingerpainting techniques, all of the following are advisable EXCEPT to

    A. have the children use only one color
    B. see that the children keep the paper as dry as possible
    C. teach the children to use the entire hand
    D. confine the painting to abstract designs

48. Permitting little children to paint on the chalkboard with clear water and a brush

    A. is time-wasting
    B. gives them a valuable learning experience
    C. teaches them bad habits
    D. is an innocuous but valueless pasttime

49. Working with art materials in the elementary grades provides opportunities for

    A. repression of emotions
    B. study of perspective
    C. constructive release of feelings
    D. periods of physical inactivity

50. Objectives of the art program for children in grades Kg-2 include all of the following EXCEPT to

    A. develop visual perception
    B. develop the child's ability to communicate ideas and feelings
    C. train children to copy the work of outstanding artists
    D. promote appreciation of aesthetic qualities

KEY (CORRECT ANSWERS)

1. A	11. A	21. B	31. C	41. B
2. B	12. D	22. D	32. A	42. D
3. D	13. A	23. A	33. D	43. A
4. D	14. D	24. A	34. C	44. B
5. B	15. D	25. B	35. C	45. B
6. A	16. B	26. A	36. C	46. D
7. B	17. A	27. B	37. D	47. B
8. B	18. A	28. D	38. B	48. B
9. B	19. A	29. B	39. B	49. C
10. B	20. A	30. C	40. C	50. C

TEST 2

DIRECTIONS: Each question or incomplete statement is followed by several suggested answers or completions. Select the one that BEST answers the question or completes the statement. *PRINT THE LETTER OF THE CORRECT ANSWER IN THE SPACE AT THE RIGHT.*

1. Which one of the following theories MOST supports the idea that learning takes place through insight?

    A. Transfer of training
    B. Reinforcement
    C. Stimulus-response
    D. Gestalt

    1.____

2. Most modern educators would accept all of the following statements about discipline EXCEPT:

    A. Emphasis should be placed on prevention of discipline problems rather than correction
    B. A properly adjusted curriculum is an important factor in maintaining good discipline
    C. To maintain a reputation for impartiality, the teacher must punish each offense in exactly the same way, regardless of who the offender is
    D. Withdrawn children frequently constitute more serious problems than aggressive children

    2.____

3. A teacher's colleague asks her to keep a child from going on a trip because he has been rude in the lunchroom.
   Of the following, the teacher's BEST response to her colleague would be to

    A. explain tactfully that it is really unprofessional of one teacher to tell another what to do
    B. try to agree with her colleague on another form of punishment
    C. honor the request in order to maintain good staff relationships
    D. let the principal adjudicate the matter

    3.____

4. Of the following, the curriculum design LEAST suited to the needs of young children is the _____ curriculum.

    A. broad field
    B. emerging needs
    C. problems-of-living
    D. subject matter

    4.____

5. Which one of the following procedures should have priority for the child who speaks little or no English?

    A. Intense individual help from a bi-lingual teacher
    B. An intelligence test in his native language
    C. Help in feeling secure in his classroom
    D. Instruction by the teacher of speech improvement

    5.____

6. Freeing the teacher for creative teaching is a major objective of the classroom designs making use of all of the following EXCEPT

    A. intensive testing
    B. team teaching
    C. telecast lessons
    D. teacher aides

    6.____

7. An *experiential* school was established in Washington, D.C. and dedicated to a teacher-directed, subject-matter approach.
   The name of this school is The _____ Elementary School.

   A. Capital   B. Washington
   C. Amidon   D. National

8. If a counselor's techniques are based on the theory that a pupil has within himself the resources for solving his own problems, but that these need to be stimulated, the counselor believes in the type of counseling known as

   A. nondirective   B. directive
   C. spontaneous   D. generative

9. The INCORRECT association of author and area of interest is

   A. Lucy Sprague Mitchell - Social Studies
   B. Gerald S. Craig - Science
   C. Emma D. Sheehy - Art
   D. Arthur I. Gates - Reading

10. All of the following are widely known for their work in the field of parent education EXCEPT

    A. Lawrence K. Frank   B. James L. Hymes
    C. Edgar B. Wesley   D. Jean S. Grossman

11. A teacher calculates the median of the results on a standardized test taken by her class by adding all the scores and dividing by the number of pupils in the class. Her procedure is

    A. *correct* because the median is the average of all scores
    B. *correct* because extreme scores are overemphasized by this method
    C. *incorrect* because the median is the most frequently occurring score
    D. *incorrect* because the teacher has really found the arithmetic mean, not the median

12. Of the following, the group of children LEAST likely to be referred for guidance is that composed of those who

    A. show troubled behavior patterns that adults are not forced to notice
    B. show aggressive behavior against other children but not against the teacher
    C. are antagonistic but outwardly appear to conform with the teacher's wishes
    D. misbehave only when the teacher is out of the room

13. Each of the following statements is true EXCEPT:

    A. The teachings of Friedrich Froebel strongly influenced some of the first American kindergartners
    B. G. Stanley Hall conducted an early study of the knowledge of children as they started schooling
    C. The child study movement led to Lewis Terman's invention of the intelligence test
    D. H.P. Bowditch began in 1879 to measure the height and the weight of the Boston school children

14. Of the following, the measure LEAST educationally effective for helping a child who has difficulty in following directions is to 14.____

    A. check on hearing difficulties
    B. send a note home to his mother about his inattention
    C. evoke the child's interest
    D. give directions slowly and clearly

15. All of the following contributed directly to an understanding of the kindergarten movement in America EXCEPT 15.____

    A. William T. Harris
    B. Harry G. Wheat
    C. Henry Barnard
    D. Josephine C. Foster

16. *When I was sick and lay abed,* 16.____
    I had two pillows at my head
    are the opening lines of the poem

    A. EVENING HYMN - Elizabeth Madox Roberts
    B. THE LAND OF COUNTERPANE - Robert Louis Stevenson
    C. LITTLE BROTHER'S SECRET - Katherine Mansfield
    D. THE FIRST SNOWFALL - James Russell Lowell

17. The title of a humorous picture folk-tale in which each character is miraculously saved from the executioner is 17.____

    A. GONE IS GONE - Wanda Gag
    B. MY FATHER'S DRAGON - Ruth Gannett
    C. THE FIVE CHINESE BROTHERS - Claire H. Bishop
    D. THE TAILOR OF GLOUCESTER - Beatrix Potter

18. Flopsy and Mopsy are 18.____

    A. ducks in the Angus books
    B. rodents in THE WIND IN THE WILLOWS
    C. dolls in RAGGEDY ANN
    D. rabbits in THE TALE OF PETER RABBIT

19. Among the following children's books, the one which is considered to be an alphabet book is 19.____

    A. THE BIGGEST BEAR - Lynd Ward
    B. ALL AROUND TOWN - Phyllis McGinley
    C. LITTLE PEAR - Eleanor Lattimore
    D. SING-SONG - Christina Rossetti

20. In the Mother Goose tale, the sparrow accidentally killed Cock Robin. His intended victim was 20.____

    A. The Cuckoo
    B. Jenny Wren
    C. Parson Rook
    D. Goldfinch

21. Rumpelstiltskin is a 21.____

    A. miller
    B. prince changed into an animal by a witch
    C. maiden with long golden hair
    D. dwarf

22. In the story FROG WENT A-COURTIN', the object of the frog's affection is a

    A. squirrel   B. fish   C. sparrow   D. mouse

23. *Little lamb, who made thee?*
    Dost thou know who made thee?
    are the opening lines of a poem by

    A. William Blake
    B. William Shakespeare
    C. Henry Wadsworth Longfellow
    D. Alfred Tennyson

24. In THE BOX WITH RED WHEELS by Maud and Miska Petersham, the barnyard animals look into the box and find a

    A. fox   B. cub   C. baby   D. red hen

25. Of the following, the MOST effective method of training children in good listening habits is to

    A. tell the class there will be a test on what is said
    B. insist that children stand when they speak
    C. talk very loudly and emphasize important points by heavier stress
    D. suit the materials and the occasion to the maturity and interest of the class

26. Parents often ask a teacher how they can help young children improve their reading ability.
    Which of the following practices should you NOT recommend?

    A. Encourage children to read the signs around them – in stores, on billboards, posters, etc.
    B. Read interesting stories aloud to the children regularly.
    C. Insist that children spend a specific minimum amount of time reading daily.
    D. Encourage and assist children in building their own home libraries.

27. All of the following are recommended procedures in teaching English to the foreign-born children EXCEPT

    A. use a great deal of repetition
    B. introduce new words in contexts meaningful to children
    C. always insist upon answers being in complete sentences
    D. avoid excessive correction of speech sounds

28. Most authorities in the field of reading would agree with all of the following statements EXCEPT:

    A. Some pupils with superior intelligence fail to learn to read satisfactorily
    B. Teacher judgment is a worthwhile criterion in assessing reading readiness
    C. Reading is one of the most complex skills taught in the elementary school
    D. Home environment bears little relationship to success in reading

29. When a teacher directs the children to *find the sentence which tells where Sally went*, she is giving practice in the skill of

   A. using contextual clues
   B. skimming
   C. determining sequence
   D. predicting outcomes

30. All of the following indicate a readiness to begin formal reading EXCEPT that the child

   A. speaks spontaneously and clearly
   B. has a mental age of at least five and a half years
   C. can distinguish similarities and differences in pictures, colors, and letters
   D. has adequate physical and motor coordination

31. The teacher of kindergarten, planning meaningful social studies experiences for her class, will regard as LEAST important the encouragement of the children to

   A. ask their fathers about the nature of their work
   B. learn to locate the place on the globe that marks the location of the United States
   C. sing the song on February 12 that they had learned about little Abe Lincoln
   D. watch the progress of the building going up near the school

32. From their science activities related to magnetism, children will discover all of the following EXCEPT that

   A. the compass is a floating magnet
   B. like poles of magnets repel each other
   C. magnets are strongest at their ends
   D. magnets attract iron, copper, and lead

33. Of the following, the demonstration which is MOST appropriate for use in an elementary school class to illustrate a chemical change is

   A. placing moistened iron filings in a dish and letting them remain there for several hours
   B. sprinkling iron filings on a piece of paper which rests on two bar magnets
   C. allowing steam from a boiling kettle to come in contact with a cold glass plate
   D. allowing a drop of ink to fall into a glass of water

34. From their science activities related to the study of wind, children will discover all of the following EXCEPT that

   A. the arrow of the wind vane points into the wind
   B. wind speed is measured by an anemometer
   C. smoke, clouds, and flags help us to detect wind direction
   D. the direction toward which a wind blows gives the wind its name

35. In teaching the numbers 7 and 8 in a grade two class, the final step should be to

   A. compare groups of pennies
   B. make change counting to 10 cents
   C. write symbols as records of addition
   D. regroup the group added

36. Which of the following is NOT true about the mathematics program for children in the early childhood grades?

    A. Young children learn mathematics best through familiar experiences.
    B. A teacher of young children can rely entirely on experiences children have in the community.
    C. Experiences differ for different children.
    D. Children must be helped to see mathematical relationships in their everyday experiences.

37. The emotional and physical development of children about 6 or 7 years of age suggests that

    A. their art work should consist of large, spontaneous, free paintings
    B. we should train their finer muscles by having them copy small pictures
    C. art has no place in little children's lives
    D. coloring pictures is the best art activity for them

38. Paper folding (origami), an arts and crafts activity popular with young children, is an ancient art form from the land of

    A. Israel   B. Peru   C. Sardinia   D. Japan

39. Holiday themes expressed through art activity are BEST realized in the primary grades

    A. by eliciting from each child an experience capable of being related to the given holiday
    B. by the teacher's drawing relevant themes on the blackboard, using colored chalk
    C. by taking advantage of the beautiful, printed materials, often available without cost and freely distributed at holiday time
    D. by a careful study of postcards in a stationery store

40. Of the following art experiences in the primary grades, all indicate a weakness in the teacher's approach to art EXCEPT when

    A. each art activity is conducted separately
    B. each pupil continues working with one art medium until he shows improved coordination of motor, emotional, and mental facilities
    C. all art experiences are carried on interdependently and are related to the curriculum as a whole
    D. the children work with the materials for art activities under the step-by-step direction of the teacher

41. Of the following, the MOST valid action for the teacher to take before the children in her kindergarten take home their simple paintings is to

    A. evaluate the paintings and drawings and select those that may be taken home
    B. encourage each child to choose his best paintings and tell why he has chosen them
    C. display the paintings in the classroom and allow all the children of the class to compare them
    D. invite the parents to a conference so that they will understand and appreciate the simple efforts of their children

42. Of the following, the song BEST suited to introduce children's names is 42.____
    A. BRIDGE OF AVIGNON
    B. PAW PAW PATCH
    C. HERE WE GO ROUND THE MULBERRY BUSH
    D. SKIP TO MY LOU

43. To develop rhythmic response to a four-beat measure, the teacher should play a 43.____
    A. waltz   B. mazurka   C. minuet   D. march

44. OVER THE RIVER AND THROUGH THE WOOD is MOST appropriately taught in connection with 44.____
    A. Thanksgiving Day   B. Halloween
    C. Valentine's Day   D. Arbor Day

45. In the rhythm band, the BEST approximation of an alarm clock bell's ringing is obtained by tapping a 45.____
    A. jingle clog   B. tambourine
    C. triangle   D. cymbal

46. Middle C on the piano is represented in music notation 46.____
    A. on a leger line below the bass staff
    B. on a leger line below the treble staff
    C. in the third space, treble staff
    D. in the first space, bass staff

47. A teacher upon detecting evidence of pediculosis should immediately 47.____
    A. arrange for a consultation with the child's parent
    B. refer the child to the principal or his representative
    C. send the child home
    D. notify the Board of Health

48. For comfort and most efficient work, the classroom temperature should be in which one of the following ranges? 48.____
    A. 60° to 65° F   B. 73° to 77° F
    C. 68° to 72° F   D. 78° to 82° F

49. All of the following are *tag* games EXCEPT 49.____
    A. CHARLEY OVER THE WATER   B. CHINESE WALL
    C. CLUB SNATCH   D. SQUIRRELS IN TREES

50. All of the following are characteristic of the average seven-year-old EXCEPT that he 50.____
    A. likes to bat and pitch a ball
    B. fits easily into organized group play
    C. enjoys alternate periods of activity and inactivity
    D. shows more interest in some activities and tries fewer new ventures than the four-year-old

KEY (CORRECT ANSWERS)

1. D	11. D	21. D	31. B	41. D
2. C	12. A	22. D	32. D	42. B
3. B	13. C	23. A	33. A	43. D
4. D	14. B	24. C	34. D	44. A
5. C	15. B	25. D	35. C	45. C
6. A	16. B	26. C	36. B	46. B
7. C	17. C	27. C	37. A	47. B
8. A	18. D	28. D	38. D	48. C
9. C	19. B	29. B	39. A	49. D
10. C	20. A	30. B	40. C	50. B

TEST 3

DIRECTIONS: Each question or incomplete statement is followed by several suggested answers or completions. Select the one that BEST answers the question or completes the statement. *PRINT THE LETTER OF THE CORRECT ANSWER IN THE SPACE AT THE RIGHT.*

1. All of the following are known for writings in the area of child growth and development EXCEPT

    A. Frances Ilg
    B. Anna B. Comstock
    C. Arnold Gesell
    D. Maria Montessori

    1.____

2. All of the following are known for their contributions to early childhood education EXCEPT

    A. Robert Hutchins
    B. Friedrich Froebel
    C. Jean Jacques Rousseau
    D. Jean Frederic Oberlin

    2.____

3. The INCORRECT association of author and title among the following is

    A. H.G. Rickover - THE DIMINISHED MIND
    B. J.B. Conant - THE EDUCATION OF AMERICAN TEACHERS
    C. Martin Mayer - THE SCHOOLS
    D. W.A. Yauch - HOW GOOD IS YOUR SCHOOL?

    3.____

4. All of the following are American educators who pioneered in the kindergarten movement before 1900 EXCEPT

    A. Elizabeth Peabody
    B. Minnie Berson
    C. Patty Smith Hill
    D. Susan Blow

    4.____

5. The arts are included in the program of the elementary school CHIEFLY because they

    A. provide an opportunity to discover artistic talent
    B. provide rest and relaxation from studies which involve mental activity
    C. provide emotional release, motor coordination, and another means of communication
    D. make it possible to illustrate and add color and interest to units of study

    5.____

6. Which one of the following educators contributed the idea of following five formal steps in a lesson?

    A. William Wirt
    B. Carleton W. Washburne
    C. Johann Friedrich Herbart
    D. Edward L. Thorndike

    6.____

7. All of the following are recent trends in education being put into practice on an experimental basis EXCEPT

    A. team teaching
    B. ungraded primary schools
    C. The Princeton Plan
    D. The Dalton Plan

    7.____

8. Of the following, the LEAST acceptable use of standardized tests is to

   A. provide meaningful standards of comparison
   B. diagnose pupils' strengths and weaknesses
   C. provide a basis for assigning marks
   D. establish a uniform basis for measuring individual growth and achievement

9. All of the following attitudes would be approved for a constructive approach to classroom living EXCEPT that the teacher

   A. emphasize the things that the children can do
   B. ignore the errors of the children
   C. protect each child's self-respect by recognizing his drive to do well
   D. establish routines which give the children a feeling of security

10. Of the following statements about a child's level of maturity, the MOST NEARLY correct is that it

    A. is the same as his mental age
    B. must be considered in teacher planning
    C. should not be discussed with his parents
    D. is the same as his chronological age

11. Of the following schools of psychological thought, the one tending MOST to treat learning as a *conditioned response* is the

    A. Behaviorist
    B. Gestalt
    C. Connectionist
    D. Sense impressionist

12. All of the following are basic guidelines stemming from the growth characteristics of children in the early childhood grades EXCEPT:

    A. Social experience for beginners in school should be timed in accordance with their short attention span
    B. Concepts should be related to the here and now and clearly tied to concrete experiences
    C. Boys and girls should play separately during the free-play period
    D. The daily program should be planned to provide for a variety of activities

13. Of the following, the natural sequence of language growth is

    A. listening, reading, speaking, writing
    B. reading, listening, speaking, writing
    C. listening, speaking, reading, writing
    D. listening, speaking, writing, reading

14. Of the following parts of speech, the one which predominates in the vocabulary of a child beginning to speak is

    A. adjectives
    B. nouns
    C. verbs
    D. pronouns

15. The Cheshire Cat is a character in

    A. MILLIONS OF CATS
    B. ALICE IN WONDERLAND
    C. THE OWL AND THE PUSSYCAT
    D. OUR BIRD NEIGHBORS

16. Of the following, the one which is a yearly prize given for the *most distinguished contribution to American literature for children* is the

    A. Medallion of the Association of American Libraries
    B. Seuss Citation
    C. John Newbery Medal
    D. Nathan Straus Award

17. All of the following books are matched correctly with their authors EXCEPT

    A. SUSIE THE CAT - Tony Palazzo
    B. STONE SOUP - H.A. Rey
    C. MADELINE - Ludwig Bemelmans
    D. PAPA SMALL - Lois Lenski

18. The animals that play an important role in Esphyr Slobodkina's CAPS FOR SALE are

    A. elephants   B. monkeys   C. puppies   D. kittens

19. In Virginia Lee Burton's book KATY AND THE BIG SNOW, Katy is a

    A. sled that has been waiting all year for the first snowfall
    B. crawler tractor that comes to the rescue when the city is visited by a blizzard
    C. pet poodle that gets lost in a week-long snowfall
    D. little Southern girl who experiences her first snowfall when she visits her grandparents in Chicago

20. All of the following were written by Dr. Seuss EXCEPT

    A. HOW THE GRINCH STOLE CHRISTMAS
    B. IF I RAN THE CIRCUS
    C. ON BEYOND ZEBRA
    D. THEODORE TURTLE

21. All of the following are noted for their poems for young children EXCEPT

    A. George Santayana   B. Walter de la Mare
    C. Hilaire Belloc   D. Edward Lear

22. The names of the human beings in Louise Fatio's HAPPY LION series give a clue to the fact that the books were written in

    A. Norway   B. Germany   C. Italy   D. France

23. A glass splinter causes little Kay to turn against his friend, Gerda, in Hans Christian Andersen's story

    A. THUMBELINA   B. THE MARSH KING'S DAUGHTER
    C. THE SNOW QUEEN   D. THE DARNING NEEDLE

24. A French child USUALLY associates fables with

    A. Racine   B. Voltaire
    C. Rousseau   D. La Fontaine

25. Which one of the following statements is INCORRECT with regard to the use of experience charts in the first grade?

   A. Frequent rereading of charts, no matter how well motivated, should not be practiced because of possible loss of interest by the children.
   B. The rules for indentation should be observed as the teacher develops the chart.
   C. Experience charts have worth not only before direct instruction in reading but also long after the child has started to read.
   D. The teacher should deliberately anticipate vocabulary to be read in the basal reading series when developing experience charts.

26. Which one of the following statements is INCORRECT with regard to reading readiness?

   A. Mental age is only one factor, and not necessarily the most important one, of the many factors which contribute to success in reading.
   B. An attempt must be made, even at the readiness stage, to teach children to become aware of the importance of the main thought of a story.
   C. Drawing inferences, authorities feel, should be left to later stages of reading development.
   D. The school library should become an integral part of any readiness program.

27. Which one of the following educators was noted for his studies in teaching nursery school and kindergarten children how to read through the use of the typewriter?

   A. Arthur Trace
   B. E.W. Dolch
   C. Donald Durrell
   D. Omar K. Moore

28. In the teaching of reading, which one of the following is an example of word attack through the use of structural analysis?

   A. Recognizing a word through its outline and shape
   B. Recognizing prefixes and suffixes attached to root words already known
   C. Combining initial consonant clues with contextual clues
   D. Distinguishing single consonant sounds

29. All of the following statements are true of modern media of mass communication EXCEPT that

   A. they present new challenges to the school
   B. they compete for the time and attention of the child after school
   C. librarians report that TV viewing can be a spur to reading
   D. the use of mass media in school encroaches on time which should be allotted to basic learnings

30. A newly appointed teacher discovers that her pupils do not speak audibly during class discussions.
   Of the following, the BEST procedure is to

   A. repeat pupils' answers to insure comprehension by other pupils
   B. establish with the class criteria for good speech and provide for consistent follow-up
   C. have a pupil secretary write all valid pupil contributions on the chalkboard
   D. establish a class rule requiring audible discussion and have offenders write the rule repeatedly until they conform

31. Of the following, the MOST important and immediate objective of the kindergarten social studies program is to develop

    A. good independent work habits
    B. a knowledge of the United States government
    C. an understanding of the nations on this continent
    D. an appreciation of American history

32. Of the following, the one which states four topics which are MOST suitable for inclusion in the social studies curriculum for early childhood classes is

    A. School, the State, Colonial America, and the American Revolution
    B. School, Explorations, Geography, and Holidays
    C. Geography, Cold Lands, the State, and Colonial America
    D. School, Home, Travel, and Communication

33. All of the following activities are recommended in the study of animals in the early grades EXCEPT

    A. arranging a bulletin board showing snapshots of the children's pets
    B. collecting birds' nests
    C. visiting a local pet shop to see the kinds of animals displayed
    D. asking a local veterinarian to speak to the children on the care of pets

34. Opportunity should be provided for growing and observing many kinds of plants in the classroom.
    From this type of activity, children should learn all of the following EXCEPT:

    A. Plants require space in which to grow
    B. The common plants in classrooms have leaves, stems, roots, and sometimes flowers
    C. A seed contains a baby plant
    D. All plants grow from seeds

35. From their science activities related to magnets, children in early childhood grades will discover all of the following EXCEPT:
    Magnets

    A. pick up objects which contain iron
    B. pick up objects which contain any metal
    C. are strongest at their ends
    D. can attract through substances such as paper and water

36. On an abacus having beads strung vertically, with white beads in the ones place, red beads in the tens place, blue beads in the hundreds place, and green beads in the thousands place, the number represented by a display of three white beads, five red beads, and four green beads is

    A. 4053   B. 534   C. 5340   D. 453

37. Of the following, the statement which is MOST accurate with reference to color blindness in human beings is that it

    A. occurs with equal frequency in males and females
    B. occurs most often in females
    C. occurs most often in males
    D. can easily be cured

38. All of the following statements are true of the game STOOP TAG except that

    A. a single circle formation is used
    B. a small ball is used
    C. several players may be *it*
    D. it appeals to elementary school children of various ages

39. The tonette is a musical instrument played by

    A. using a bow
    B. striking with a drum stick
    C. blowing
    D. shaking

40. Of the following songs, the one NOT included in the opera HANSEL AND GRETEL by Humperdinck is

    A. SUSIE, LITTLE SUSIE
    B. BROTHER, COME AND DANCE
    C. PRAYER
    D. WHISTLE WHILE YOU WORK

41. Of the following, the one on which a teacher can sound the starting note for a class song is the

    A. cymbal
    B. tambourine
    C. xylophone
    D. tom-tom drum

42. Sand blocks, rhythm sticks, and a triangle played by the children would BEST contribute a suitable rhythm-band setting to a children's song about

    A. THE RAILROAD TRAIN
    B. THE MUFFIN MAN
    C. THE PUNCH AND JUDY SHOW
    D. CLIP-A-DEE CLOP

43. Eighth notes are BEST demonstrated to young children as

    A. half of a quarter beat
    B. part of a divided pie
    C. *running* notes
    D. the count of *one and two and* etc.

44. A musical production which has been a favorite of children in recent years contains the songs OVER THE RAINBOW and

    A. LAVENDER'S BLUE
    B. DING DONG, THE WITCH IS DEAD
    C. THE OWL AND THE PUSSY CAT
    D. DEEP IN THE HEART OF TEXAS

45. The singing range of young children is CORRECTLY described as   45.____

    A. about an octave, treble staff
    B. about half an octave to below treble staff
    C. about an octave and a half to above treble staff
    D. so flexible as to defy precise description

46. To help him sing on pitch, the teacher should encourage the out-of-tune singer to   46.____

    A. listen but not sing
    B. listen, then sing
    C. sing freely without special guidance
    D. engage in other types of self-expression

47. In a regular classroom without built-in provision for art activity,   47.____

    A. it would be best to conduct no art activity
    B. painting activity should be avoided
    C. only crayon or pencil drawing should be planned
    D. the art teacher and classroom teacher should confer regarding an art program capable of being conducted in a classroom with ordinary facilities

48. In displaying children's art work, the BEST practice for the classroom teacher is   48.____

    A. to hang only the work of the best pupils
    B. not to hang any work that the teacher deems unworthy according to accepted standards
    C. to hang the work of all the children on a rotating plan if space is a consideration
    D. to touch up the work of some pupils in order to be able to hang all

49. In the absence of accumulated experiences, young children in art activity should   49.____

    A. trace simple pictures
    B. copy the teacher's drawing
    C. seek help from parents
    D. be taken on trips to secure first-hand experiences

50. Of the following expressions in art, the one in which young children would probably be MOST successful is   50.____

    A. an etching   B. a collage
    C. an illuminated manuscript   D. cloisonne

KEY (CORRECT ANSWERS)

1. B	11. A	21. A	31. A	41. C
2. A	12. C	22. D	32. D	42. A
3. A	13. C	23. C	33. B	43. C
4. B	14. B	24. D	34. D	44. B
5. C	15. B	25. A	35. B	45. A
6. C	16. C	26. C	36. A	46. B
7. D	17. B	27. D	37. C	47. D
8. C	18. B	28. B	38. B	48. C
9. B	19. B	29. D	39. C	49. D
10. B	20. D	30. B	40. D	50. B

CHILD DEVELOPMENT

I - MIDDLE YEARS: AGES 6-12

The ages six to twelve are commonly known as the middle years of childhood. This is the time when children are in full bloom: they are no longer babies but the demands of adult life are still far away. All through this period children continue to develop their special personalities. They are getting to know more about themselves and the world in which they live, and their slow, steady growth can be observed. They grow in independence and are more able to take care of themselves. They also are eager adventurers who learn from their explorations but who often find, to their dismay and to the dismay of the adults around them, that they still have a lot to learn.

Each child is different and there are no set rules for rearing or teaching children. How children grow depends on the characteristics they inherit from their parents and, to a great extent, it depends on the guidance provided by parents and other adults. It also depends on the experiences they have inside and outside of their homes.

Although each child's temperament makes her special, certain guidelines of child growth apply to most youngsters, and parents and other caregivers may find these guidelines helpful when working with the middle-years child.

Physical Development

Growth is of many different kinds and a child's development during the middle years includes increases in height, weight, and strength. The different rates of growth of various body parts account for the awkwardness of the youngster in the late childhood years. Height and weight increase much more slowly and evenly during the middle years than in early childhood. Children usually gain about two or three inches in height each year. Just as height increases at a slow steady pace, so, too, does weight. At the age of six, a child will be about seven times his birth weight. For example, a child who weighed seven pounds at birth will weigh almost fifty pounds at age six. Body proportions also change. The trunk becomes slimmer and more elongated in contrast to the chunky body of the preschooler. The chest becomes broader and flatter, causing the shoulders to droop. Arms and legs become long and thin with little evidence of muscles. It is this thinning-out of the trunk, combined with the elongation of the arms and legs, that gives the middle-years child the "all arms and legs" gawky appearance.

Sexual Differentiation

During the middle years, boys and girls gradually become aware of sexual differences in behavior, attitudes, and manners. These sex differences still can be seen in many play activities. Fortunately, however, both boys and girls now receive more encouragement to try activities traditionally reserved for the opposite sex. This helps to break down sex-role stereotypes. For example, girls learn that they can be good at tasks requiring physical skill, and boys learn that they can be caring young persons without losing their "masculinity." Opportunities for different kinds of play also mean that children develop a variety of skills to carry with them into adulthood.

Psychological Development

Middle-years children can find themselves in conflict with the need to grow up and the desire to remain a child forever, a conflict known as the Peter Pan fantasy. They want to grow up so that they can enjoy the prerogatives of adult life: staying up late, driving the car, wearing adult-styled clothes, and being privy to adult secrets. They want to be able to understand and laugh at adult jokes and be accepted into adult confidences and discussions.

On the other hand, they also want to hold on to all the privileges of childhood. Boys who quarrel, fight, and roughhouse and girls who dress up in their mothers' clothing and makeup are regarded as amusing by adults who would not tolerate such behavior in teenagers.

Social Development

There is a culture of childhood that is passed on solely by oral tradition. Many childrens' games, like hopscotch, marbles, kick-the-can, and blindman's buff, are passed down verbally from one generation to the next. Jokes, riddles, and sayings also are transmitted orally.

Georgie Porgie, pudding and pie Kissed the girls and made them cry.
or
Sticks and stones may break my bones, But names will never hurt me.
or
Ladybug, ladybug fly away home. Your house is on fire your children are gone Except for the little one under the stone Ladybug, ladybug fly away home.
or
Rain, rain go away
Come again another day.

This culture of childhood that finds itself rooted in the past gives a clue to the child's relationship to her family. In contrast to the upheaval an adolescent experiences, the young child may appear to be a staid traditionalist who accepts the authority of the family just as she accepts the games and superstitions of previous generations of children. The middle-years child is more likely to defend than attack her family and what it stands for. The family is the main base of security and identity and is still more important than the child's peer group.

Ages and Stages

Information presented here about the ages and stages of children is only a *guide* for adults working with children. Physically, emotionally, and intellectually, each child grows and develops at his own rate. Some youngsters may be early bloomers. That is, they may have reached a stage of emotional or physical development beyond their chronological years. It is not unusual for a six-year-old to be as tall as a ten-year-old. But when interacting with this child, adults must remember that he *is* six and not ten and they should not expect him to behave as though he were a ten-year-old. Another example is an eight-year-old with an extensive vocabulary who can converse with adults as though she were twelve. In a relationship with this child, it is important for adults to remember that although she may be conversationally mature, she may be mentally, physically and emotionally still an eight-year-old.

Understanding the characteristics of an age can be helpful to adults who work with or care for children. But, if adults are to foster optimal growth and development in children, they also must remain sensitive and responsive to children as individuals.

Six-Year-Olds

General
The sixth year is the age of transition.
• At this age, children are active, outgoing, and self-centered. Their own activities take precedence over everything else.
• They are in constant motion: jiggling, shoving, and pushing. They like to roughhouse and their play may go too far because they don't know when to stop.
• They can play organized games with rules, but only at beginning levels because strategy and foresight are not highly developed at the age of six.
• Six-year-olds may be clumsy and tend to dawdle. For example, they may be slow at dressing to go to school or other places. On the other hand, they want their needs met at once and get upset when adults do not drop everything to do their bidding.

Self-Concept and Independence
• They want to be the center of everything to be first and to win. They are the center of their very own universe and their way of

doing things seems the best and only way. They do not lose gracefully or accept criticism.
- They are assertive, bossy, and extremely sensitive to real or imagined slights. They dominate every situation and are always ready with advice.
- Growing up may be a strain at times for six-year-olds and there may be a period of regression during which they engage in baby talk and display babyish behavior.
- Six-year-olds are extremely possessive of their belongings.
- When the outside world impinges adversely upon them, they are stubborn, obstinate, and unreasonable.
- They tend to project their own feelings onto others and then criticize other people because of this. "She thinks she's-everything" or "He's so fresh."
- They are ashamed of their mistakes and fears and of being seen crying and are careful not to expose themselves to criticism.

Relating to Other Children and Adults
- Six-year-olds often pair up and have best friends with whom they spend a good deal of time. Such pairs often take pleasure in "keeping out" a third child who wants to join them.
- Friendships are erratic and may change many times. Lots of tattling and putting-down of other children goes on, for example, "He's dumb."
- Boys and girls occasionally play together at this age, but the movement toward same-sexed friends has already begun.
- Six-year-olds can be highly sensitive to their parents' moods. For instance, they are quick to notice changes in facial expressions.

Although the six-year-old is most loving of his mother, he is also building his sense of self by trying to break away from her. Many temper tantrums are directed at her and the six-year-old may often refuse to obey his mother's directions. On the other hand, the six-year-old can be sympathetic toward his mother when she is not feeling well.

Parents can find the six-year-old trying. Adults working with six-year-olds need to keep a sense of perspective and their sense of humor. If parents and other caregivers remember the transitional nature of this age, six will become a more manageable and less trying age.

Games and Activities
- Their activities center on the physical. Riding a bicycle is an activity they enjoy. Roller skating and swimming also are favorites.
- They are poor at games requiring strategy and foresight like chess, checkers, and tic-tac-toe, but like running games such as tag and hide-and-seek.
- Six-year-olds like making things as well as cooking activities. They also like to paint, color, and draw.

Seven-Year-Olds

General
Seven is the age of quieting down.
- Toward the beginning of the seventh year the child begins to assimilate the wealth of new experiences and information she learned in first grade.
- They begin to sift and sort information into categories and link the bits of information that they have acquired. Seven-year-olds begin to reason and may at times appear serious and reflective.
- Seven-year-olds can be moody and brooding and pensive and sad because their assimilation of knowledge is not always smooth. Action has shifted and may now take place within their minds rather than within a physical space.
- Although they are self-absorbed they are not isolationists. They are becoming more aware not only of themselves, but of others as well.

Self-Concept and Independence

- The increased introspection of seven-year-olds also means that they have an increased sense of self and are acquiring sensitivity to the reactions of others. This sensitivity is to what others do and say, but not to what other people think. To the seven-year-old, thinking and doing are the same thing.
- They are sensitive about their bodies, which they do not like to have exposed or touched, and they may refuse to use the bathroom at school if it has no door on it.
- Because the physical self and the psychic self are so closely related at this stage, seven-year-olds are reluctant to expose themselves to failure and criticism. They often leave the scene rather than put themselves in a position where they might be subject to criticism or disapproval.

Relating to Other Children and Adults

- They want to be helpful and to become real members of the family group.
- They can take on tasks and responsibilities. When performing chores, they are careful and persistent, and they will demand guidance from adults as to "What do we do now?" or "How do we do this?"
- They can be polite and considerate toward adults. Seven-year-olds are less resistant and less stubborn than six-year-olds.
- They play easily with other children and seem to be in control. Although they are active and boisterous, they know when to stop before someone gets hurt.

Games and Activities

- Seven-year-olds have more capacity to play alone than they had at six, and they enjoy solitary activities such as reading and drawing.
- Group play is still not well organized and is carried out to individual ends.
- They like building things but need to know where things go and where they end. They can understand a simple model and a blueprint.
- Seven-year-olds continue to skate, swim, and are better at bike riding.
- They are avid collectors of anything and everything from stones to bottle tops.
- Seven-year-olds are fond of table games and jigsaw puzzles and can tackle a complicated game like Monopoly.

Eight-Year-Olds
General

Eight-year-olds are expansive, but on a higher level than when they were six.

- They are outgoing, curious, and extremely social and self-confident.
- They tend to be critical of themselves and judgmental of others.
- They now concern themselves with the why of events, and they are active and expansive as they seek out new experiences.
- Eight-year-olds talk constantly and love to gossip.

Self-Concept and Independence

- Eight-year-olds have a greater awareness of self; they are less sensitive, less introspective, and less apt to withdraw. They are becoming individuals who are aware of themselves in the social world.
- They are able to judge and appraise themselves and are conscious of the ways in which they differ from other people.
- Eight-year-olds are concerned about how other people feel about them, and they can be demanding in their efforts to get information about themselves.
- They can work independently, but need direction.

Relating to Other Children and Adults

- Eight-year-olds are mature in their social relationships with others. Relationships with friends are positive. Friendships are closer and very important.
- There is a noticeable separation between boys and girls and both play at games that tend to exclude the opposite sex.

• They are usually friendly and cooperative, preferring mature jobs that resemble adult-like activities.

• They are more polite with strangers than they are at home and are able to hold their own in conversations with adults.

Games and Activities

• Eight-year-olds dislike playing alone. They prefer to be with an adult or another child. Action becomes the focus of all their play.

• Both boys and girls like cooking and baking and show an interest in foreign places and children from different times.

• The collections they began at seven now become more organized and classified.

• They tend to make up their own rules for games and they may even invent new games.

• Eight-year-olds like dramatic play, especially where they take the role of characters they have read about, seen, or heard about.

• Table games such as cards, parchesi, checkers, and dominoes are very popular.

When working with eight-year-olds, adults must remember that they are very social and like to be with peers. They gossip and talk constantly, passing notes from one to the other. This often gets out-of-hand when they are in group situations. In addition to their tendency to judge others, eight-year-olds are increasingly self-critical. For example, many children who liked artwork at six or seven may give it up at eight because they see the difference between the quality of their drawings and those of a friend.

In Summary

Children are individuals with their own special temperaments and idiosyncracies. The ages and stages children go through can vary tremendously from one child to the next and, by respecting the variousness of children, parents and other caregivers can help them develop strong and healthy self-concepts.

II - MIDDLE YEARS: AGES 9-11

The ages six to twelve are commonly known as the middle years of childhood. This is the time when children are in full bloom; they are no longer babies but the demands of adult life are still far away. All through this period children continue to develop their special personalities. They are getting to know more about themselves and the world in which they live and their slow steady growth can be observed. They grow in independence and become more able to take care of themselves. They also are eager adventurers who learn from their explorations but who often find, to their dismay and to the dismay of the adults around them, that they still have a lot to learn.

Each child is different and there are no set rules for rearing or teaching children. How children grow depends on the characteristics they inherit from their parents and, to a good extent, it depends on the guidance provided by parents and other adults. It also depends on the experiences youngsters have inside and outside of their homes.

Although each child's temperament makes her special, certain guidelines of child growth apply to most youngsters, and parents and other caregivers may find these guidelines helpful when working with the middle-years child.

• **In physical development,** height and weight increase slowly and evenly. Children gain about two or three inches in height each year. Body proportions also change. In contrast to the chunky body of the preschooler, during the middle years the trunk becomes slimmer, the chest becomes broader, and the arms and legs thin out.

• **In psychological development,** middle-years children can find themselves in conflict between the need to grow up and the desire to remain a child forever. They want to grow up so that they can enjoy the prerogatives of adult life, but they also want to hold on to all the privileges of childhood.

During the middle years, boys and girls gradually become aware of sexual differences. Fortunately, children now are encouraged to try activities traditionally reserved for the opposite sex-a trend that is helping to break down sex-role stereotypes.

• **In social development,** the middle-years child may appear to be a staid traditionalist who accepts the authority of the family. The family is the main base of security and identity, although around the age of eleven the child begins to place more and more value on the peer group.

Ages and Stages

The information presented here about the ages and stages of children is only a *guide*. Physically, emotionally, and intellectually, each child grows and develops at his own rate. Some youngsters may be early bloomers. That is, they may have reached a stage of emotional or physical development beyond their chronological years. Understanding the characteristics of an age can be helpful to adults who work with or care for children. But, if adults are to foster optimal growth and development in children, they also must remain sensitive and responsive to children as individuals.

Nine-Year-Olds
General
Nine is a developmental middle zone.

• The nine-year-old shows a new maturity, self-confidence, and independence from adults.

• There is an increase in maturity and refinement of behavior. Judgmental tendencies are more discerning and objective. Nine-year-olds can evaluate themselves, find that they are lacking, but not feel guilty about it.

Self-Concept and Independence

• Nine-year-olds tend to be inner-directed and self-motivated.

• They have occasions of intense emotion and impatience, but their outbursts are less frequent and they show greater self-control. The inner-directed quality of their behavior allows nine-year-olds to become intently involved in activities.

• If forced to interrupt an activity, nine-year-olds will usually come back to it on their own.

• They can think and reason for themselves.

• They can be trusted.

• They may withdraw from surroundings to get a sense of self. They do not, however, retreat as much as they did when they were seven.

• Nine-year-olds do not feel impelled to boast and attack to protect themselves.

Relating to Other Children and Adults

• In their relationships with both adults and peers, they show consideration and fairness beyond that shown at a younger age.

• They can accept their own failures and mistakes, and they are willing to take responsibility for their own actions.

• Nine-year-olds have an increased awareness of sex and sex-differentiated behaviors.

• Girls can become concerned about their clothing and appearance. They take more interest in the "right" fashion.

• Friendships tend to be more solid, but occasionally nine-year-olds can have an intense dislike of the opposite sex, preferring to be with children of their own age and sex. Boys and girls both may begin to form clubs around various activities.

• Although their independence can be trying at times, they are often easier to work with than younger children who make great demands on adults.

• They are anxious to please and love to be chosen.

- Most of the mother-child conflict of the eight-year-old has disappeared, and the nine-year-old makes fewer demands on parents.
- Nine-year-olds usually have no problems with young children or older brothers and sisters. In fact, they can be very loyal to siblings.

Games and Activities
- Nine-year-olds spend much time in solitary activities of their own choosing.
- Bicycling, roller and ice skating, and swimming are physical activities they enjoy.
- They continue to enjoy the advanced table games they learned at eight.
- Materials and information attract the nine-year-old. Organized games or activities such as baseball, football, and basketball are popular. Many children at this age also have mastered basic reading and arithmetic and can use these skills to gain information, to solve problems, and to participate in games and recreation.

Ten-Year-Olds

General
Ten is the high point of childhood. Ten-year-olds have worked through the difficulties of home, school, and community. They now can take pride in their ability to fit in at home, at school, and at play with their peers. On occasion, there can be outbursts of anger, depression, or sadness, but these moods are short-lived and soon forgotten.
- Girls are slightly more advanced sexually than boys and already there is some evidence of the rapid sprint to maturity that will make them taller and heavier than boys their own age in a couple of years. Their bodies are rounding out and the softening of contours may begin. Some girls may even experience the first stages of breast development. Girls become concerned about their bodies and menstruation and about sexual activity in general.
- For boys physical changes are less marked, thus concern for the body and physical maturity is much less noticeable.

Self-Concept and Independence
- Ten-year-olds accept themselves as they are without worrying too much about their strengths and weaknesses. They are much less interested in evaluating themselves. They like their bodies and like what they can do both athletically and academically. Their self-acceptance is heightened by the acceptance accorded them by peers, families, and school.

Relating to Other Children and Adults
- Ten-year-olds like and enjoy their friends. Boys may move into loosely organized groups. Within these groups, boys may have particular friends, but there is a lot of switching around. Girls usually move in smaller groups and are likely to form more intense friendships and have more serious "falling outs" with their friends being "mad" and "not playing" or "not speaking" to one another as a result. There are times when ten-year-olds may seem to value their peer group more than their families.
- Teachers and other adults who interact with this age group are popular if they are fair and not partial to particular children in the group. Adults working with ten-year-olds need to be firm but not strict. At this age children like adult leaders to schedule activities and like to keep to the schedule.

Games and Activities
- They like outings and trips.
- They like organized games and belonging to clubs and groups.
- When working on a project they may need to get up and move about.

Eleven-Year-Olds

General
At this age, there is an accelerated growth pace.

• The eleven-year-old's activity level increases; energy and appetite also increase.

• There is a tendency at this age to forget manners, to be loud, rude, and boorish, and to take unnecessary chances as a means of defying adult authority. Riding bicycles in heavy traffic is an example of this kind of behavior.

• Eleven-year-olds quarrel a good deal with adults and lack emotional control although they can be cooperative and friendly with strangers. They need firmness and understanding from adults.

Self-Concept and Independence
• They can be belligerent because of their high energy level, which pushes them toward activities, but which sometimes leads to carelessness.

• The eleven-year-old is looking for new self-definition.

• They will often confront others with criticism in an effort to get attention. They can, however, admit faults.

• They will sometimes differ with parents on careers and have dreams of being famous while their parents try to temper such fantasies.

• An eleven-year-old, on occasion, will challenge parents and other adults on child-rearing practices.

Relating to Other Children and Adults
• Boys and girls have best friends and a group of other friends who are selected because of common interests and temperaments.

• Both boys and girls admit to being interested in the opposite sex and show their interest by teasing, joking, and showing off.

• Eleven-year-olds like to quarrel with others, but don't like others to argue with them.

• They can be cooperative, friendly, and pleasant with adults, but they need to be treated with understanding and firmness.

• Eleven-year-olds can feel left out from their peer group.

Games and Activities
• They don't like to work with materials that are complex, but they do like things that show off their rote skills.

• Eleven-year-olds have trouble understanding relationships and the complex combinations of events.

In Summary

Children are individuals with their own special temperaments and idiosyncracies. The ages and stages children go through can vary tremendously from one child to the next and, by respecting the variousness of children, parents and other caregivers can help them develop strong and healthy self-concepts.

III - ADOLESCENTS

> *The young are prone to desire and in regard to sexual desire they exercise no self-restraint. They are changeful, too, and fickle in their desires. They are passionate, irascible, and apt to be carried away by their impulses. They are slaves, too, of their passion.*

A distinguished scientist and philosopher made this observation over 2000 years ago. To some, Aristotle's lament might suggest that adolescents haven't changed much since the days of ancient Athens, but recent research indicates that what hasn't changed is adults' *perceptions* of adolescents. Surveys of adolescents and their parents show that their values and attitudes are generally quite compatible. The famous "generation gap" appears to be an invention of the news media in response to a small but highly visible group of adolescents whose challenge to the older generation in the 1960s was mistakenly interpreted as representative.

What is it about the stage of life between childhood and adulthood that makes it so difficult for adults to understand? Although adolescence is not equally troublesome in all societies and for all families, adults' reports of its stressful nature are sufficiently widespread to warrant attention.

Change-physical, mental, and social change-is the most notable quality of adolescence and accounts for a good deal of the difficulty.

Physical Changes

The most obvious physical change during adolescence is rapid acceleration of growth. Within two years before or after age 12 for girls and age 14 for boys, a growth spurt occurs. The rate of gain in height and weight typically doubles for a year or more. Physical growth takes place in a fairly consistent sequence, beginning at the extremities and moving inward. Head, hands, and feet enlarge first, followed by arms and legs, then trunk. The broadening of male shoulders and female hips that characterizes adult body form occurs last. Overall growth is accompanied, though not always in the same order or at the same rate, by maturation of the reproductive organs and glands and by the appearance of pubic and underarm hair, and facial hair in males.

Together, these physical changes accomplish the biological aspect of adolescence, which is known as pubescence: they transform a child into an adult, one who is able to have children.

But this physical transformation is not as simple for the person going through it as it sounds when described in the abstract. For one thing, the ages at which pubescence begins and is completed vary as much as four years among different young people. Furthermore, the period from beginning to completion may be as little as 18 months for some and as much as six years for others. As a result of this variation, any group of early adolescents is likely to include young people who are at very different points in pubescence. Because girls enter pubescence, on the average, two years earlier than boys, the greatest variation among girls' physical maturation occurs during ages 11-13, while in boys it is during ages 13-15.

Rapid change combined with wide variation among individuals tend to make adolescents extremely sensitive to their appearance. At no other time in life are feelings about the self (self-esteem) so closely tied to feelings about the body (body image). Physical appearance also affects the ways in which other people treat an adolescent. Adults tend to expect adult behavior from a 15-year-old boy who is six feet tall and shaves regularly, but they will readily excuse childish behavior on the part of his classmate who, though the same age, has not yet begun his growth spurt. Perhaps even more importantly, peers judge one another on the basis of physical size and appearance. Early maturation can be an advantage for boys but often is not for girls because it puts them out-of-step with their peers.

The physical changes of pubescence, therefore, have direct effects on adolescents' social relations. They also affect emotions. The maturation of the gonads reproductive glandschanges the balance of hormones in the body, which can result in new sensitivities to the environment. For example, an adolescent may have a heightened sensitivity to loss of sleep, which results in moodiness or outbursts of temper. Cyclical changes in hormonal balance, especially among girls but also to some extent among boys, are associated with changes in emotions, behavior, and thinking. Since these cycles are new to adolescents, they may not be handled well.

Mental Changes

The most important mental change during adolescence is the growth in capacity for abstract thinking. Before age 11 or 12, children think in terms of concrete objects and groups of objects. Their reasoning is simple and direct. It does not allow for much complexity or subtlety. Given a problem to solve, the child tends to plunge into it with first one possible solution and then another until she either finds the correct solution or gives up. Confronted with a moral dilemma, she responds on the basis of a rule, which may or may not be appropriately applied.

By age 16, most adolescents have transcended this simple way of thinking, though not all of them adopt the most complex forms of reasoning. Nor do all use the same types of reasoning about all issues, any more than adults do. Adolescents begin to achieve the capacity to approach a problem systematically. Instead of moving immediately into the trying out of an assortment of solutions, they can analyze the problem and arrive at some tentative conclusions about what sorts of solutions probably will and will not work. Then they can proceed in a logical fashion to test and evaluate solutions, gaining a greater understanding of the problem along the way.

Moral issues become much more complex than they are for young children because adolescents are able to understand that two sound rules or principles might conflict in some cases. For example, they will understand that in certain situations, the values of friendship and honesty conflict, and they will struggle with a question about whether someone should report a friend for breaking a rule. Younger children are more likely to choose either one principle or the other without recognizing the dilemma. Furthermore, adolescents outgrow the childish belief that only evil people do bad things. They understand accident and circumstances involve even the best-intentioned people in undesirable actions. They are, therefore, likely to be more understanding and forgiving of human frailty than young children, though their interest in principles can also make adolescents morally rigid at times.

Along with the capacity to think abstractly comes the realization that what exists is only one of many possibilities. Thinking about those possibilities becomes a fascinating activity. The real is frequently compared to the ideal and found wanting. Because they can conceive of a more ideal worJd without having to bother themselves with all the details of how it might be achieved and what drawbacks it might have, adolescents are often impatient with the real world and with the failure of adults to have made it better already.

This capacity to think about many possible realities is important, given the momentous choices adolescents will make as they move into adulthood and choose career directions, educational paths, and mates. Without it they are likely to drift into the first opportunities that arise without considering what the other possibilities might be, which are most desirable, and which are feasible.

Similarly, the ability to reason about moral issues is necessary if a person is to establish a personal moral code. Rules and principles simply accepted from parents and other authorities are essential to children, but adolescents need to think through rules and principles and consider the alternatives in order to adopt or adapt them for themselves. An adolescent who does not go through the process of questioning principles and values may be without guidance when confronted with a new and complex moral dilemma or when one or another of his/her basic principles is seriously challenged.

Social Changes

Because of their physical and mental growth, adolescents are no longer treated like children. The expectations adults and peers have of them change and their behavior changes. Thus the social world in which they live changes in important ways.

One of the most obvious social changes is the initiation of serious interest in and interactions with young people of the opposite sex. The physical and emotional changes of pubescence described above lead to strong new feelings between girls and boys. Even before they begin to act upon these feelings by dating and engaging in other heterosexual activities, many adolescents begin to have "crushes" on opposite-sex peers, and sometimes on same-sex peers and on adults. These one-way emotional attachments simply indicate the presence of new emotional capacities, but they can be difficult for the adolescent to understand and deal with. Learning to handle the emotions and behavior that go along with attracting and forming emotional attachments to members of the opposite sex can be stressful, in addition to being terribly exciting.

The social world of the adolescent changes in other ways as well. A sixteen-year-old may notice that adults are treating her more like one of them, engaging in real conversation, for example, instead of saying "My, how you've grown," and asking about school. She may also notice that she enjoys this adult conversation when just a year or two before she would have preferred to go out and play.

By the age of sixteen, adolescents are being given many privileges formerly reserved for adults. In most places they can drive a car, quit school, and hold a job. Although it is usually against the law, they can fairly easily smoke and drink alcoholic beverages.

Relations with parents change too. As they grow more mature, adolescents are less dependent on their parents than they were earlier. They might be able to live on their own. They have ideas of their own and are reconsidering some of the beliefs and values their parents have taught them. They receive emotional support from peers. Sometimes their peers' values are inconsistent with their parents'. For all these reasons, they become less deferent to their parents' wishes and opinions, adopting a more independent and often a more aggressive stance.

Modern industrial societies demand highly educated workers and do not need the labor of children. Therefore, most young people experience a long gap between the attainment of physical adulthood and adult status. Marriage, parenthood, and full-time paid employment are the principal indicators of adult status in our society. At least two ambiguities arise from this social definition of adulthood. One is that young people are expected to postpone marriage and to remain economically dependent on their parents for several years after they are physically capable of reproduction and full-time employment. A second is that while many young people "prolong their adolescence" by enrolling in college and then in graduate or professional school, many of their peers are entering full-time employment, getting married, and starting families. Although adolescence can be an enjoyable stage of life because of the freedom from adult obligations, it can also be a frustrating time because adult privileges are withheld.

Difficulties for Parents

Adolescents are no longer children; they and their parents have to work out new ways of dealing with each other that recognize their growing but not yet complete maturity. Parents must realize that they can no longer control their offspring in many important areas. Adolescents simply have too many opportunities to do as they please. Young people, who are often adamant in demanding relief from parental control, need to understand that freedom demands responsibility. They cannot expect their parents to give them adult privileges regarding their social activities and then excuse them from household obligations because they are only children.

One of the reasons adolescents often seem to be a burden to their parents is that parents have to change the way they treat their adolescents. Parental behavior that has developed over several years and has been rather effective becomes obsolete. New behavior, a new parental style, is called for.

Being required to deal with new challenges and to behave in different ways is always difficult, but it can be especially difficult for parents of adolescents who are simultaneously experiencing stress in other parts of their lives. The term "midlife crisis" has become popular in recent years in recognition that many people go through a period of self-examination and often of serious readjustment in middle age as they realize they have relatively few years left to accomplish what they aspire to. Two life cycle changes in the family are associated with this midlife crisis: one is the death of one's own parents and the other is the maturation of one's children. People at this point frequently have to accept the fact that they will not achieve the prominence in their careers that they might have wanted. Common responses to this "crisis" include career and marital changes.

Parents who are experiencing crises of this magnitude are likely to feel overwhelmed by the challenges of dealing with their rapidly changing adolescents. But even parents who feel satisfied and secure in most aspects of their lives may have difficulty coping with their adolescent children.

What Adults Can Do for Adolescents

There are times when the adolescent says, "Why don't you just leave me alone!" and the adult wants to say, "Alright, I will." That is not a solution, however, because adolescents need adults to help them achieve adulthood themselves. The following suggestions may prove helpful to adults who work with adolescents, but they cannot be treated as a cookbook. Just as adolescents refuse to follow many adult "recipes" for proper behavior because they need to work out their own behavioral code, adults must be flexible and resourceful in responding to adolescents. There is no single way to do it.

1. Be honest. With their newly developed capacity for abstract thinking, adolescents become fascinated with principles and with consistency. They are severe critics of adults they think are hypocritical or two-faced. Most adolescents are sophisticated enough to see through dishonesty or pretention in adults who are close to them. They tend to be skeptical at what adults tell them and to welcome any confirmation of that skepticism.

2. Be open. Adolescents want and need to talk about things with their parents and other adults close to them. But they also need to maintain their privacy and their independence. Therefore, adult-adolescent conversations cannot be one-sided, with the adolescent baring his soul and the adult listening and offering advice. Adolescents need to know that some of the same concerns they struggle with are concerns of adults too.

Sexuality is one of the most insistent concerns of adolescents because it is a new one, brought out by their sexual maturation. Adults cannot be very helpful to adolescents about sexual issues unless they, as adults, are comfortable with their own sexuality. They must be willing to acknowledge the complexity of the issues and the strength of the social and emotional pressures. In our society the "official" morality is that sexual relations are limited to marriage, yet television, movies, magazines, songs on the radio, and even billboards bombard us constantly with the message that sexual attractiveness is the most important personal quality and that unrestrained sexual behavior is good. Like adolescents, adults can find this contradiction confusing, and they should be willing to discuss it.

3. Set clear and consistent limits. Most children will abide by rules their parents or other adults set down just because they are rules, at least as long as the adult is looking. Adolescents are much more likely to want to know why a particular rule or expectation has been stated. Adults should respect this need for explanation and should allow for some negotiation regarding rules for behavior. But, consistent with the recommendation to be honest, adults should not hesitate to say what they believe is absolutely essential and is not open to negotiation.

There may be some rules or limits set by parents that adolescents continue to violate because they are independent enough to do so. Parents may have to acknowledge that they cannot control what the adolescent does away from home but make clear that they will not allow it in the home and then follow through with that prohibition.

4. Remember that growing up means becoming independent. Effective parents, and other adults who succeed in helping adolescents become adults, are able to accept young people making choices that they would not have made and behaving in ways they do not approve of. That is what independence means. Young adults who still do as they are told all the time are immature and unprepared to face a world in which they are constantly required to decide for themselves. Most adolescents become adults who are a source of pride and happiness for their parents and for the other adults who worked with them. But for this to happen, they must first establish some independence, and that can require a painful break.

Adolescents undergo dramatic physical and mental changes in a short period of time, and they are given a confusing in-between place in our society. The period can be painful for the adolescents and for the adults who are close to them. But it is a necessary process both for the adolescents to come of age and for our society to renew itself through the questions, the new perspective, and the new talents that each group of young people brings into adulthood.

www.ingramcontent.com/pod-product-compliance
Lightning Source LLC
Chambersburg PA
CBHW081807300426
44116CB00014B/2263